Redeeming the Screens

The House of Prisca and Aquila

Our mission at the House of Prisca and Aquila is to produce quality books that expound accurately the word of God to empower women and men to minister together in a multicultural church. Our writers have a positive view of the Bible as God's revelation that affects both thoughts and words, so it is plenary, historically accurate, and consistent in itself; fully reliable; and authoritative as God's revelation. Because God is true, God's revelation is true, inclusive to men and women and speaking to a multicultural church, wherein all the diversity of the church is represented within the parameters of egalitarianism and inerrancy.

The word of God is what we are expounding, thereby empowering women and men to minister together in all levels of the church and home. The reason we say women and men together is because this is the model of Prisca and Aquila ministering together to another member of the church—Apollos: "Having heard Apollos, Priscilla and Aquila took him aside and more accurately expounded to him the Way of God" (Acts 18:26). True exposition, like true religion, is by no means boring—it is fascinating. Books that reveal and expound God's true nature "burn within us" as they elucidate the Scripture and apply it to our lives.

This was the experience of the disciples who heard Jesus on the road to Emmaus: "Were not our hearts burning while Jesus was talking to us on the road, while he was opening the scriptures to us?" (Luke 24:32). We are hoping to create the classics of tomorrow: significant and accessible trade and academic books that "burn within us."

Our "house" is like the home to which Prisca and Aquila no doubt brought Apollos as they took him aside. It is like the home in Emmaus where Jesus stopped to break bread and reveal his presence. It is like the house built on the rock of obedience to Jesus (Matt 7:24). Our "house," as a euphemism for our publishing team, is a home where truth is shared and Jesus's Spirit breaks bread with us, nourishing all of us with his bounty of truth.

We are delighted to work together with Wipf and Stock in this series and welcome submissions on a wide variety of topics from an egalitarian inerrantist global perspective.

For more information, visit www.houseofpriscaandaquila.com.

Redeeming the Screens

*Living Stories of Media "Ministers"
Bringing the Message of Jesus Christ
to the Entertainment Industry*

Edited by
JEANNE C. DEFAZIO
and
WILLIAM DAVID SPENCER

WIPF & STOCK · Eugene, Oregon

REDEEMING THE SCREENS
Living Stories of Media "Ministers" Bringing the Message of Jesus Christ to the Entertainment Industry

Copyright © 2016 Wipf and Stock. All rights reserved. Except for brief quotations in critical publications or reviews, no part of this book may be reproduced in any manner without prior written permission from the publisher. Write: Permissions, Wipf and Stock Publishers, 199 W. 8th Ave., Suite 3, Eugene, OR 97401.

Wipf & Stock
An Imprint of Wipf and Stock Publishers
199 W. 8th Ave., Suite 3
Eugene, OR 97401

www.wipfandstock.com

PAPERBACK ISBN: 978-1-4982-3446-7
HARDCOVER ISBN: 978-1-4982-3448-1

Scripture quotations marked NIV are taken from the New International Version, copyright © 1984, 2011 Zondervan.

Scripture quotations marked NRSV are taken from the *New Revised Standard Version of the Bible*, copyright © 1989, 2015 Thomas Nelson.

Scripture quotations marked NLT are taken from the New Living Translation, second edition, copyright © 2013 Tyndale House Publishers.

Scripture quotations marked NKJV are taken from the New King James Version, copyright © 1990 Thomas Nelson, Inc.

Scripture quotations marked TNIV are taken from Today's New International Version, copyright © 2005 Zondervan.

Manufactured in the U.S.A.

This book is dedicated to my mentor in Hollywood ministry, Michael P. Grace II. Thank you, Michael.

—Jeanne DeFazio

I thank all the saints past and present who have been working to make this entertainment industry revival happen. Whether we have been able to mention you in our book or not, the Lord knows who you are, and from us we send a grateful thank-you.

—William David Spencer

Contents

Acknowledgements ix
Other Works by the Editors xi
Introduction: Jeanne DeFazio xiii

1 Transforming the Mass Media of Entertainment   1
   —Ted Baehr

Actors and Performers

2 Out of the Claws of the Predator: How to Avoid Being a Victim of the Entertainment Industry   25
   —Olga Soler

3 When the Wheel Stopped   43
   —Susan Stafford

4 Hollywood's Circus of the Stars Stuntman   53
   —Bob Yerkes

5 The Hula Hoop Queen   62
   —Jozy Pollock

6 Heavenly Manna, Inc.   73
   —Mel Novak

7 The Flight of a Butterfly   81
   —Sheri Pedigo

8   Healing through Faith and Compassion   90
    —Martha Reyes

9   Ambassador of Prayer Ministries: From
    Show Business to God's Business   96
    —April Shenandoah

**Producers, Directors, Consultants, and
Pastors to the Entertainment Industry**

10 Amazing Grace   108
    —Beulah "Bee" Beyer Wenger

11 Unity   115
    —Gemma Wenger

12 Caretakers of the Future   127
    —Charlene Eber

13 Christ in You the Hope of Glory
    International Ministry   135
    —Joanne Petronella

14 Uniting the Nations through Media   142
    —LeaAnn Pendergrass

15 Media Fellowship International   152
    —Bob Rieth

16 The Cathedral of Love of the Seven Golden
    Candlesticks Church and World Outreach   159
    —Larry Abernathy

17 All Things Work Together for Good   165
    —Linda Bair Smith

18 Following Our Rebel Lord   174
    —William David Spencer

Conclusion: William David Spencer   189

Bibliography   199

Acknowledgments

Jeanne DeFazio

THIS BOOK WAS INSPIRED by the creative genius of William David and Aída Besançon Spencer of the House of Prisca and Aquila Series, published by Wipf and Stock. Thanks to Jen Creamer, Mary Huckstep, Kris Johnson, Lydia Somang Lee, and Gina Zurlo for careful correcting, and William David Spencer for brilliantly editing the manuscript. Aída Besançon Spencer and Deb Beatty Mel diligently oversaw the final stages of the manuscript. This book exists because of all of those who added their stories to mine: Larry Abernathy, Ted Baehr, Charlene Eber, Mel Novak, Sheri Pedigo, LeaAnn Pendergrass, Joanne Petronella, Jozy Pollock, Martha Reyes, Bob Rieth, April Shenandoah, Linda Bair Smith, Olga Soler, Susan Stafford, Beulah Bee Wenger, Gemma Wenger, and Bob Yerkes.

Special thanks to Lili Baehr for being a great role model for women in media ministry, and to Peter S. Lynch, Fred and Suzi Wehba and Morgan Grace for their support of Christian ministry. Thanks also to Michael P. Goodman, oncologist William R. Grace, Patrick P. Grace, Edward Keazirian, Gerald A. Maguire, and Congressman Ed Pease for their encouragement; to Paul, Michelle, and my amazing niece Ella Louise Ryan, who hosted me during the editing process; and to Hollywood stuntwoman Tree O'Toole, who gave great advice. Elaine Madera-Jean has been a great blessing to me through this process. I am beholden to Monica "Happy" Castro Valdivieso, who served as a theatrical consultant for the book, and I owe a debt of gratitude to

Michael A Sullivan, Cambridge Clerk of Court, and to Jennifer Dever Wood for their support. Many thanks to Father Andrew Green, Canon David Caffrey, Canon Victoria Hatch, Brother John Westaway, Kevin Kirkpatrick, Harvey and Suzanne Trackman, and Church Vestry Alan Zimmerman—all angels of mercy at St. Paul's in the Desert Church. Ronald O. Perelman has been a great inspiration to me.

Thanks to my brothers, Bill, Jim, Mike, Tom, Joe, Peter, and my sister Anne, and my niece Francesca for their valuable input over the years. Special thanks to Caleb Loring III for his support of this project. Most of all, I thank Jesus for his heart to serve that made this work possible.

Other Works by the Editors

BY JEANNE C. DEFAZIO

Creative Ways to Build Christian Community (ed. with John P. Lathrop)
How to Have an Attitude of Gratitude on the Night Shift (with Teresa Flowers)

BY WILLIAM DAVID SPENCER

Name in the Papers (a novel)
Mysterium and Mystery: The Clerical Crime Novel
Dread Jesus
God through the Looking Glass: Glimpses from the Arts (ed. with A. B. Spencer)
Marriage at the Crossroads: Couples in Conversation about Discipleship, Gender Roles, Decision Making, and Intimacy (with A. B. Spencer, S. R. Tracy, and C. G. Tracy)
Joy through the Night: Biblical Resources on Suffering (with A. B. Spencer)
The Prayer Life of Jesus: Shout of Agony, Revelation of Love (with A. B. Spencer)
Global Voices in Biblical Equality: Women and Men Serving Together in the Church (ed. with A. B. Spencer and M. Haddad)
Reaching for the New Jerusalem: A Biblical and Theological Framework for the City (ed. with S. H. Park and A. B. Spencer)
The Global God: Multicultural Evangelical Views of God (ed. with A. B. Spencer)
The Goddess Revival: A Christian Response (with A. B. Spencer, D. G. F. Hailson, and C. Kroeger)
Chanting Down Babylon: The Rastafari Reader (ed. with N. S. Murrell and A. A. McFarlane)
2 Corinthians: A Commentary (with A. B. Spencer)

Introduction

Jeanne DeFazio

"IF YOU SURVIVE, YOU will make a lot of money!" This was famed stuntman Bob Yerkes's advice to me shortly after I arrived in Los Angeles. Bob was renowned for dangling multiple stories up as a stunt double for Hollywood's most famous leading men. His advice was not metaphorical. He was offering to teach me to jump off buildings into airbags. In many ways, this observation describes the whole experience of working in the film and television industry—a daily risk of life and limb for many, but for all, a risk of the soul!

Our book, *Redeeming the Screens*, written or dictated by active participants in the entertainment industry, reflects on the impact of "the screen" in our contemporary world and consists of autobiographical accounts of Christians actively bringing Christ's message to the entertainment industry. The premise of this book is that people may argue with theology, but they cannot argue with a personal testimony, because it is what it is. *Redeeming the Screens* offers testimonies from world-class relational media evangelists telling their own stories of what brought them to receive Jesus and how the power of his death and resurrection on the cross helped them through the challenges in their lives.

When House of Prisca and Aquila co-founder William David Spencer suggested that I follow up my book *Creative Ways to Build Christian Community* with a book on how we are trying to build Christian community in Hollywood, it brought my ministry concerns and my own life experience together. "I'll do it if you help me edit it," I offered.

"It's not the usual academic kind of book I edit these days," he responded, "but it sounds really worthwhile. I can see it would serve God's reign, and these are fascinating stories to tell. It promises to be an entertaining and edifying book, and, Sister Jeanne, we also owe you a tribute for all the help you've been giving our at-risk students in the theology classes here at the Center for Urban Ministerial Education of Gordon-Conwell Theological Seminary, Boston, so I'll do it with you," and he added, "but please begin it with your own story. It's interesting and would start the book off well."

So, here it is.

I was reared in a large Italian/Spanish Roman Catholic family. I felt the love and presence of Jesus when I was a child attending Roman Catholic Schools and the Catholic Church. As a junior at the University of California, I said the "sinner's prayer" with a born-again friend, expecting nothing at all like what happened. As C. S. Lewis described in his autobiographical *Surprised by Joy*,[1] I felt Jesus's presence and

---

1. Lewis, *Surprised by Joy*, vii.

great joy, and I began attending both Catholic charismatic as well as Protestant evangelical services. After graduating from the University of California at Davis in 1974, I joined the high-profile ministry to the counterculture, the Christian World Liberation Front (CWLF).[2] As a member of CWLF's street theatre, I performed on Sproul Plaza on the University of California at Berkeley campus, as well as on the UC Davis campus, during its Whole Earth Day while, a hundred feet away from our performance, young women were dancing topless to a bongo drum beat. This was such a mundane sight in the early 1970s that CWLF street theatre drew a larger crowd.

During the 1976 American bicentennial celebration in New York City, Charlie Lehman and I recruited and directed InterVarsity Christian Fellowship members to perform CWLF's street theatre production *Registration* at the Queens College and Hunter College campuses and at Greeley Square Park as the Democratic National Convention nominated Jimmy Carter for president in nearby Madison Square Garden. I then enrolled in Lee Strasbourg's master class at Lee Strasbourg's Acting Institute in New York City in 1977 and performed in Eric Bentley's *Are You Now or Have You Ever Been*, directed by Frank Gero, off Broadway (1978). Established Broadway stars, including Liza Minnelli, Colleen Dewhurst, Tammy Grimes, Rosemary Murphy, and Frances Sternhagen rotated the play's cameo role of Lillian Hellman. Peggy Vanek-Titus and I, two former CWLF street theatre actresses, found ourselves captivated by the world of theatre while sharing a walk-on and a production assistant job. In 1980, James Goldstone directed the Emmy Award–winning television film *Kent State* at a Gadsen, Alabama, campus in which, once again, Peggy Vanek-Titus and I worked together, portraying young student radicals from UC Berkeley. An actor portraying a National Guardsman hit me in the face with a bayonet in a riot scene on camera, causing me severe sinus problems due to a deviated septum and several breaks in the nose. Interplanetary Productions, owned by the Osmond Family, paid for a painful surgical reconstruction. Acting can be hazardous to your health! But I was young and in love with acting and was, despite this experience, certain of greater success in Hollywood.

Arriving in Los Angeles in 1981, I made the rounds while attending a Vineyard Christian Fellowship Church, where I was baptized in the Holy Spirit. Wendy Gilmore, a Christian friend from the Vineyard,

2. "The Jesus Revolution," Time Magazine, 21 June 1971.

was a high school friend of Corey Allen, director of *Hill Street Blues*, and was able to get me on the HSB set twice.

Then, I became acquainted with Michael P. Grace II, CEO of Grace Motion Pictures, at Hollywood producer Peter Engel's prayer meeting in his West Los Angeles home. There, I also met top Hollywood agent Lee Mimms, Linda Surgenor, and Hollywood's top stuntman Bob Yerkes, who made that offer to teach me how to jump off buildings into an airbag. Quick-witted as ever, Bob joked, "If you survive, you will make a lot of money." Not wanting further injuries on Hollywood sets, I thanked Bob, but I accepted Mr. Grace's offer to work as a "script girl" for Grace Motion Pictures—and the rest, as they say, is history. I subsequently became secretary of MPG Energy Corporation, overseeing much of Mr. Grace's gas and oil interests, legal matters, and banking, as well as organizing his Christian ministries internationally and nationally, until his passing in 1995. From 1995 to 2015, I worked as a part-time administrator to Mr. Grace's estate. During this period, in 1996–1997, I also assisted Harriet Nesbitt, writer of the column "Politics and Such" at the *Murray Hill News*.[3] In 1998, I canvassed and fundraised for the Clean Air Act for Ralph Nader's US Public Interest Research Group in Washington, DC. In 1999 to 2001, I staff-assisted at the Environment and Public Works Committee of the US Senate. In 2002, at the advice of Caleb Loring III, trustee of Gordon-Conwell Theological Seminary, I pursued seminary education at Gordon-Conwell, completing a Master of Arts in Religion in Theology in 2004. To complete the English learners program of Cal State Teach[4] in 2008, I student-taught in the barrios of San Diego in 2006 and 2007. Since 2009, I have returned each year to Gordon-Conwell's Boston Campus Center for Urban Ministerial Education (CUME) as an Athanasian teaching scholar in William David Spencer's summer and fall Systematic Theology 1 and 2 courses, advising the English learners in the classroom. In 2011, I co-authored a book with Teresa Flowers, *How to Have an Attitude of Gratitude on the Night Shift*, and, in 2013, I co-edited, along with John P. Lathrop, *Creative Ways to Build Christian Community*.

3. The Murray Hill News was founded by Congresswoman Dorothy Frooks and published by her husband Jay Vanderbilt. "Politics and Such" author Harriet Nesbitt interviewed celebrities at New York City benefits reflecting on matters of social significance.

4. Cal State Teach is the official name of a top English-learners teaching program in the California State University system: www.calstateteach.net.

Through all the twists and turns of this journey, the Holy Spirit impressed upon me the words of Exodus 23:20: "I am going to send an angel in front of you, to guard you on the way and to bring you to the place that I have prepared" (NRSV). I realize now that these contributing authors were "angels" God sent to guide me.[5] I met and ministered to several of them through my work with Michael Grace, either directly or via networking. Like the man in Jesus's parable (Luke 14:12–24), Mr. Grace held banquets for those from the highways and byways to share the word of God and help them receive Jesus. Like the servant in this parable, I notified guests, worked with caterers for these events, and prayed for the Holy Spirit to bring people to Jesus.[6]

In this parable, Jesus declared that God's kingdom had arrived and was ready to receive everyone who accepted his invitation. The master in this parable sent his servant into the streets to invite guests to his feast. Each contributor to this present book sees herself or himself as a faithful servant extending the invitation of Jesus, inviting everyone along the highways and byways of the media and beyond to sit at the table and feast from a banquet of God's great love and mercy.

Through the ministries of these contributing authors, Jesus calls everyone to the wedding feast of the Lamb (Rev 19:6–9),[7] the culmina-

---

5. Hebrew malak, a messenger specifically of God, "angel." The word occurs 213 times in the Old Testament.

6. Luke 14:16–24: "Then Jesus said to him, 'Someone gave a great dinner and invited many. At the time for the dinner he sent his slave to say to those who had been invited, "Come; for everything is ready now." But they all alike began to make excuses. The first said to him, "I have bought a piece of land, and I must go out and see it; please accept my regrets." Another said, "I have bought five yoke of oxen, and I am going to try them out; please accept my regrets." Another said, "I have just been married, and therefore I cannot come." So the slave returned and reported this to his master. Then the owner of the house became angry and said to his slave, "Go out at once into the streets and lanes of the town and bring in the poor, the crippled, the blind, and the lame." And the slave said, "Sir, what you ordered has been done, and there is still room." Then the master said to the slave, "Go out into the roads and lanes, and compel people to come in, so that my house may be filled. For I tell you, none of those who were invited will taste my dinner"'" (NRSV).

7. Rev 19:6–9: "Then I heard what seemed to be the voice of a great multitude, like the sound of many waters and like the sound of mighty thunderpeals, crying out, 'Hallelujah! For the Lord our God the Almighty reigns. Let us rejoice and exult and give him the glory, for the marriage of the Lamb has come, and his bride has made herself ready; to her it has been granted to be clothed with fine linen, bright and pure'—for the fine linen is the righteous deeds of the saints. And the angel said to me, 'Write this: Blessed are those who are invited to the marriage supper of the Lamb.' And

tion of human history when God and his beloved church will be joined forever.

In 2013, in *Creative Ways to Build Christian Community*, which I co-edited with John Lathrop, I wrote the chapter "Building Christian Community through Meetings and Meals," wherein I highlighted creative networking in various communities where I had served, sharing my experience of building hospitality and relational community across cultural lines. My chapter explained the impact of networked communities.[8] To demonstrate the impact of relational evangelism on building Christian community, I noted and quoted extraordinary lifestyle evangelists in Christian media with whom I had been privileged to work. Our vision became creating another book with each of these wonderful Christians modeling through testimony effective ways to bring people to Jesus. This book is the fulfillment of that vision.

Bill Spencer suggested we set up each chapter with a brief introduction that I would write, followed by the first-person accounts of each of these powerful ministers of Jesus's redemptive love. Our intention as editors is that each chapter provide a model of how to create Christian community in the media, with original contributions by (in alphabetical order) Pastor Larry Abernathy, producer of evangelical television programs and founder of Cathedral of Love of the Seven Golden Candlesticks Church; Ted Baehr, chairman of the Christian Film and Television Commission, publisher of MOVIEGUIDE®, and executive producer of the MOVIEGUIDE® annual Faith and Values Awards Gala and Report to the Entertainment Industry; Charlene Eber, Hollywood producer, director, and founder of World Alliance for Peace and Caretakers of the Future; Mel Novak, award-winning actor, prison chaplain, and skid-row minister; Sheri Pedigo, internationally known actress, vocalist, and composer; LeaAnn Pendergrass, host of the *Uniting the Nations* broadcast, pastor, and founder of My Gathering Place International; Joanne Petronella, television personality and founder of Christ in You the Hope of Glory International Ministry; Jozy Pollock, the UK's hula hoop queen, a magician's assistant, song lyricist, and former chaplain to the Los Angeles County Jail; Martha Reyes, musician, psychologist, author, and founder of Hosanna Foundation; Bob Rieth, founder of Media Fellowship International; April Shenandoah, actress,

---

he said to me, 'These are true words of God'" (NRSV).

8. DeFazio and Lathrop, *Creative Ways*, xx, xxi.

author, columnist, producer/director, and founder of Ambassador of Prayer Ministry; Linda Bair Smith, Christian television talk-show host and ordained minister in the global live-stream outreach of the Cathedral of Love of the Seven Golden Candlesticks Church; Olga Soler, director, writer, and performer for Estuary Ministries; Susan Stafford, pioneer for women in television, original hostess of *Wheel of Fortune*, and founder of Wheel of Grace Unlimited; Beulah "Bee" Beyer Wenger, producer of *Cooking around the World* and *The Bee Beyer Show*, president of the Hollywood Easter Sunrise service, televised internationally by Trinity Broadcasting Company, former editor of *The Hollywood Times*, and, most recently, former senior vice president of the Southern California Motion Picture Council; Gemma Wenger, actress, producer of *Gemma Wenger's Hollywood* and *Beauty for Ashes,* and founder of Gemma Wenger Ministries Inc.; and Bob Yerkes, Hollywood *Circus of the Stars* award-winning stuntman.

These chapters present effective lifestyle evangelism in lives that are connected by the power of the Holy Spirit in unique ways. Chapters do overlap, although the perspectives may vary, as these Christians together have been building community across the disciplines of the entertainment industry. Paul, in 1 Corinthians 12:13, explains that, by one Spirit, we are baptized into one body.[9] These collective chapters demonstrate a spiritual truth in that verse, identifying how the body of Christ is empowered by the Holy Spirit.

In the time I spent interviewing and editing these chapters, I encountered so many circumstances that were clearly the Holy Spirit's way of working anonymously. Charlene Eber's testimony explains how the Spirit led actress Joan Caufield to call Charlene's Video Ventures studio requesting that Charlene produce and direct a video for Michael Grace and Breath of Spirit Ministry. Charlene was a believing Christian who, via Michelle Corral and Joanne Petronella's ministry, became baptized by the Holy Spirit into the body of Christ, where her directorial skills brought media recognition to several ministries and, through them, many to Jesus.

Bob Yerkes provided hospitality for Ted Baehr while Ted was raising the bar of excellence in the entertainment industry with his now highly influential organization, MOVIEGUIDE®. While editing his chapter, I

---

9. 1 Cor 12:13: "For in the one Spirit we were all baptized into one body—Jews or Greeks, slaves or free—and we were all made to drink of one Spirit" (NRSV).

interviewed stuntman Bob Yerkes at his Northridge, California, home and met Nashville's Sheri Pedigo, who gladly contributed a chapter. Bob has a photo of LeaAnn Pendergrass on his refrigerator. I asked him if she might be willing to contribute a chapter to this book, and she agreed. Recently, Bob brought me to Billy Davis and Marilyn McCoo's Soldiers for the Second Coming worship service, where I met Jozy Pollock, who then contributed a chapter. Bob Yerkes is humble, witty, kind, and a bit of a rascal, but the Holy Spirit uses him mightily.

The Holy Spirit moved on my life the day I met Susan Stafford, then hostess for Merv Griffin's *Wheel of Fortune*. New to Los Angeles, I was invited by Michael Grace to attend a Christian luncheon hosted by Bob Rieth's Media Fellowship International. Susan Stafford emceed the event. Despite wanting to be very impressive, I lost my contact lens on the carpet. Susan Stafford walked into the room, introduced herself, and proceeded to help me find the lens. Kindness to the non-A-list Hollywood wannabe is a remarkable trait of Susan Stafford, herself a friend to the rich, famous, and celebrated. She shows God's love and treats everyone with Jesus's mercy. True to her nature, Susan kindly contributed a chapter to this book.

While I was living in New York City in 1996, the Holy Spirit brought April Shenandoah, actress and author of *Your Tongue Determines Your Destiny*, into my life. April visited New York often and encouraged me from the word of God, speaking positively in every challenging situation. Her chapter is characteristic of her innate understanding of positive thinking and speaking.

The Holy Spirit prompted Mel Novak to visit our mutual friend Mayrita Varna's Beverly Hills home twenty years ago and to give me what he calls his "Arsenal prayers." These prayers have become the daily backbone of my intercessory prayer ministry.

The Holy Spirit led Pastor Bob Rieth to meet with me over the past twenty years in New York City, Los Angeles, Washington, DC, and London to encourage and support my ministry through prayer and God's word.

The Holy Spirit prompted Martha Reyes to be a compassionate role model in my life during a missionary tour of Israel in 1987, while I was struggling with my faith as a young woman.

Charlene Eber was moved by the Holy Spirit to bring me into community with Larry Abernathy and Linda Bair Smith of the Cathedral of Love of the Seven Golden Candlesticks Church.

Prompted by the Holy Spirit, Gemma Wenger broadcast a series of interviews of these great evangelists that aired on her *Beauty for Ashes* program globally via The Cross TV and Isaac Television. Gemma's mother was Beulah "Bee" Beyer Wenger, who died just after approving the initial editing of her chapter for this book. Bee was a close friend of Michael Grace, hosting me while I was in need of a place to stay while editing this work. The Holy Spirit brought Olga Soler to perform with me in the film *Christ's Message to the Media*, produced to fulfill requirements of my Master of Arts in Religion degree at Gordon-Conwell Theological Seminary, when Bill Spencer was my supervising professor.

I am blessed to be able to present the stories of these media insiders who have been great role models to me. I have seen their love and sensitivity to the Holy Spirit that enabled each to bring Jesus's message through each one's chosen medium. I know that they will be a blessing to you as you meet them in this book, or deepen your relationship with them if you have already enjoyed their work. May Jesus serve all of us together at the wedding feast of the Lamb as we have served him on this earth.

RESOURCES

View LeaAnn Pendergrass's *Uniting the Nations* interview with Jeanne DeFazio: https://www.youtube.com/watch?v=nSFMoAJuPRk; LeaAnn Pendergrass's interview of Gemma Wenger: http://www.thecrosstv.com/media-gallery/918-uniting-the-nations-6-16-15?category_id=237. Email me at jcdefazio55@gmail.com. I will be happy to speak at events.

Transforming the Mass Media of Entertainment

Ted Baehr

THE MINISTRY CONGLOMERATE GOOD News Communications Inc.–The Christian Film and Television Commission® MOVIEGUIDE® is dedicated to redeeming the values of the mass media according to biblical principles, by influencing media executives to adopt higher standards, and by informing and equipping moral people who work in the industry to create more family-friendly productions.

With only a small budget compared to the organizations it is influencing, and fewer than fifteen fulltime workers, this not-for-profit is making big waves in Hollywood and around the globe.

Each year, around Oscar time, the MOVIEGUIDE® hosts its Annual Faith and Values Awards Gala Celebration and Report to the Entertainment Industry in Hollywood. At this event, the best family-friendly movies and television shows of the previous year and the most moral and Christ-centered films for mature audiences are awarded more than $200,000 in prize money. MOVIEGUIDE® also sponsors the $50,000 Kairos Prize for spiritually uplifting screenplays by first-time and beginning screenwriters, as well as the inaugural $50,000 Chronos Prize for inspiring screenplays by established filmmakers. Both prizes reward scripts that "increase love or understanding of God."

MOVIEGUIDE® is able to influence the top studios through its presentation of a statistical economic analysis based on the 150 criteria used in MOVIEGUIDE® reviews. The analysis consistently shows that family-friendly content, and even Christian-friendly and conservative content, can significantly increase a movie's profitability. For families, MOVIEGUIDE® reviews nearly every movie released nationally in the United States in 100 theaters or more and alerts families about their positive and negative content. The ministry's website, movieguide.org, is the largest faith-based movie review website on the Internet. Each year, the website publishes more than 325 movie, video, and television reviews. It also sends out two weekly e-newsletters to more than 300,000 subscribers, including many families and churches.

MOVIEGUIDE®'s radio program reaches more than 23 million people per month with two-minute daily, 60-second weekly, and five-minute biweekly movie review programs, making the ministry's reach one of the largest in the faith-based radio market. It also telecasts a weekly television show on seven cable and satellite networks, several Internet television outlets, and six independent television stations, plus YouTube and its own website. The cable, satellite, and local telecasts of the television program average more than one million viewers in the United States and overseas.

Another important aspect of MOVIEGUIDE® and its sister organization, the Christian Film and Television Commission ministry, is teaching media wisdom to parents, grandparents, children, grandchildren, teachers, and students. Every year in the United States and overseas, the founder, premier movie critic, and entertainment industry advisor Dr. Ted Baehr speaks more than forty times to various groups about media wisdom, introducing audiences to the MOVIEGUIDE® websites, and he participates in the Annual Faith and Values Awards and Report to the Entertainment Industry. His speaking tours have become so popular that he now has affiliated organizations and partners in Japan, Germany, Russia, South Korea, Australia, and India. He and his staff offer a six-week course in media literacy and wisdom for churches and family groups. Five times per year, he teaches an intense four-day workshop on filmmaking, including scriptwriting.

Daily, Dr. Baehr is in contact with studio and television executives, producers, actors, writers, and other artists, helping them reach the Christian or family audience and guiding them to craft better, more successful movies and television programs and to adopt higher standards reflecting Christian, biblical principles.

Over the years, Dr. Baehr's ministry has had impressive results. When MOVIEGUIDE® started in 1985, only 6 percent of the movies were aimed at families; today, more than 35 percent of the movies released in theaters are aimed at families. Those family-friendly movies grossed an average 200 percent higher than movies aimed at the adult marketplace. In 1991, the year before Dr. Baehr began analyzing box office statistics for the Annual Faith and Values Awards Gala, the number of major movies with at least some Christian-friendly content was only twenty-seven. In 2013 and 2014, more than 60 percent of the movies analyzed contained at least some Christian-friendly content, an increase of 511 percent. Since the annual report to the entertainment industry began, the average domestic earnings of movies with strong Christian content and values have increased from $21.14 million per movie to $90.78 million, a 329 percent increase—and that does not include what such movies earn overseas or on home video.

The effectiveness of this ministry is quite astounding. MOVIEGUIDE® is clearly helping create a shining culture of truth and beauty in an industry often tarnished by degrading depictions of extreme violence and depraved behavior. In 1854, Alexandre Dumas, the author of *The Three Musketeers* and *The Count of Monte Cristo*, reportedly introduced the proverb, "Nothing succeeds like success." Now, 160 years later, Christians are seeing the truth of this saying. Faith-based movies have been among the top five at the box office every week, sometimes at number 1, 2, or 3. Recent examples include *Son of God, God's Not Dead,* and *Heaven Is for Real.*

In addition, a faith-friendly film such as the science fiction movie *Divergent* (written by a Christian and featuring Christian themes) led the box office the weekend it opened. The second entry of Marvel Studios' Captain America movie series, *The Winter Soldier,* developed a Christian theme, showing the hero risking his life to save "a lost sheep" and undergoing a symbolic baptism, itself a metaphor of death and resurrection. All this good news is, to a large degree, the result of God's calling the son of 1930s Hollywood stars to redeem the mass media of entertainment. Here is the Ted Baehr story:

In 1946, at the height of the Golden Age of Hollywood, I was born to Theodore Baehr (whose stage name was Robert "Tex" Allen) and Evelyn Peirce. Both of my parents were successful stage, screen, and television actors. For example, along with the Golden Age Westerns featured in his stage name, such as *The Revenge Rider* (1935) and *The Unknown Ranger* (1936), my father starred or was the romantic juvenile lead in such noted films as the archetypal serial *The Perils of Pauline* (1934), Joseph Von Sternberg's version of Dostoyevsky's *Crime and Punishment,* and the classic screwball comedy *The Awful Truth* with Irene Dunne and Cary Grant (1937).

Growing up in New York with extended times in Hollywood and on location with movie productions in which my father was acting, I followed reluctantly in my parents' footprints, performing in commercials, movies, television, and on stage, but I was neither fond of waiting in the background nor of being in front of the camera.

What I did enjoy from a very, very young age was living the high life, which included everything from horse shows to fancy trips to self-indulgence. After my mother died in 1960, when I was a young teenager, I renounced the concept that I thought was God and dove completely into a sordid life of drugs and looking for love (of course, "in all the wrong places").

I even tried to bring as many people as I could with me on the road to perdition by throwing parties with lethal concoctions, from which some never recovered and ended their precious lives. The fun was always appealing and always a mirage.

After studying abroad, I graduated with high distinction in comparative literature and as a Rufus Choate Scholar from Dartmouth College. I then received the Juris Doctor from New York University School of Law, where I served as the editor of the NYU Law School newspaper, editor of the *Drug Law Review*, and editor of the *Environmental Law Review*. At the same time, I was involved in radical causes, including leading the Law School Coalition to End the War in Vietnam, the National Lawyers Guild, and starting the environmental movement at the US Attorney's office in the southern district of New York and the environmental studies at New York University Law, motivated by a particular disdain for big business.

In 1975, God rescued me from the bondage to sin. I had begun financing independent movies for Canon Films when an older friend who had come to know Jesus Christ at the Billy Graham Crusade in New York City in 1957 suggested that I read the Bible to show her what was wrong with it. Reading God's word in order to refute it changed my perspective both professionally and personally. God rescued me. Suddenly, life made sense. Chasing after empty promises lost its appeal. Hedonism relinquished its hold on me by God's grace alone. There was no withdrawal from stopping the addictions, only the peace that comes from a personal encounter with Jesus Christ. Immediately, I was compelled to marry my beloved. The week before the wedding, a friend asked me if I wanted to accept Jesus Christ as my Lord and Savior and be filled with His Holy Spirit. I did. Filled with the Holy Spirit through my new faith in Jesus Christ, I decided to attend seminary at the Institute of Theology at the Cathedral of St. John the Divine.

To support myself through seminary, I was offered a position miraculously as the director of the television center at the City University of New York (CUNY) and was hired at the same time to head the television and radio ministry of Trinity Church at Broadway and Wall Street.

During my tenure at CUNY, I worked closely with academia, researching the impact of the media. I joined with more than sixty professors to develop and test the first intergenerational media literacy course. Being troubled by my previous financing of salacious and violent movies, I started the Good News Communications ministry in 1978 to redeem the mass media of entertainment. Again, miraculously, I was elected president of the Episcopal Radio and Television Foundation in 1979 and began conceptualizing another ministry, the

Christian Film and Television Commission. During my tenure, the Episcopal Radio and Television Foundation won an Emmy Award for Best Animated Special for *The Chronicles of Narnia: The Lion, the Witch, and the Wardrobe*, which aired on the Columbia Broadcasting System (CBS) and was watched by more than 37 million viewers. I was nominated for another Emmy Award for one of the programs in the Public Broadcasting System (PBS) Perspectives Series: *War and Peace*, for which I served as the executive producer, creative director, and host.

In 1983, while I was serving on the communications board of the National Council of Churches and working with National Religious Broadcasters, the great movie producer Ken Wales (*The Pink Panther*, *Christy*, and *Amazing Grace*) introduced me to George Heimrich and his work at the Protestant Film Office. Ken and George informed me about the history of the church film offices and the Motion Picture Production Code that had been used to improve movie content. George recounted the story of the breakdown of morality in the entertainment industry. He said that part of the reason for the breakdown of morality in movies and television today, and in the culture at large, is that people of faith retreated from being salt and light in the culture.

From 1933 to 1966, Christians comprised one of the predominant forces in Hollywood. During that period, the Roman Catholic Legion of Decency and the Protestant Film Commission (which started several years after the Legion of Decency) read every script to ensure that movies represented the largest possible audience by adhering to high standards of decency. As a result, *Mr. Smith Goes to Washington*, *It's a Wonderful Life*, and *The Bells of St. Mary's* rang out across the land. It had taken ten years and God's grace acting through three dedicated Christian men to position God's people as such a powerful moral influence on Hollywood. As the documentary *Hollywood Uncensored* all too clearly demonstrates, in 1933, prior to the involvement of these Christians, American movies were morally bankrupt—full of nudity, perversity, and violence. From 1922 to 1933, churchgoing men and women tried everything, including censorship boards, to influence Hollywood to make wholesome entertainment. Nothing succeeded until Christians volunteered to work alongside the Hollywood studios to help them reach the largest possible audience.

When the Protestant Film Office closed its advocacy offices in Hollywood in 1966 (in spite of many pleas to continue by the top

Hollywood entertainment industry executives), not only did it open the floodgates to violence (*The Wild Bunch*), sex and Satanism (*Rosemary's Baby*), and perverse anti-religious bigotry (*Midnight Cowboy*), it also caused a severe drop in movie attendance from 44 million tickets sold per week to about 17 million. Inspired by George Heimrich and George's beloved wife, Lucille, I began contacting prominent members of the entertainment industry and formed the Christian Film and Television Commission ministry and, in 1985, MOVIEGUIDE®: A Family Guide to Movies and Entertainment.

In his will, George Heimrich donated his Protestant Film Office files to the Good News Communications, where they are now archived. My ministry uses the same vision for positive change to redeem the values of the mass media of entertainment according to biblical principles by influencing key entertainment executives to adopt higher moral standards and by informing and equipping the public, especially parents with children and extended families. Based on these principles, MOVIEGUIDE® has been analyzing movies in depth since 1985. Over the years, we have developed a comprehensive method that helps us pinpoint which movies will succeed and why.

Adam Smith, the father of free-market economics, broke with the tradition of his peers not by studying failure, but by studying success. In the process, he came up with the most successful economic model ever. This is exactly what MOVIEGUIDE® tries to do.

To understand the economic viability of a movie, we look at its entertainment and artistic value and then, beyond that, at its production value, content, worldview, philosophy, theology, politics, economics, genre, themes, characters, and actors. Each film is viewed aesthetically, thematically, morally, biblically, cognitively, and spiritually in more than 150 different categories. Through its annual analysis, MOVIEGUIDE® has consistently chosen 25 to 40 percent of the winners at the box office, whereas other groups and critics have consistently chosen only zero to 8 percent of the winners. In 2013, 52 percent of our award winners were among the top twenty-five movies at the box office in the United States and Canada. MOVIEGUIDE® has found that movies that adhere to traditional Christian values and biblical morality consistently outperform all other categories. We bring this comprehensive system to bear on film finance to help give a better experience to those who want to improve the entertainment industry. Box-office figures are the truest measure of what the public chooses to see in movies. For instance, in 2013, nine of MOVIEGUIDE®'s top picks for best family movies and best movies for mature audiences made it into the top ten movies at the box office for North America—more than ever before! In contrast to this, none—or, at most, only two—of the top choices of most other major film critics made it into the top ten. The MOVIEGUIDE® critics and judges' prognostications were also more accurate that those of such renowned critic associations as the American Film Institute, National Board of Review, and Broadcast Film Critics.

To do all these things properly not only takes a knowledge of basic critical standards and movies, including understanding the history of movies and film theory, but also involves a philosophical knowledge that takes into account what has been called the queen, or handmaiden, of philosophy: theology. That is the level of knowledge I expect of the editors and writers who work at MOVIEGUIDE®, and that is the level of knowledge that all Christians should demand from MOVIEGUIDE® and from all other Christian leaders in the burgeoning mission field of mass media ministries.

Parents, children, and other moviegoers write us to say that they trust MOVIEGUIDE®, because we use these comprehensive critical tools to review movies. Entertainment industry executives also call to tell us how helpful and important our reviews are because we give them accurate, verifiable information based on objective standards, not subjective whims. A Wheaton College graduate told us, "College students raised with MOVIEGUIDE® grew in discernment and Christian faith. Those I saw raised with other so-called faith-based reviews drifted into theological and moral liberalism." The good news is that concerned and discerning moviegoers trust MOVIEGUIDE®, demonstrated by the fact that our website, movieguide.org, has more than 15 million hits per month and is still growing. In summary, MOVIEGUIDE®'s aesthetic standards match the aesthetic standards of the general movie-going public; the movies we commend do much better at the box office. Thus, the better the quality rating from MOVIEGUIDE®, the more money a film made at the box office. Also, our MOVIEGUIDE® awards gala tends to pick the best movies appearing in the top ten and top twenty-five at the box office and at the home video store, while many other film critics are picking the worst movies seen by the fewest number of people.

As a result of an unexpected and miraculous telephone conversation with Sir John Templeton, beginning in 1988, the Christian Film and Television Commission ministry initiated the Annual MOVIEGUIDE® Faith and Values Awards Gala and Report to the Entertainment Industry in 1992 in Los Angeles. The gala now features two prestigious $100,000 Epiphany Prizes for the most inspiring movie and TV program each year, supported by a grant from the John Templeton Foundation, rewarding the movie and the television program that help people know God and understand him better. Other prizes include the Faith and Freedom Award for promoting positive faith and values; the $50,000 Kairos Prize for spiritually uplifting screenplays by first-time and beginning screenwriters, again supported by a grant from the John Templeton Foundation; the $50,000 Chronos Prize for spiritually uplifting screenplays by established screenwriters, supported by the John Templeton Foundation; the annual Grace Award for the most inspiring performances in movies and television, given to the two actors whose performances best display God's grace and mercy toward us as human beings; the MOVIEGUIDE® Teddy "The Good News" Bear Award for the ten best movies for families, and the MOVIEGUIDE® Papa Bear Award for the ten best movies for mature audiences. We seek to acknowledge movies, TV programs, and actors truly deserving of praise and those persons responsible for bringing them to the screen. To add glamour to the event, actors and actresses are invited to host and to present the awards. Music and entertainment are also added to make it a memorable event. We even hand out Bibles and other redemptive materials to make certain we carry out our mission to reach Hollywood for Christ. Within this context of elegance, I present MOVIEGUIDE®'s *Report to the Entertainment Industry.* Through careful analysis of box office figures and MOVIEGUIDE® criteria on all the major movies released (nearly three hundred each year) by the six studios controlling the industry, I present valuable and unique information to the highest-level Hollywood leaders through a high-impact report.

The purpose of the gala and the report is:

- To encourage filmmakers to continue to make movies with moral and spiritually uplifting values
- To share the concerns of the majority of the American public in regard to the negative influences of today's movies

- To present an in-depth study of annual movie box-office receipts and not only dispel myths that extreme sex, violence, and nudity sells, but also show that family movies and movies with morally uplifting, Christian values and positive Christian content make the most money by far.

By God's grace, this *Report to the Entertainment Industry* is having an impact. When we started MOVIEGUIDE® in 1985, the major studios in Hollywood released few movies with any positive Christian content or values—less than 3 percent! By the time we started the annual gala and report in 1992 and 1993, however, there were 27 such movies, or about 10.38 percent of the market share. Twenty-two years later, in 2013, at least 179, or 65.57 percent, of the movies released by the movie industry contained at least some positive Christian, redemptive content. This is a numerical increase of almost 563 percent and a percentage increase of nearly 532 percent! Also, when we started in 1985, less than 6 percent of the major movies were aimed at families. In the past several years, movies marketed to families have increased to nearly 40 percent of the top movies released in local movie theaters. Finally, when we started in 1985, there were only about one or two movies being made with strong, explicit Christian content or values, but, now, there are sixty-five or more such movies each year! That is at least a 3,150 percent increase.

The former chairman of a major Hollywood studio told me he attributed all these positive shifts directly to MOVIEGUIDE®'s influence as well as the Christian Film and Television Commission's box office analysis and *Annual Report to the Entertainment Industry*. Many major movie studios now have a Christian, faith-based film division, and several studios are producing major movies with strong and overt Christian or biblical content. Also, now, all the major studios, not just Disney, are creating movies for young children and families. Additionally, there is an increasing number of positive faith-based and family-friendly independent films, even though these movies do not garner a significant share of the box office, which is dominated by the major entertainment industry studios.

This does not mean, of course, that the studios are not making morally bad and sadistically violent movies any more, but it does mean there are fewer and fewer of such bad movies and an increasing number of good ones. It is our prayer that the movie industry will make more and more commendable movies and remove offensive elements from all of them.

All along the way, we have been helping and encouraging Christian filmmakers and even non-Christian filmmakers to put faith-based, family-friendly content in their scripts, movies, and television shows and improve their storytelling abilities so they can reach and influence as many people toward the good as possible.

By God's grace, we have seen an explosion of inspiring, faith-friendly family movies being produced, including some of the potential Epiphany nominees listed above. Many of these movies are animated and reach the top of the box office charts, such as *Frozen*, which MOVIEGUIDE® picked as the best movie for families in 2013. *Frozen* promotes a Christian, biblical view of love and has grossed more than $1.16 billion worldwide so far as of this writing. The success of faith-based and faith-friendly movies and television shows such as *Son of God*, *Heaven Is for Real*, *God's Not Dead*, *The Bible*, *Duck Dynasty*, *Frozen*, *Captain America: The Winter Soldier*, *Noah*, *Despicable Me 2*, and *The Blind Side* is no fluke. It is a miracle from God.

When Christians abandon the mass media, they abandon their culture and their compatriots. When Christians become involved in the mass media, God honors that commitment with success.

The mass media creates the culture that shapes the hearts and minds of children and teenagers. By the time they reach seventeen, average children will have spent up to 60,000 hours or more with the mass media, according to recent figures from the Motion Picture Association of America, the Kaiser Family Foundation, the US Census Bureau, and other groups—but only 800 hours in church, if they attend a church service once every week. The goal of MOVIEGUIDE® and the Christian Film and Television Commission is to redeem the values of the mass media and, thereby, redeem the character of children and teenagers, our future leaders. That is the mandate God has given this ministry.

Here are some developments that have encouraged us in our ministry:

- In the ten years from 2004–2013, movies with very strong Christian, redemptive worldviews have averaged $74.89 million at the North American box office, up from $21.14 million in 1995, the year we began the Epiphany Prize competition for most inspiring movie of the year (a 254 percent increase).

- In 2013 alone, movies released with very strong Christian worldviews averaged $87,073,022, generating ticket sales of about $10,710,089 per movie, totaling $1,567,314,394 for all eighteen movies with very strong Christian worldviews, or about 192,781,598 ticket sales (the average ticket price in 2013 was $8.13). And this doesn't include what such movies earned in 2014, 2015, and so on. (There are always a few movies with very strong Christian, redemptive worldviews at the end of the year, such as *Frozen* or *Les Miserables*, that earn millions after the New Year's holiday.)

The above numbers only calculate the cost and cost effectiveness for what is called the domestic theatrical box office in the United States and Canada. They do not include box office figures overseas or home video sales figures.

Between 1991 and 2013, the number of movies with at least some positive Christian content has increased from 10.38 percent of all major movies to nearly two-thirds, 65.57 percent, an increase of 532 percent. This impact is not only evident in the big blockbuster or "tent pole" movies released by the top decision makers and opinion leaders in Hollywood, it also affects the small, independent movies distributed by these key players in Hollywood.

Thus, in the wake of the success of such Christian, redemptive blockbusters such as *The Passion of the Christ*, *The Chronicles of Narnia* movies, and *The Lord of the Rings* movies, two of the top three small, independent movies in limited release at the box office from 2007 through 2013 were also Christian: *Fireproof*, with $33.46 million in earnings in the United States and Canada, and *Amazing Grace*, with $21.25 million in earnings. MOVIEGUIDE®'s support of such movies is clearly making a big difference.

The success of these independent films led to Christian movies such as *Soul Surfer* (earning $43.85 million) and *Courageous* (earning $34.52 million), released in more than 2,200 and 1,200 theatres domestically in 2011, respectively. Consequently, in 2014, the Christian movie *Heaven Is for Real* earned $90.8 million, with *God's Not Dead* and *Son of God* not far behind with $60.7 million and $59.7 million, respectively.

In fact, dollar for dollar, *God's Not Dead* is now one of the five most successful independent movies ever produced.

Since the mass media creates the culture that shapes the hearts and minds of future generations—our children and grandchildren—ministries like MOVIEGUIDE® and the Christian Film and Television Commission, including the annual Faith and Values Awards Gala and *Report to the Entertainment Industry*, are indispensable and deserve the support of every concerned citizen and group that cares about the future of our children and grandchildren, the future of the United States, and the future of the whole world.

When Hollywood releases more movies like *Captain America: Winter Soldier*, *God's Not Dead*, *Heaven Is for Real*, and *Son of God*, many children living in a vast cultural wasteland are given new hope in Jesus Christ. Clearly, the entire world needs more movies like these and fewer or no movies that inspire vulgarity, violence, and sex outside of marriage. That is why our mission is focused on inspiring key people in Hollywood to make morally and aesthetically good movies.

In 2013, studios were inspired to put at least some positive Christian content in nearly 66 percent of Hollywood's major theatrical movie releases. In fact, 68 percent of the top twenty-five movies at the box office actually had strong or very strong Christian, biblical, redemptive, or moral worldviews, while none of the top ten movies at the box office, either in North America or overseas, was R-rated. Also, the stronger the Christian content, the more money a movie made at the box office. Finally, since the awards gala began in the early 1990s, the percentage of major motion pictures with at least some positive Christian content, including positive references to Jesus or the New Testament, has gone from 10 percent to nearly two-thirds of the major movies released, from only 10.38 percent in 1991 to 65.57 percent in 2013! This is a 532 percent increase!

Since the John Templeton Foundation and MOVIEGUIDE® together have been sponsoring the Epiphany Prize for most inspiring movies, motion pictures with very strong Christian content have gone from earning only $21.14 million per movie to about $90 million or more per movie each year, with each movie reaching an average of at least 11.4 million people. A clear example of such success is *The Blind Side*, the strongest Christian blockbuster movie within a five-year span.

- In 42, Branch Rickey told Jackie Robinson that Jesus Christ was the strongest man who ever lived because he was strong enough to turn the other cheek.

- Tony Stark in *Iron Man 3* talked about people going to heaven and hell and he took the villains to church.

- Clark Kent, aka Superman, went to church to confess and, under the guise of Superman, manifested many Christological, allegorical characteristics in *Man of Steel*.

- Love and self-sacrifice became the spiritual weapons against socialist tyranny in *The Hunger Games: Catching Fire*.

- Bilbo the humble Hobbit, Dwarf King Thorin, and their twelve dwarf companions confronted the evil dragon who had seized the kingdom of the dwarves in the visual trilogy adaptation of the devout Roman Catholic Christian J. R. R. Tolkien's *The Hobbit*, as Gandalf brought the light to fight the evil necromancer who was conquering the world under the cover of darkness (despite good people ignoring what was happening).

- Gru found love thanks to the prayers of his adopted daughters in *Despicable Me 2*.

- Christian hymns lifting up Jesus Christ were sung in Old Norse, as real and Christian self-sacrifice triumphed in *Frozen*.

- Free enterprise, an aspect of the Protestant work ethic, was lauded in *Monsters University* and *Turbo*, as Mike and Sulley worked their way up the ladder of success from the mailroom and Tito saved the taco stand he owns with his brother by creating and executing a well-conceived marketing plan.

- Oscar Diggs, the future Wizard of Oz, confessed and cried to God for help in *Oz, The Great and Powerful*.

- Stranded in space, NASA astronaut Dr. Ryan Stone asked for prayer and help from God while looking at a picture of Jesus Christ carrying a child in *Gravity*.

- Thor learned from his father, Odin, that they are not gods, but mortal, in *Thor: The Dark World*.

- *The Croods* took a leap of faith to follow the Light.

- *Captain Phillips* was willing to sacrifice his life to save his crew.
- The prodigal daughter came home to her family and Jesus Christ in *Grace Unplugged*.
- *Jack the Giant Slayer* discussed heaven and hell, finding God, obeying God, and wanting to find God, while monks, king, queen, princess, and others prayed to God and monks fashioned a crown of glory to defeat evil (1 Pet 5:4).
- A young outcast teenage boy found salvation watching a church *Black Nativity* Christmas musical.

Movies with very strong Christian, redemptive, biblical, and moral content and values also did much better at the box office in 2013 than movies with excessive or graphic foul language, sex, nudity, violence, alcohol use, and illegal substance abuse. Thus, movies with strong biblical and Christian worldviews and content were some very big moneymakers.

Statistically, 100 percent of the top ten movies in the US and Canada in 2013 had strong or very strong Christian, redemptive, moral, or biblical content and worldviews. Also, 100 percent of the top ten movies overseas had strong or very strong Christian, redemptive, biblical, and/or moral worldviews, earning 100 percent of $4.951 billion. Finally, 80 percent of top ten home video sales in 2013 mentioned by the Digital Entertainment Group in its preliminary study in early January were honored by MOVIEGUIDE®'s Awards Gala.

There were, however, some new lows in filmmaking in 2013, such as the anti-free-market *Inequality for All* and *The Wolf of Wall Street*, which also featured perverse sex; *White House Down*, which accused Christians of terrorism; and *Jackass Presents: Bad Grandpa*, which presented an abhorrent role model. A couple of these movies made a lot of money, but most of them flopped.

Assessing the major movies released by the entertainment industry in 2013, we noticed that positive acceptability ratings from MOVIEGUIDE® (+1 to +4) earned about twice as much money as those with negative acceptability ratings (−1 to −4). This statistic means that the most family-friendly movies in 2013 were also the most successful movies of the year. Also, movies with the most positive acceptability ratings from MOVIEGUIDE® (+1 to +4) earned more than three times as much money as those with the worst ratings (−4). In addition, R-rated movies made less money than movies with other ratings. According to an eighteen-year old study by *The Numbers*, G-rated movies earn more than twice as much per movie as R-rated movies. Furthermore, since the annual MOVIEGUIDE® Faith and Values Awards Gala and *Report to the Entertainment Industry* began, the percentage of movies with at least some positive Christian biblical and/or moral content has increased overall from an average of 18.27 percent in 1991 to an average of 74.55 percent in 2013, a 308 percent increase. Major Hollywood executives are finally getting the message that movies with positive Christian moral, biblical, redemptive content are great for business.

According to *The Numbers* website, the ten top home video sales of their year included *Despicable Me 2*, *Monsters University*, *Wreck It Ralph*, *The Hobbit: An Unexpected Journey*, *Fast and Furious 6*, *The Little Mermaid*, Part 2 of *The Twilight Saga: Breaking Dawn*, *Skyfall*, *Man of Steel*, and *Hotel Transylvania*. Out of those ten titles, 80 percent contained strong or very strong Christian, redemptive, biblical, or moral content.

In MOVIEGUIDE®'s 2012 *Report to the Entertainment Industry*, we found that 72 percent of the top twenty-five home video sales in 2012 had strong or very strong Christian, redemptive, biblical, moral, and/or heroic (good conquering evil) content.

In 2013, *The Bible*, one of the most Christian television programs ever produced in the United States, earned more than $43.44 million on home video, making it the top-earning TV program on home video that year. These figures show that the vast majority of DVD buyers and watchers prefer family-friendly movies containing strong Christian, moral values and biblical principles.

Hollywood can't afford to ignore the 2.376 billion Christians around the world, including America's 238.61 million Christians, the 212.6 million people in America who say they have a personal relationship with Jesus, the 149.75 million Americans who say they go to church monthly or more, and the 123.75 million or so Americans, including children and teenagers, who go to church weekly. Neither can Christians afford to ignore the influence that Hollywood has on our children and grandchildren and on the society in which they live. This is a mission we cannot afford to abandon.

The MOVIEGUIDE® staff prays that God will raise up people in the body of Christ who will support our vision and join the movement to clean the screens. If we want to turn society right-side up, we have to stop simply discussing worldviews and be willing to act on a Christian worldview and disciple the nations, as Jesus commanded us. That action requires not only a personal faith in the gospel of Jesus Christ, it also requires a commitment to the values that Jesus and his disciples taught in the New Testament, empowered by the baptism of the Holy Spirit through Jesus Christ, as happened on Pentecost in chapter two of the Book of Acts and as described elsewhere in the New Testament Scriptures.

We can turn the perverse culture right-side up. A small group of Christians did just that in England during the early 1800s. Led by William Wilberforce, John Newton, and other Christians, they brought revival to England, which reformed faith and values throughout the fabric of their society.

By God's grace, acting on a consistent biblical view of the world, our small team at the Christian Film and Television Commission has helped to turn a significant portion of the entertainment industry right-side up. A former head of one of the six top Hollywood studios once told us personally, "You have shown through your *Report to the Entertainment Industry* that producing good movies is morally responsible and financially lucrative." We could not have done this, however, without properly understanding and using the values taught in Scripture, nor without the power of the Holy Spirit that comes through faith and trust in our Lord and Savior, Jesus Christ. We welcome and greatly appreciate your support in helping us to carry out this mission to redeem the values, as well as the worldviews, of the mass media of entertainment. Together, with God's help and direction, we can ensure that the good, the true, and the beautiful will continue to spread throughout Hollywood and throughout the nations.

Our MOVIEGUIDE® television program has improved considerably and we upload small video reports to many different sites, including movieguide.org. The two-minute MOVIEGUIDE® TV program is carried around the world, however, and so are our two-minute and five-minute MOVIEGUIDE® radio programs. Our outlets for all these programs have grown tremendously. In fact, a major cable network is currently running the television program. Every episode mixes our weekly movie reviews with exclusive interviews with the filmmakers, family tips on media wisdom, and insights on current cultural events.

In a pluralistic society where some of the mass media water down absolute moral truths, promote sexual hedonism, push rampant liberalism, and constantly attack the gospel of Jesus Christ, the need for teaching media wisdom is absolutely essential. Our *The Culture-Wise Family* book and six-week DVD course provides just that. We at MOVIEGUIDE® are completely dedicated to protecting your children and grandchildren from the risks and dangers of the media of entertainment.

Even though you and I have seen the number of movies and other entertainment with positive, morally uplifting, Christian content increase tremendously in the past thirty years, we have also witnessed an increase in special interest groups that would seek to kill, steal, and destroy the Christian moorings of our nation. These groups work tirelessly to put more graphic violence, more explicit sex, more same-sex content, and more corruption into our entertainment media. Wise viewers do not need me to remind them how negatively these harmful elements affect your children and grandchildren. Even though these groups work to change your children's thinking, at MOVIEGUIDE®, we work to protect your children and grandchildren from the harmful effects of the media. As our Lord Jesus said, "Whoever causes the downfall of one of these little ones who believes in me—it would be better for him if a heavy millstone were hung around his neck and he were drowned in the depths of the sea!" (Matt 18:6 CSB). You and I must oppose this vicious onslaught against our children. If we do not take a stand for righteousness in order to protect them, then we will be as responsible for our children's downfall as those who attack and destroy our children's hope and faith. As Proverbs 25:26 warns, "If the godly give in to the wicked, it's like polluting a fountain or muddying a spring" (NLT).

As a result of our work, an increasing number of entertainment companies are now asking us to become active in guiding their future. As Dave Clark said to me several times, "Never have so few done so much with so little." That, of course, is because God is doing it, and we are just participating in His Grace, and because supporters have donated time, energy, and resources to the Christian Film and Television Commission and MOVIEGUIDE® to redeem the values of the mass media.

BOOKS: EQUIPPING FAMILIES AND FAITHFUL INDIVIDUALS

How to Succeed in Hollywood (without Losing Your Soul)

For everything you wanted to know about making or understanding faithful, blockbuster, mass media entertainment, a great place to start is learning from those who are making it in Hollywood and are making a difference. *How to Succeed in Hollywood (without Losing Your Soul)* will show you how to use your God-given and God-ordained gifts and talents to make significant creative contributions to the entertainment world.

Learn from industry professionals—the brightest and best people of faith in the entertainment industry—how they developed their screenwriting, acting, directing, producing, and behind-the-scenes interests to make Hollywood and the world a better place.

The contributors you will read include:

- Richard Cook, former chairman of Walt Disney Pictures
- Bill Fay, executive producer of many movies, including *Independence Day* and *The Patriot*
- Al Kasha, Academy Award–winning songwriter and composer for many movies and television programs, including *The Poseidon Adventure*, *The Towering Inferno*, and *The Rugrats Go Wild!*
- Andrew Stanton, the scriptwriter for *Toy Story*, *Toy Story II*, *A Bug's Life*, *Monsters Inc.*, and *Finding Nemo* (which he also directed and produced).

The Culture-Wise Family

The Culture-Wise Family: Upholding Christian Values in a Mass Media World by Pat Boone and me is a clear, concise, comprehensive guide to becoming more than overcomers in the midst of an increasingly toxic culture. While most books focus on the almost apocalyptic problems facing believers in an increasingly neopagan society with its secular news theology and fear mantra, "If it bleeds, it leads," *The Culture-Wise Family* helps concerned readers understand the problems and develop discernment and wisdom. This wisdom guides them to be able to live within the neopagan world without being corrupted by it, while being also able to lead others out of the darkness into the transformational light and truth of the gospel of Jesus Christ.

Building on the proven principles presented in the related *Media-Wise Family* book, tapes, and videos, *The Culture-Wise Family* helps the reader understand the social ills we face from a biblical perspective and how to be media-wise in the midst of the conflicting and often toxic messages from the mass media of entertainment and contemporary culture. It looks beyond the so-called culture wars to help readers acquire the skills to recognize and decipher what is being communicated to them. It is a helpful book that every parent, teacher, and person of faith and values will want to read and reread.

The Culture-Wise Family helps Christians understand the clash of worldviews, the influence of the entertainment industry, and how to develop media wisdom. Designed to be more than just another book about the media and the culture, this study aims at helping turn parents' and children's hearts away from the negative and addictive influences bombarding them and bending their hearts toward God and family. Readers learn step by step how to teach their children to develop discernment and understanding about movies, television, electronic games, and other media of entertainment and communication. This will enable children to use and enjoy entertainment media without succumbing to the vain imaginings and temptations of the media mindset. The approach in *The Culture-Wise Family* has been tested on children and parents for more than two decades, and more than 90 percent of those who have been taught this method of discernment have found it effective.

The Amazing Grace of Freedom: In the Life, Times, and Movie of William Wilberforce

The Amazing Grace of Freedom by Susan and Ken Wales and me is a high-quality, faith-enriching, inspirational coffee-table book. It is filled with profound, enlightening, inspiring, and discerning information and stories about Wilberforce, including articles and interviews with leading Wilberforce scholars focused on faith in action and the need for Christian influence in addressing social issues today. The book enlightens readers and the audience about the influence of Wilberforce then and now while inspiring readers to look at how they, too, can grow in faith, knowledge, and understanding. Coauthor Ken Wales produced the movie *Amazing Grace*, which brings to life the extraordinary impact and influence of William Wilberforce on our culture. Our book, *The Amazing Grace of Freedom: In the Life, Times, and Movie of William Wilberforce*, helps the reader understand the pivotal and powerful faith aspect of the story: how Wilberforce's faith transformed his life and how God's grace can transform the reader's life.

Above all, the story is a testament of how one person can make a difference in the world when called by God. *The Amazing Grace of Freedom* shows that you can change the world. Whether you are six or sixty, rich or poor, sick or healthy, if you have been called to fight the good fight for truth, justice, faith, and values, you can be more than a conqueror through Jesus Christ who loves you so much. A heroic Christian reformer who illustrates the power of one plus God in an amazing way, William Wilberforce, who lived from 1759 to 1833, suffered mightily all his life from painfully poor eyesight, serious digestive problems, and a very weak spine. Even so, when he came to faith in Jesus Christ, he dedicated himself to, and succeeded in, stopping the lucrative slave trade and reforming the morals of a debauched society. William Wilberforce and his small group of reformer friends, joining many other saints throughout history, demonstrated not simply what they themselves could do, but what anyone can and will do if empowered by God's call and his Spirit.

Narnia Beckons

Narnia Beckons is a beautiful gift book that will help you and your families understand *The Lion, the Witch, and the Wardrobe*. With articles by the best C. S. Lewis scholars, the response to *Narnia Beckons* has been overwhelming:

> An elegant coffee-table book rich with photos related to Lewis's stories. . . . This is a compilation of essays on his entire life. There are rare photographs of his English childhood haunts and profiles of family and friends. Interspersed throughout are rich illustrations and back stories of his brilliant characters, special interviews with a variety of associates, and a unique look at the

television and film adaptations of *The Lion, the Witch, and the Wardrobe*. (Jean Peerenboom, *Green Bay Press-Gazette*)[1]

Anyone who is reading any of the Narnia books of C.S. Lewis, or is viewing a film of one of his works, will be greatly blessed and enlightened by the wonderful insights and information of *Narnia Beckons*. I highly recommend it to you. (Paul Cedar, chairman and CEO, Mission America Coalition)

I feel that *Narnia Beckons* is one of the most beautiful, well written and necessary books of our time. I wish everyone could have a copy. I don't like it, I love it! Bravo!" (Susan Stafford, former Wheel of Fortune hostess, chaplain, and psychologist)

When my kids were younger, we took turns reading the *Chronicles of Narnia* while we traveled. We still remember those times. I wish this book would have been available to us in those days to help us with the deeper, theological insights. I highly recommend *Narnia Beckons* to every person who is reading, or has read *The Lion, the Witch, and the Wardrobe*, or who has seen the movie versions. (Jerry Rose, president and CEO, Total Living Network)

Thank you so very much for your new book, *Narnia Beckons*! My family and I have been devouring and discussing it enthusiastically. My oldest daughter, Andrea, has read all of the *Chronicles of Narnia*, and I have read some of them aloud to our younger children. With the coming of the new film, your book has been a tremendous blessing in bringing some of the rich Christian symbolism and deeper messages of C.S. Lewis's works back into focus. The release of *The Lion, the Witch, and the Wardrobe* has provided us with a wonderful evangelistic tool, as we are able to speak to our friends, neighbors, and colleagues of the deeper significance and meaning of Christ, the devil, and the Bible. We always greatly appreciate MOVIEGUIDE®, and each of your books has better equipped us to be more selective and discerning, and to use films as springboards for evangelistic conversations with our neighbors. May the Lord continue to bless, guide, and multiply the effectiveness of the Christian Film and Television Commission. We are so very grateful that you are

---

1. Jean Peerenboom, "New Books Chronicle Works of C.S. Lewis," Green Bay Press-Gazette, Green Bay, WI, 20 Nov 2005. Online: http://archive.greenbaypress-gazette.com/article/20051120/GPG07/511200437/Jean-Peerenboom-column-New-books-chronicle-works-C-S-Lewis, accessed 27 Nov 2015.

our missionary to Hollywood. (Peter Hammond, founder and director, Frontline Fellowship, South Africa)

I teach kids who come from all parts of the globe. Many have little or no Christian background in their lives. Recently, I taught a class of students who were given the assignment to read C.S. Lewis's *The Lion, the Witch, and the Wardrobe*. Their thirst to learn challenged me. I wanted to give them something more than just the text, and so I brought *Narnia Beckons: C.S. Lewis's The Lion, the Witch, and the Wardrobe—and Beyond* to class with me. Written by Dr. Ted Baehr and James Baehr, *Narnia Beckons* is a short, clear, and beautiful elaboration of C.S. Lewis as an author and of the Narnia series. By using the Baehrs' explanations, I was able to show some of the deeper meanings within Lewis's masterpiece, *The Lion, the Witch, and the Wardrobe*. Their pictorial and verbal illustrations of characters supplemented Lewis's words far better than I ever could. The authors explore many of the didactic themes of *The Lion, the Witch, and the Wardrobe* in a way that attracts adults and students alike. While using this book, I had the opportunity not only to help my students improve their reading skills, but also to show these kids the beauty of the gospel. To my great joy, one of the students I had from China became so interested in what she had read that she then proceeded to read *The Magician's Nephew* and *The Screwtape Letters* on her own time. I value my copy of *Narnia Beckons* over most of the other books in my library. I have recommended it to other teachers and will continue to do so. If ever I have the opportunity to teach from the Narnia series again, I plan to make sure that my copy of *Narnia Beckons* is close by. (Rosemary Thoburn, dean/teacher at Fairfax Christian Academy and author of *Exploring Narnia in the Classroom*)

Frodo and Harry

There is a tremendous amount of confusion in the discussions regarding the Harry Potter movies versus *The Lord of the Rings* movies. *Frodo and Harry: The Lord of the Rings versus Harry Potter* will help people of faith and values understand the arguments and the differences between the two movie series adapted from popular literary works. *Frodo and Harry* provides audiences with the tools not only to exercise discernment, but also to make wise choices. The book contrasts the fictional "real world" of *The Lord of the Rings* with the nominalistic "occult world" of Harry

Potter. The book helps the audience ask the right questions and understand that *The Lord of the Rings* focuses on honor, truth, loyalty, and valor, whereas Harry Potter suggests that evil is not really evil, actions do not have real consequences, and rebellious behavior, including lying and subversion, are to be commended. Considering the influence that both of these works have had on our culture, *Frodo and Harry* is an extremely important and helpful tool for families and churches, as well as an interesting and captivating read in its own right.

Faith in God and Generals

Faith in God and Generals will help you understand the true story behind the epic feature film *God and Generals*. It is filled with accounts of the key historical figures in the movie. In effect, *Faith in God and Generals* presents the heart and soul of the movie. This book will help you learn more about the motivating faith and values of the key participants in the story and the history behind the story. More good news is that *Faith in God and Generals* made it to the top ten general interest Christian Booksellers Association bestseller list and was the top selling book for the publisher Broadman and Holman for the first quarter of 2003.

2

Out of the Claws of the Predator

*How to Avoid Being a Victim of
the Entertainment Industry*

Olga Soler

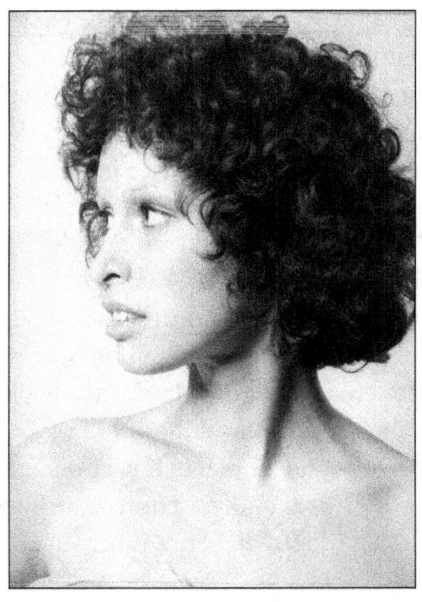

OLGA SOLER IS DIRECTOR/WRITER and performer for Estuary Ministries, a Christ-centered performing arts ministry dealing with biblical themes, inner healing, abuse, and addictive problems. The art forms used include drama, dance, storytelling, mime, comedy, graphic arts, writing, film, and song. Olga attended the High School of Performing Arts (*Fame*), the Lee Strasberg Theater Institute, and the Herbert Berghof Studios, all in New York City. She has performed widely at conferences, churches, prisons, coffeehouses, support groups, youth groups, and retreats, and has even performed on the streets, at secular colleges, and in worship services across the United States and the United Kingdom. She holds degrees in education and communications with equivalent studies in theology and psychology. She studied for two years at Gordon-Conwell Theological Seminary. She has designed and conducted the workshops "Dance Alive" and "Trauma Drama" at many Christian Recovery conferences. She wrote the curriculum and conducted Discovery Groups for addicts at the Boston Rescue Mission, using the arts to help them process aspects of their recovery. She also conducts workshops for Christian drama and dance in many churches of all denominations. Using Paulo Freire's *Pedagogy of the Oppressed*, she wrote a script for the "Mosaics" group of parents helping their children, who were victims of sexual abuse, through the courts system, and she assisted them in filming the script for a documentary. She performed and coauthored scripts for four years with the "Team" Christian ministry in Massachusetts and conducted eight full-scale multimedia presentations out of the Rio Ondo Arts Place in Woburn, Massachusetts, including *Voice of the Martyrs*, *Techno Easter*, and *Clean Comedy Night*. She has directed and choreographed entire productions at universities and colleges, including *A Man for All Seasons*, *Jane Eyre*, *Amahl and the Night Visitors*, and (by permission of the author) Calvin Miller's *The Singer*. She wrote and illustrated the book *Epistle to the Magadalenes* and has conducted retreats for women using the book accompanied by dramatic presentation. She is the author of other books and assorted screenplays. She is the proud mother of three wonderful children Cielo, Reva, and Ransom. She lives in Massachusetts with her husband Chris and her Japanese Chin (dog), Kiji.[1] Here is her story:

I know the media tells us to shun age and glorify youth, but I defy that idea by beginning with the fact that I have been forty years a believer. My father was no longer aware of that fact when he died this year. I

---

1. DeFazio and Lathrop, *Creative Ways*, 86–88.

miss him a great deal. Just before he passed, I asked him if he wanted me to read to him, and he asked me to read Deuteronomy 8, specifically this verse:

> Remember how the Lord your God led you all the way in the wilderness these forty years, to humble and test you in order to know what was in your heart, whether or not you would keep his commands. (Deut 8:2–3 NIV)

When he had me read this, he said, "Don't forget." He punctuated that with his gentle goodbye. I was engaged in this remembering when I was asked to write this chapter. So, I will share a little of what I remember and learned in the Spirit and in the media, arts, and theater.

Dad and I watched a lot of TV interspersed with his narration. He could not just watch it; he had to comment. Because of this, I became a critical thinker. After his conversion, Dad became a wonderful, transparent, honest man of God. Like many of us, though, he did not start out that way. He grew up in a Catholic orphanage, and things that happened there twisted his sexual ideas. What he thought of intimacy became very disturbed and, as a parent, he passed on a lot of good things, but he also passed on a lot of error. I became a believer when I was nineteen and told him about Jesus. Then I had to pray for twelve years before those prayers bore fruit.

When he came to his knees before the Lord, the transformation was genuine and he passed every test of authenticity. He became a person of prayer. He would pray and God would answer. His faith was fueled by his sincere gratitude. How sincere was he? Most perpetrators will not confess when confronted. My dad did. He confessed and begged my forgiveness, even though I could have pressed charges. It was more important to him to be right with God and me than to be free. I did not press charges, but neither of us could speak to each other for years. The shame deafened us with its silence. Then the Lord said, "Go ahead and see your father," and we started over as father and daughter as if we had never had an abnormal day in our lives. I had a real earthly father for the first time. This is a fantasy that many survivors of abuse have, but never live. I lived it by the grace and the power of God.

I know this chapter is supposed to highlight my background in the media, and I will get there, but this is part of that. Before Dad became a believer, he was addicted to a certain type of "media," so this story means a lot to one who knew how addicted he was. Not long before his death, he walked up to an "adult media" store. He turned his head away, placing his hands on the window, then prayed, "God, let this place be cursed." Two days later, this store, which had been a thriving establishment for years, closed its doors and went out of business. Like I said, He would pray and the Lord would answer. He prayed with similar faith for hundreds of people who came to the Christ. He taught many of them personally from the Bible. He was a humble elder, but no one could doubt who his Lord was. The "media" did not rule him anymore.

Most of us do not even think about the arts and media, though we live with its effects daily. The influence is profound but subtle. As the air we are breathing, many of us in modern society "breathe in" the influence of the media and it moves us. Media is a force to be contended with. It touches and shifts the masses in deep places, though we hardly realize how profoundly our lives are molded and shaped by it in every way. It tells us where to go and what it wants us to think is going on in the world. It dictates what we should buy and what we should believe. It tells us who we should allow to rule us and what we should fight and die for. It conditions us in what we should eat and what we should wear. Media lifts us up when we are down or disturbs us when some moguls of media choose to vomit their madness upon us. It stimulates us and pacifies us then numbs us and excites us. It helps us and teaches us, but it can also distract us from what is really important: our relationships with each other and the actual things we need to be doing.

Some of us cannot remember the last time we had a conversation with people who were not simultaneously interacting with screens (phones, computers, television, tablets). Many gatherings, including meals, have screens for each individual person or a large screen monopolizing the attention of the whole gathering. Those who exploit the media intend to have it everywhere, influencing every person at all times. They are succeeding. We can find cell phones on the Kalahari and in the Brazilian rainforest. The media educates us and gives us a lot of good information, but, if we trust it too completely, we may "learn" the wrong lessons, take the wrong paths, and never know it was the media that took us there. If we doubt this fact, we need merely to shut off all the media for one day each week and see what happens. How alone we feel. Children especially will have very intense reactions. They act like we were cutting off their air supply; it is that important to them.

Media is now also a two-way stream. We can find anything and, if we have a transmitter/receiver with us, anything can find us.

My mother has become a victim of the media. Recently, we spoke on the phone on her birthday. She told me about the nursing home she lives in near my brother and how she likes her new wheelchair. We never intended for her to live in a nursing home, but media had a part in putting her there. You see, my mother was easily the most unforgiving and critical person I ever knew. I prayed for her for forty years before I (just recently) witnessed her conversion. She made a lot of enemies through her bitter years and, in the end, her only "friends" were on television. She became so "focused," for lack of a better word, on the TV that she did not want to go anywhere or do anything. She was in bed for a couple of years by her own volition. Though her musculature was normal, her doctors declared her legs atrophied through disuse to the point of being crippled. She had become a true "couch potato." No one thought she would walk again.

The media can have real casualties, but, unlike other useful but potentially dangerous things, it does not generally carry a disclaimer that educates its fans sufficiently of potential dangers. My mother's story has a happy ending, however. She accepted Christ a few weeks ago, and all the bitterness and her inability to forgive went away. She is so happy that no one at the nursing home recognizes her. Like Scrooge in Dickens's *Christmas Carol*, she has seen the edge of the abyss she was about to go over and has turned back. She is taking tentative (physical) steps, and there is a good chance she may walk again. She is reading . . . of all things. She wants to do so and may even be able to move back in with family.

Media is neutral. It can be used for good or ill. And those who love influence recognize its power. Baron Nathan Mayer Rothschild's observation about money—"Give me control of a nation's money and I care not who makes the laws"[2]—could be said today about media. Those who control the media have the means of influencing a great number of people for their own agendas. Righteous or sinful, media is at the hub of modern life because it is that significant. If you are a mover or a shaker,

---

2. Baron Nathan Mayer Rothschild: "I care not what puppet is placed on the throne of England to rule the Empire. . . . The man that controls Britain's money supply controls the British Empire. And I control the money supply," http://quotes.liberty-tree.ca/quotes/rothschild.

you have the media in your pocket. Those who have the most control of it have greatest power and keep that power through their control of others by means of vehicles like the media. Generally speaking, the control follows the money. And there is a lot of money to be made with and through the media. But there are two sides to it: the producing and the receiving ends. If we are on the receiving end only, we are the ones who are molded by media. If we are a part of those who make the media, we cash in on its power and we get to mold the masses. This is the agenda of the world, but God has his own agenda—and media can be a useful tool to advance God's goals.

As an artist, I have been involved with the media for a long time, and this is what I know. Before the internet, few of the "little people" had an opportunity to use the media. Now, *temporarily*, the masses have *some* leverage. Before this time, when I was young, I saw the power in the media and I did not like being a "sheep led to slaughter," so I wanted to be in the group that called the shots. This is why I went into the theater. I naively thought it played fair and that I could make my own opportunities with hard work and talent. But the media, as I said, is at the hub of modern life, and life, as we all know, is not fair.

Well, what did I find in the theater? Let me give you some background first. I am Puerto Rican and lived in the South Bronx most of my youth. Everything you have heard of the South Bronx is probably true, but you may not know what it does to a kid who lives there. Besides forcing you to live in fear and poverty and robbing you of identity and resources, it makes you envious. You live in one of the greatest cities in the world, and you have to compete with a lot of wealth that you can never come close to having yourself. I suffered from this envy. What made it worse for me was that I tried out for Performing Arts High School and was the only one of five hundred candidates for freshman class that made it from the Bronx. I was really proud, but I had no idea what I was getting into. I ended up in a school with six hundred students, most of whom had parents who had been grooming them for fame since they were "Gerber Babies." Those kids not only had traveled the world and tasted the cream on the upper crust of life, but they had dance lessons, speech lessons, braces, acne specialists, and money that could buy them an agent. They were also endowed with parents who were motivated to see their kids succeed and who had the money to back that motivation. These kids had been around people who knew what they were doing in business as well as the arts and who could protect them in the seamy world of the theater. They also had talent.

I was determined, but also depressed. Part of me said, "Why not me? Why can't I have a piece of the pie of fame and fortune?" The other part said, "Give up while you are ahead and don't look back. You can't compete with this." I was told repeatedly by many people in the business that I had "something," a quality that made me interesting to watch. Did this mean I had a shot? It was a toss of the dice, but I did not have any idea what I could go back to. I was a good student, but I had no passion outside the arts. My parents did not even go to high school. They did not direct me much and certainly could not help me.

I also heard all the rumors, such as that 80 percent of the people in theater are bisexual. Whether you knew someone or not, sooner or later, you would have to sleep with someone (of either sex) to get a shot at a good part. Fifty thousand other talented actors out there (at the time, but now more) are your competition, and there are no free rides. I heard that people needed to be ruthless and step on the face of a best friend to get to the top. I was prepared to do that—maybe. But, when others did it to me, it was unbearable. I could not take betrayal. I also wanted to be loved so badly. That was a bad liability. It was better to be desired than loved in the theater. The vulnerable would be picked off. All the rumors were, by the way, essentially true.

The lifestyle was fine with me. I had no morals per se. My upbringing was very double-standard, so I abandoned ideas of morality. But those universal laws get in there somehow and plague a conscience, don't they? This is why I believe the Spirit of God speaks to every person. I know he was speaking to me even though, for the most part, I learned to shut that voice out.

I wanted to be an atheist, but just couldn't convince myself the universe was that sterile. I thought I was smart, but I had been reared with Santeria and other superstitions. There were things outside of our reality I could not account for. I began reading Plato and Shakespeare when I was twelve and I also explored many spiritual philosophies from the I Ching to Satanism. All of them said the same thing I was hearing in the theater: "You are your own god; embrace that and make your own heaven here on earth." It seemed the loneliest of propositions to me. If every person has her own religion, who would be left to worship?

At some point, I got tired of telling lies and of listening to them. I also felt like there had to be more than "me, me, me, and money." I became obsessed with finding that elusive thing called truth, whatever that was. After all, if there were so many lies, there had to be a truth. As day follows night and light breaks up darkness, truth would come in and out of my focus, taunting and drawing me. My search for truth, however, had to be secondary to survival. I had to deal with Performing Arts. I must have been a good actress, because I felt crushed and fragile inside, though my teachers said I was a "hard seed." I guess they thought no one could get to me. How wrong they were.

Right about that time, the civil rights movement and the Vietnam War were vying for media attention and I learned another great lesson: you cannot believe all you hear on the news. My generation began to march for everything from jeans in school to peace, civil rights, Black power, gender equality, gay rights, and free love, but what we saw on the nightly news was not, for the most part, what was happening. There were our pictures and words, but the slant given to them and what was shown (or not) painted a certain picture. Much of the time, it was not true and did not favor us. Still, we marched, we sang, and we rioted. At that time, I began to think there might be something just as good as art and that might just be politics. We were making a difference too. I will say it was good to move the government with the will of the people. I obviously do not agree with all we said and did back then, but I think it is sad we, as the people, do not have the influence today to be heard as we once did.

Pursuing the political phase of my youth, I left Performing Arts in my junior year and joined the Young Lords. This was a Hispanic communist group fighting for the rights of the poor. They were tired of marching peacefully with little result and a lot of risk. So, like the Black Panthers, they decided to get violent. They took a church in Harlem at gunpoint, and I was with them in my neighborhood when they took over the rat-infested medical center called Lincoln Hospital. The Lords did not really hurt anyone in that offensive, but they stood guard, allowing the people to rise up and say they needed a decent facility and better care. We were proud things were moving at last. I never carried a gun, but I went to a lot of meetings carrying Mao Zedong's little red book in my military jacket's pocket and proclaimed the gospel of violence while smoking a lot of dope. I was close to happy. I felt like I had some kind of history and identity, like I was somebody. With the Young Lords, I felt close to something meaningful.

Then, there was a riot I attended that turned me around. In the Lords, we were encouraged to read about past overthrows and revolutions, and it all sounded good on paper until you were there with glass and metal exploding and brother smashing in the head of brother. I grew up with gang violence, but had never seen war. These riots were how I imagined war to be. If the French revolutionaries saw blood washing down the streets by the gallons while the people cheered, could we become as calloused? That day, I believed we could. Violence was not the way. I also began to see fallacies in a lot of other things the "comrades" were teaching.

I saw what happens when good intentions meet the sinful human heart. Here were people who were speaking of equality for all, but practicing inequality for some. Women were still being treated badly "in the name of equality." Women still had to do the menial tasks in addition to the "manly" ones while the brothers took things easy. We hated rich people. Love was not for everyone, apparently. The thing I loved the most about the party's promises was the hope of real community. But communism is not community. It is void of the spiritual nature of true community. It is forced, and, therefore, can never be community. Without the spiritual component, there is no power for people to live together in harmony, whether we call it a collective or a church. The movement also masked many neurotic, perverse, and selfish behaviors behind the ideal of liberation. But even this equality they spoke of was, of course, a smokescreen. Some were more "equal" than others. There were the comrades at the top, pocketing lots of money in the name of the movement. It was George Orwell's *Animal Farm* all over again. I became very disillusioned. I crawled back to the theater, thinking, "To blazes with it, nothing matters but me, and I'm not even sure of that."

On the home front, my mother collapsed mentally, and she blamed her children as the cause of her trouble. The state considered her an unfit parent, and my brothers and I were told we could not live with her. Apparently, foster homes were not available, so youngest brother, Sam, went away to school on scholarship and got into cocaine. My brother Frank went to the streets to become a heroin addict, and I was granted emancipated minor status and left to my own resources. I got a job and an apartment with a guy I met and cried every moment I was alone. If

I was awake, I was high. I was sixteen. Sam later became a pastor, and Frank now works with the Salvation Army ministering to the homeless in Sacramento, California. God is good, but we all went through some dark times.

Once students left Performing Arts, it was not customary to let them back in. They made an exception for me. I asked, and they said I could come back, but I was so emotionally unstable I never showed up. I really did not know what to do or where to go. So I went back to the old neighborhood and I got involved with local school politics. I was persuasive and stopped a few riots, so the teachers sought me out when there was trouble. But, I also attacked my English teacher and my sweet little old guidance counselor, so they assigned me to the truant counselor who was three hundred pounds, six feet tall, bald, and sporting a Fu Man Chu goatee and mustache. He was scary looking, but turned out to be a nice guy, and he was the only reason I stayed long enough to graduate.

My boyfriend got involved with cocaine, and I decided to leave without having anywhere to go. I ended up on drugs myself, and homeless. I became pregnant and, after hearing the heartbeat of my child at the doctor's office, I cold-bloodedly decided to terminate it. I never quite recovered from that, even though I had convinced myself it was just a thing and not a baby. I had an IUD put in for birth control at the clinic and began hemorrhaging. I didn't care. I wanted to die. I hemorrhaged for a month and crashed in hovels wherever I could. A fellow druggie found me bleeding to death in an abandoned apartment on a freezing New York January day, and he was kind enough to drop me off at a local emergency room. They removed the IUD, and I survived, but I left the hospital alone and not caring what happened next.

Then, I bumped into an old friend from Performing Arts who lived in a spiritualistic community. She said I could stay with them. They were heavily into the occult, but that is another story. I almost stabbed myself to death there, but was stopped by a voice I heard, which I believe now was God's. Despite the darkness I was in at the time, I am glad I listened to the voice and lived.

My involvement with theater continued. I did some community theater and some summer stock and some film, but my life needed more structure. Thanks to a scholarship from the New York Yankees and the Martin Luther King foundation, I ended up at the Lee Strasberg

Theater Institute. I thought I would find more freedom in the arts, but saw that, like all human endeavors, my experience was that most of those involved were driven by overwhelming need and heartless greed. There is no real freedom when one is enslaved to these things. At the same time, there were some good people there too, including one of my teachers who told me he had visited an Amish community and experienced peace there. He said I was very emotionally fragile and needed to get out of the theater and go find some normalcy somewhere else. He was thinking of getting out too. I hope he found his way. Meanwhile, another teacher forty years my senior got me drunk and took advantage of me one night. He told me what he did was part of being actualized and free. I could not see it, but I had no absolutes to controvert what he said. I certainly did not feel very liberated by it.

I started dating a man who helped me to become healthier. In the end, he left me for a man, but I thank him for his lessons on exercise and good health at least. I knew I had to compete to continue my pursuit of the arts. All I had was my talent and my looks, which healthy living would help me maintain. I could not afford to neglect either one. My teachers at Strasberg's encouraged me for the most part. They said I was in the top five students there. If I got a break, anything could happen. I might make it. I could be the next Jane Fonda, but it was plain I had to eliminate any outdated morals I had skirting around the edges of my consciousness. I was told to let myself become a "turned-on woman" willing to do or portray anything. Sexual harassment in the theater was not a concept back then. If you wanted into the club, you had to be ready to pay any price. What is being said about Bill Cosby and all his victims is not unusual. Sex is still part of the stock and trade of any industry where there is a lot of money and power. Why he is being painted as "the only dirty old man in Hollywood" is a question, but it is proof that the media can protect or punish whomever it wants to.

The man who helped me get healthy and then broke my heart had a Baptist mother. It was my first exposure to any kind of real Christianity. What I had been told about Jesus for the most part was hateful. The only Christ I knew was condemned as the perpetrator of papal wealth, inquisitions, crusades, and bigotry: a monster who exacted severe penance for small infractions and one whom I could never hope to please with my history. My friend's mom had a different Christ. He was humble and poor and forgiving.

I started thinking about the whole Christ thing, but took to the New Age eclectic view. Exclusivity was so not cool. Even as a critical thinker, I was, after all, a product of a lot of media, including the Beatles' Magical Mystery tours, Yes's universalism, King Crimson's in-your-face rebellion, the class struggle of Janice Ian, the drug culture of Jefferson Airplane/Starship, Eastern mysticism in so many movies and books such as *2001: A Space Odyssey* and *Slaughterhouse 5*, the eclectic Christian Science of *Jonathan Livingston Seagull*, the fashion and art of people like Andy Warhol, Peter Max, and Roger Dean, the movies of Zeffirelli and Polanski, and the sci-fi culture.

The atomic terror of our generation's childhood was anesthetized by science fiction and drugs. We began to feel that it would not produce Armageddon, but that it would bloom into one great psychedelic mandala and get "beamed up" in a light-speed future. If there was no God, we could look to ourselves and technology, and maybe some cool aliens, for a future in the stars. The *Star Trek* religion was alive and well under the influence of Isaac Asimov, Gene Roddenberry, Ray Bradbury, Aldous Huxley, and many other "gods" of the sci-fi world—and many of their educated predictions have come to life in today's technology. Where it will lead we shall see, or our descendants will. The science community claims we are short years away from placing human consciousness into a machine. The book *That Hideous Strength* by C.S. Lewis needs to be reread and given some serious attention.

Right about then, three things happened. I started attending a Buddhist meditation group, I got a job at a health restaurant owned by Christians, and I met a photographer who had some impressive connections. He set me up with an agent who had worked with Richard Hamilton. The agent jokingly told me he would protect me by getting me a stunt girl to sleep with my prospective employers so that I could be all his. In the end, he did not get me work. So my photographer got me an appointment to see "Guy," one of the wealthiest men in the world whom I will not name for many reasons. He owed a prominent magazine in the industry, and I was sent to his private penthouse at the age of eighteen in my best mini-dress and high heels. I was told to do whatever he wanted me to do, because it would be worth my while. I went to his New York penthouse and obeyed, but only to a point because of what had been happening to me.

You see, the Christians at the restaurant had invited me to their devotional sessions before work, and I went. I told them it was fine. Mohammed, Buddha, Christ—it was all good, right? And I had a trunk full of religious and philosophical books of all persuasions that I had been carrying around since forever, and there was a Bible in it right next to the *Book of Mormon*, the *Bhagavad Gita*, and Sophocles's works. Some girl had given it to me when I was twelve, and I could never read it, even though Shakespeare's plays were no problem for me. I brought it to work and asked if there was a trick to reading it. They told me I needed to pray to the Spirit who inspired the Bible and humbly wait on his guidance to understand it. I thought that was, as we used to say, "far out." I went home, sat in a lotus position, lit up a joint, and prayed, "O, Spirit of the Bible, help me to understand this book." I was amazed at every page from then on. Things I read started speaking to me at odd times, as they did on the day I went to see Guy.

I had done a lot of things I am not proud of in my life, and what Guy wanted me to do would just have been one more with a promise of great possibilities. But, while I waited for him in his living room and observed this wealthy but decrepit man being lavished with hypocritical attentions from models and photographers, I began to get a queasy feeling inside. He made me wait at least an hour, then popped over to where I sat and squeezed my thigh like a grapefruit at a market. Why did that shock me? This was after all a market of flesh as far as he was concerned, with lots of people willing to be his pickings. He told me he would be right with me. I waited another hour.

Finally, everyone went about their business. He hardly looked at me, then told me to follow him up the red velvet spiral staircase to his private office. This turned out to be his bedroom. It had a wall-to-wall bed the size of two king-sized beds. I can only imagine why he needed so much sleeping space. The room was festooned with his magazines everywhere, and I saw disturbing things on the covers and opened pages. He locked the door behind him. I swallowed hard and held up my portfolio. He rolled his eyes at my naiveté and said, "We don't need that. I will do a two page spread with you in the magazine and I will take the pictures myself." He tossed my portfolio aside and said, "I need you to fix my zipper, it seems to be broken."

At that point, the phone in his room rang. He answered it and it was Mrs. "O" of "O" ballet. I cannot mention her name either. My astrology teacher's son was the pianist for Mrs. O's ballet, and he often came home with many horror stories about her. She was wealthy enough to tell presidents and kings where to get off and was known as the dragon lady of ballet. She was sixty-seven, but she looked twenty-seven, and, it was rumored, that this was due to a certain injection therapy that involved serum from human placentas. Now, it was said, most people of the times (including Ronald Reagan) who used this kind of therapy used sheep placentas. Mrs. O was said to have believed this was not good enough. I had heard that she promised young dancers fame and invited them to her home. There, she would have them seduced by a handsome young man and impregnated. When the girl would come to her in tears, she would promise to "fix" it, but would wait till she was six months along so that a placenta was developed. Then the child would be destroyed, the placenta obtained, and the girl would be black-balled from the theater. Mrs. O did not want anyone around reminding her of her actions. She did this at a time when this kind of abortion was illegal. I tell you this because, during that conversation, as I heard Guy speaking to her and "kissy poohing" her over the phone, I understood that this was his kind of person. I heard a voice in my head saying, "This is the club you will be joining. Do you like it?" I did not.

He hung up the phone and approached me again. I began to feel sick at this point, when he touched me. Then, I guess I prayed my second prayer. I promised, "If you get me out of here, I will go to church at least once." The phone rang again. This time it was a private line he had in the bathroom. He apparently reserved that for special calls, and he did not want me listening. He said he would be right back, but shut himself away in the soundproof bathroom to talk. I heard the voice in my head again: "Will you gain the whole world and lose your soul?" That was it. I did not hesitate. I started throwing magazines around looking for the key and finally found it in the top drawer of his dresser. I had been so scared that I did not see when he placed it there. I unlocked the door, nearly broke my neck running down the stairs in my heels, and jumped into the private elevator. When I got to the ground floor, I ran for a solid four or five city blocks before I found a phone and called my friend from the restaurant to tell her I would go to church with her the next day. I was not impressed with the idea of church, but I went. I had promised.

Years later, I learned on good information that this man I had run away from had a sexual proclivity toward sadomasochism. He was into beating women up pretty badly. As a relatively unknown person, I could have been maimed or worse if I had stayed. It seldom occurs to us that our choices for good or evil may mean imminent life or death. God sees everything, and he saved me in more than one way that day. I am so glad the Lord is in my life.

The day after, my photographer called me laughing and said Guy was sorry to have kept me waiting. He wanted me to go back. I said I would not. I told him I had decided to try to make it on my own talent. He said sarcastically, "Good luck," and I never heard from him again. I did, however, get an interview with the advertising company Batten Barton Durstine and Osborne (BBD&O), which promised to use me in a few commercials at the end of the summer. My job at the restaurant would hold me till then.

The man who owned the restaurant was Rick Shorter. He had been one of the early producers of *Hair* on Broadway. I had gotten a part in that play when I was sixteen, but my mother would not let me do the nude scene, so I had to drop out. Rick had now retired from the theater to pursue the way of the Lord and was praying that I would "retire" from it too. He had held cast parties at the restaurant for *Jesus Christ Superstar* and other shows, and he knew that the theater, for the most part, was not God-friendly.

While I waited for BBD&O, I auditioned for an off-Broadway rock musical. I really wanted the part, but weeks passed, and I heard nothing. At that point, my guru at the meditation center stopped a session in the middle of it and told everyone he saw airplanes around me and a boy leading me out of New York. The next day, a young man came to the restaurant and told me I needed to accept Christ as my savior and go to his Christian college in Tennessee to study nursing. I had been thinking about nursing as a possible quick education for a day job, but it just never had worked out. I said I did not know about Christ yet, but the young man was cute and I thought that, if I went to Tennessee with him, I could see the sights and then come back in time for the commercials at BBD&O. I had no intention of staying, but he was a very resourceful man and, within three days, he had raised the money for me to go and the financial aid for me to start school. I was on a plane with a boy just as the guru had said. I often wonder why this message came from a

Buddhist, but I think the enemy guessed this would happen and wanted to confuse me. It did not work. On the contrary, I was moving in the direction of Jesus. Then the day after I left, the off-Broadway musical called the restaurant looking for me. I had gotten the lead role. But Rick did not pass that information on to me, and I am glad he did not. I might have come back, and who knows how that might have turned out.

When I arrived in Tennessee, I began a class called "Teachings of Jesus" by a professor named Robert Francis, who had been a lawyer, but was now a minister. His arguments were cogent and forceful. I put him through a lot of hard questions, but he gently answered them all. He was bringing me around with the help of the Holy Spirit, but I was not quite ready to give in. The denomination this school belonged to was very conservative. Not a peep of "Amen" or "Halleluiah!" was heard during service. Everyone wore their best clothes, and only hymns were sung. It was still easy for me to say, "I can get into Jesus, but this church stuff is a bore."

Then, one day, a black brother who had been convicted of murder, saved, and was paroled came to church and gave his testimony. Remember, I had been in the theater, did a little modeling as well, and now abhorred it when my nails chipped or I got a zit on my face. I dressed to the hilt and I did not like to look like anything but in vogue. But, when that brother started preaching, something came over me. I went to my knees when no one else was kneeling. Tears mixed with mascara rolled down my face like mud. I sobbed from deep in my chest and could not breathe. The preacher was weeping too and telling us how he had been a "filthy, nasty, dirty sinner," but Jesus had made him clean. I wanted that: he was talking to me. When he called for people to come forward, a few hesitant souls walked up, but I had to crawl. Everyone stared, but I was beyond embarrassment. I needed Christ, and I did not care who knew about it. I did not care what I had to do to get him in my life.

Dr. Francis had convinced me, but still my feelings had been lagging. After that brother's testimony, all of me was ready to come before the throne and surrender. Later, when I told the doctor my decision, he smiled as if he had won, but I got even with him: I made him baptize me in a cold river instead of a comfortable sanctuary! I was a drama queen and wanted to tell everybody, "I love the Lord who made sense of my chaotic world." This time, I think the Lord approved.

I was so serious about God that I was willing to submit to the rules of the church I joined. This denomination was, however, of the unscriptural opinion that art itself was egocentric and anti-Christian. They have changed their policies since then. But, because of their views, I did not create for ten years after my conversion. I became a teacher. I believe it was a period of detoxification for me, much like Moses's experience as a shepherd in the wilderness, and I do not regret it. I had to be purged from the way the world creates to learn what real creativity is for. Now, I am glad to be a believing artist who does not depend on a muse, but who has the infinite creative power of the Lord God to inspire my work. I have achieved much more artistically as a believer than I did as a worldly performer. What you have read is not all my testimony. My testimony of the Lord's interaction with me happens every day. I am amazed daily at where his inspiration leads me. The wilderness into which I embarked after my conversion is the nursery for the people of God. He teaches us to grow up in such places. The story of that spiritual growth is much more interesting than the one I have just told. I am becoming more and more fearless in my art and, as I do it, it resembles more and more the work of the prophets who used any and every medium to portray the truths God gave them. It is, after all, the Lord's intention that we be a nation of prophets and priests before him. May his inspiration fill all his people and may light shine through whatever medium he chooses for the increase of his kingdom.

RESOURCES

If you have any questions about what you read in my chapter, or if you would like to hear, as Paul Harvey used to say, "the rest of the story," I am available to you. I speak publicly about intentional community, healing, support and recovery (from abuse and addiction), domestic violence, the media (the blessings and the curses of), and the arts from a biblical perspective. I punctuate all my talks with what I have just mentioned, demonstrating how these are used well and advocating for their use in worship, teaching, and evangelism. I do workshops on dance (Davidic and liturgical), drama, storytelling, mime, and the arts as a healing or community-building medium. I also speak to school and home-school groups about alternative methods for help with dyslexia, ADD, and ADHD. I have traveled all over the United States and the United Kingdom speaking, and am available for a small stipend, travel, and board expenses. If anyone in your congregation does not mind a house guest for an evening, I am happy to fellowship with my brothers and sisters anywhere.

I also have many books available, which I can send you in e-book format for a donation. These include: *The Body* (illustrated, book about the church from Genesis to Revelation); *Primer for Home Fellowship*; *Tough Inspiration from the Weeping Prophet* (about domestic violence); *Who Am I?* (about children); *Epistle to the Magdalenes* (illustrated); and *Adoni*, the psalms of a woman (illustrated book of deep spiritual poetry). I have collaborated on two other books: *Just Don't Marry One*, edited by Yancy and Yancy, and *Creative Ways to Build Christian Community*, edited by Jeanne DeFazio and John Lathrop (available at Amazon.com).

Contact me by email at fleursavag@aol.com, or by phone at 774-261-3815.

3

When the Wheel Stopped

Susan Stafford

Written by Tammy Files[1]

Susan Stafford and Chuck Woolery were the original hostess and host of *Wheel of Fortune*, and, during the seven years they teamed up, Susan and Chuck enjoyed phenomenal success and made the show

---

1. Tammy Files has been Susan Stafford's personal assistant for twenty-nine years. Susan Stafford was interviewed in person March 12, 2015.

number one on daytime television.[2] Susan Stafford broke new ground as the first woman to be given a microphone on a game show (which made a major difference in pay), the first woman on a game show to make her own clothing deal (with Giorgio's), and the first woman to be nominated for an Emmy on a game show. America came to know Susan Stafford as a pioneer for women in the game show world.

While on the show, Susan began working with prostitutes, bringing them into her home, helping them build their confidence and find a better direction for their lives. Susan became one of the top ten highest paid women on daytime television. When Chuck left, Susan continued the show for the next seven months with Pat Sajak. When Susan's contract came up to go nighttime, Merv Griffin thought that Susan was seeking more money by not wanting to sign for another seven years. Though the fame and the money had been exhilarating, after answering fan mail from so many people with cancer, Susan knew she had to do something more meaningful with her life than just turn letters. Before leaving the show in October of 1982, Susan passed the baton to Vanna White, who has enjoyed great success as well. Vanna was more than happy to take that baton.

Long before it was fashionable for celebrities to be concerned about issues overseas, Susan worked in Calcutta, helping Mother Teresa's nuns care for leprosy[3] (Hansen's disease) victims. By spreading the word, she helped secure the funding that financed the discovery of a cure for this disease.[4] That first trip to India, seeing the devastating poverty firsthand, working with leprosy patients, providing comfort and encouragement to the dying, stirred something deep inside. Susan could no longer be comfortable with a life of indulgence. Susan spent a year as a chaplain intern in pastoral care education at St. Joseph's Hospital in Houston, Texas, and received her credentials by caring for terminal cancer patients. Interns were not allowed to wear makeup, and there was no audience to applaud her efforts. Instead, Susan found a satisfaction in her heart and soul that nothing else could match. She

2. Susan was the first lady of daytime television game shows. After testing for the Wheel of Fortune pilot at NBC with Edd (Kookie) Byrnes, the producers selected Chuck Woolery and Susan Stafford.

3. In the Num 12:10 account, Miriam, Moses's sister, was a leper.

4. American Leprosy Missions received a check from President Ronald Reagan during the time Susan worked with lepers (wet or dry). Don Baer and Susan Stafford produced a documentary on leprosy.

learned that sometimes the Lord says no because the tapestry is woven by his will not ours.

Susan continued to work with American Leprosy Missions as an international correspondent, making documentaries with former Surgeon General C. Everett Koop and Merlin Olsen in Paraguay, the Himalayas, Nepal, Ethiopia, India, the Philippines, Brazil, and Liberia. Then, she returned to television to write, produce, and host 130 health shows, along with co-hosting *The 700 Club* with Pat Robertson and Ben Kinchlow. Susan became known for her crisis ministry after helping her friend Rock Hudson deal with "America's leprosy"—AIDS. The Lord had prepared Susan for dealing with AIDS by her previous experiences caring for lepers. For serving in these areas of need, Susan was honored with the World Unity Award for Humanitarian Service along with Edward James Olmos and Martin Luther King, III.

Because of her expertise in the world of entertainment, Susan was elevated to vice president of public relations for Barry and Enright Productions. Years ago, Susan served on a board called Mid-East Communications with Casey Kasem and Dan Enright, among others. The goal was to help establish good relations among the various faiths. Susan has made numerous trips to Israel and especially loves the Jewish people.

While getting her master's and PhD in clinical psychology, Susan served a one-year internship (three thousand hours) at the Chabad Chassidic House in Los Angeles, working with drug addicts and the homeless, and was co-president of the Chai Circle. As a member of an emergency response team with Media Fellowship International (Pastor Robert Rieth), Susan was called to Columbine and Virginia Tech to counsel survivors and affected families in the aftermath of the mass shootings there. She is a motivational/inspirational seminar speaker and spiritual counselor who is often called to help with confidential crisis situations in the Hollywood community (as well as in other areas) and continues to serve as a chaplain. She received a star on the Palm Springs Walk of Stars given by the Rock Hudson estate for her humanitarian efforts and her work with cancer and AIDS.

Susan formed a nonprofit organization called Wheel of Grace Unlimited and continues to reach out as she is called on daily. When the wonderful actor Ed Lauter was making his final journey, his wife Mia called Susan, and she came within the hour. Since Ed was Catholic,

Susan called on her longtime friend former Jesuit priest Fr. Terry Sweeney, and they were both with Ed and his wife as he passed on. Providing comfort through the grief process for many months, Susan assisted his wife with the memorial, where she also spoke.

Wherever she is, Susan's goal is to lift people up, offering a hope through her faith in Christ that this world can never give. She has learned that, while the world's ladder of success leads to pretty thin air at the top, there are no limits to what our Lord can provide.

Recently, Susan Stafford was honored at a special gathering by the Hollywood Prayer Network. The focus of the evening was honoring the trailblazers who have continued to serve the Lord faithfully throughout their careers. Others honored were Charles Cappleman, Shirley and Pat Boone, Ken Wales, Michael Warren, Rosey Grier, Bob Yerkes, and Carol Lawrence. These individuals' quality work and spiritual walks inspire young people never to give up, never to surrender, as they pursue their careers as Christians in Hollywood. Susan Stafford's book, *Stop the Wheel, I Want to Get Off!*, received five stars on Amazon.com. Here is her story:

I was born in Lynn, Massachusetts, on January 27, the sixth child of Louise Vignone and George W. Carney. My mother's mother, Katherine, moved to America with her bridegroom, Joseph Vignone. Her noble Austrian family disowned her when she fell in love with an Italian. Class distinction meant everything to them and Joseph's family was not pleased with the union either. While they did not disown Joseph, they did their best to make Katherine's life miserable. My Italian grandfather was a top musician who, under the stage name of Joe Pino, played several instruments and opened for Jack Benny at the Palace in New York City. My grandmother Katherine was heartbroken when her beloved husband Joseph died at thirty-nine of a heart attack while performing on stage at the Palace Theatre. Katherine went into shock, was put in a mental institution, and eventually died there. Her three daughters—Ida; my mother, Louise; and Geri—were moved from place to place. Mama, along with her sister Geri, ended up in an orphanage. Her sister Ida contracted polio and was placed in a special facility.

Mama was a beautiful devout Catholic who married her first husband at sixteen. She and her husband started a family immediately. Unfortunately, her husband was irresponsible and unfaithful, and Mama struck out alone facing in the 1930s the stigma of being a divorced woman with two small children. She waited tables at a popular restaurant in Lynn where my father, George Carney, regularly came for dinner. My dad embraced my two eldest sisters, Jackie and Carol, adopting them when he married Mama. Even after fifty years of marriage and seven children, however, my father's upper-crust Southern family never accepted my mother: a Roman Catholic of Italian descent and a divorcée. Despite the ill feeling, Mama and Daddy moved from Massachusetts to Rolla, Missouri, where my father's family had relocated. Rolla was near the army base Fort Leonard Wood, where my father ran the base commissary. Mama and Daddy became the proud owners of C&B Café, a popular venue for the boys who attended Rolla School of Mines. My parents provided the locals with great food and warm hospitality. Oftentimes, the boys at Rolla could not pay for their meals, and my parents fed them for free.

When I was two, my parents allowed Dr. Davis and his wife, Laura, to take me into their home so I could recover from an illness. My parents both worked in the café, and, since the Davises had no children, Laura had the time to devote to me. In the process of our time together, they came to love me very much, and I loved them as well. Dr. Davis was a trusted and respected physician in the community. I lived in their beautiful brick house, and people began to call me "the Davis girl." I was given everything money could provide and visited my parents and family at the C&B Café each week. I think my mother allowed the arrangement because it gave me what she had always dreamed of in her Depression-era childhood in an orphanage. While I knew my parents had good intentions, I felt confused and devalued by being separated from my family as a child. The arrangement caused me to develop abandonment issues, with which I would deal for the better part of my life. Regardless of the fact that I had everything a child could want in the Davis home, I cried myself to sleep often, wanting my mother to hold me.

When I was nine, I left the Davis family and moved along with my family to Kansas, where my father managed the commissaries and PX stores at military bases. It was a tearful goodbye. Dr. Davis and his wife were distraught and offered my parents a lot of money to keep me as their child. My father insisted that he wanted to keep his family unified, and that I would move to Kansas with everyone else. I felt a conflict leaving the Davis home, in part because I knew the money could bring a better life for my sisters and brothers, and partly because my privileged life was over.

In 1958, my parents leased a small family café in Grandview, Missouri, where I worked part time as a waitress during high school. For free lunches at Grandview High School, I worked in the cafeteria scraping the dirty dishes. When I turned fifteen, Colonel Ripple's wife entered my name in a pageant for Miss Richards-Gebaur Air Force Base. At sixteen, I was named Sweetheart of the Air Force Academy Ninth Squadron via Cadet Sam Westbrook, who was my sweetheart (now General Samuel Westbrook). I eventually became Miss Kansas City Photographer. This led to a television appearance on KCMO-TV in Kansas City. The interview revealed that I was underage for the contest. I was disqualified and had to return my crown, trophy, and cash prize. In spite of the devastation I experienced, the publicity over the disqualification brought offers for modeling and my first television appearance on *The Art Linkletter Show*. As an eighteen-year-old newlywed to my highway-patrolman-officer husband G.K., I continued my modeling career and worked as a hospitality hostess at Showarama in Kansas City.

Mel Gold hired me at eighteen as the lead hospitality hostess for National Screen Service, which made all the movie trailers. This job was my entrée into the celebrity world: I met Sean Connery, Peter Fonda, Frankie Avalon, and Ann-Margaret, among others. On my second visit to California, I found a note from my husband that read, "Dear Susan, I know you won't be coming back, I am sorry, I will always love you, G.K." Living with my sister Catherine in Los Alamitos, I began sending postcards to agencies and started getting offers for work in the entertainment industry. The first summer, I was cast in national commercials for Alberto VO5 and Borden's milk. I met many celebrities, and my life in Hollywood began. I got my Screen Actors Guild card via a term contract with 20th Century Fox and my first acting job with Irwin Allen.

At thirteen, I had gone to the Billy Graham Crusade in Kansas City on a Baptist church bus trip. I took my walk up the aisle and gave my life to the Lord. More than twenty years later, I was a syndicated radio broadcaster with the McLendon radio stations and interviewed Hal Lindsey, author of *The Late Great Planet Earth*. Hal suggested I find a church, so I began attending Pastor Jack Hayford's Church on the Way.

As an adult, and understanding more about the Lord, I recommitted my life to Him on May 7, 1972.

I began hosting Bible studies in my home for Rev. Kenn Gulliksen, which evolved into what is now The Vineyard. This was my introduction to born-again Christians (Gavin and Patti MacLeod, Pat and Shirley Boone, Billy Davis Jr. and Marilyn McCoo) who have become lifelong friends. Rev. Bob Reith of Media Fellowship International baptized me in the Jordan River in the early 1980s.

I met George Nader, Mark Miller, and Rock Hudson in the 1970s, and we remained fast friends. They were homosexuals and I was a Jesus freak, but friendships do not always follow a set pattern. We all had fears and hopes as well as a willingness to set aside our differences to care truly for each other. And it was my sincerest conviction that Jesus died for all of us.

My marriage in the 1970s to tycoon Gordon McLendon lasted just over a year. Gordon's family members wanted me to remain in the marriage, but I was so unhappy, I left taking no divorce settlement. Returning to Hollywood, I did the pilot for *Wheel of Fortune* at NBC studios and became the show's first hostess. Two years after *Wheel of Fortune* began, I married Dick Ebersol, NBC's Wonder Boy, who, with Lorne Michaels, was responsible for the early success of *Saturday Night Live*. I remained legally married to Dick Ebersol for five years, but I was not able to find balance in my faith and my personal life. This marriage was the epitome of "circus Christianity." Kenn Gulliksen of The Vineyard married us on the beach in Malibu. John Belushi[5] and Chevy Chase from *Saturday Night Live* attended the ceremony. Soon after we married, geographical conflicts occurred. Dick wanted to live in New York City, and I wanted to remain in Los Angeles. Dick decided he did not want my parents to live in the home (my home prior to our marriage). It was a breach of trust, since he had promised they could continue to live there after we were married. My abandonment issues resurfaced when my parents had to move back to Missouri. My lack of forgiveness toward my husband at the time was enormous. There was mutual grievous infidelity in the relationship on both our parts. Despite it all, as God would have it, we remain friends to this day. Many years later, after Dick's son, Teddy, died in a plane crash, I finally felt love for Dick in the way it was meant to be: unselfish and pure.

---

5. John Belushi was making advances on Kenn Gulliksen's wife, Joni.

Divorced and disenchanted with *Wheel of Fortune* after Chuck Woolery left the show, I had a great void in my life. My "self" was dying. I visited India with Father Herbert DeSouza and ministered with Mother Teresa among the lepers and the dying and felt God's special calling upon my life. I left *Wheel of Fortune* on October 22, 1982. My popularity on *Wheel of Fortune* had engaged me in a life relating to fans, many of whom were writing to me about their battles with cancer. Leaving *Wheel of Fortune*, I began to minister to cancer patients at the Dr. John Stehlin Cancer Center in Houston's St. Joseph Hospital in 1982. Subsequently, I cared for Rock Hudson during his much-publicized death from AIDS in the mid-1980s. The fear of contagion at Rock Hudson's deathbed was great. Shirley and Pat Boone, Gavin and Patti MacLeod, and I were the only outsiders who came in to minister at Rock's deathbed. We called in Father Terry Sweeney S.J. because Rock was a Roman Catholic. The loss of Rock as a friend was heartbreaking. I am grateful that Rock came to Jesus on his deathbed, and I have the promise of seeing this beloved friend again in heaven.

In the early 1990s, I became vice president of public relations for Barry and Enright Productions. Dan Enright and I shared a love and devotion as deep as any I had ever known. In the 1990s, my relationship with Dan grew closer while I completed a PhD in psychology and served three thousand hours as an intern at Chabad, becoming cochair of Chai Circle. This training helped prepare me for the chaplaincy. Dan was the love of my life, and, before he died, Dan came to Jesus. I so look forward to the day I see him again in heaven.

I grew up in the Midwest in a time when virginity was valued by gentlemen who wanted to marry. I was a Missouri girl who never intended to become a Hollywood girl. Despite my every failed marriage, God touched each of my husbands' hearts through our continued relationships and my fervent prayers and brought all three of them to Jesus. God has a way of taking our failures and using them for his glory.

During my time in Hollywood, I journeyed through the fast lane and survived to realize that, when the wheel stopped, my greatest fortune was found in the love and mercy and grace of Jesus Christ. A Scripture I often share is Matthew 16:24–26: "Then Jesus said to his disciples, 'Whoever wants to be my disciple must deny themselves and take up their cross and follow me. For whoever wants to save their life will lose it, but whoever loses their life for me will find it. What good will it be for someone to gain the whole world, yet forfeit their soul? Or what can anyone give in exchange for their soul?'" (NIV). I do not want to know Christians who have not suffered. If we try to save our physical life from death, pain, or discomfort, we risk losing eternal life. If we protect ourselves from the pain God calls us to suffer, we begin to die spiritually and emotionally. Our lives turn inward, and we lose our intended purpose. When each of us gives our life in service to Jesus, we discover the real purpose of living. I lived a life of self, and my "self" died. God placed a call on my life, and I have found great satisfaction in serving the Lord Jesus Christ.

Life on earth is, in essence, an introduction to eternity. When we do not know Jesus, we make choices as though there is no afterlife. In reality, how we live in this life determines our eternal state. I understand from personal experience that earthly accomplishments have no value in my gaining eternal life. My highest social or civic honors will not earn me entrance into heaven. Speaking from personal experience, I explain often what it is like as a Christian to take up my cross daily and follow the saints who have preceded me.

I mentioned that my childhood left me with abandonment issues that took a lifetime to work out. I have learned to view life from an eternal perspective and find value because I am loved and accepted in my beloved Jesus, whose love has brought the greatest emotional healing in my life. The experience of being accepted in the Beloved, which Paul expresses in Ephesians 1:6,[6] reminds me constantly of the wonderful kindness God has poured out on me because I belong to his dearly loved Son, Jesus. God brought me into unmerited favor through Jesus's death and resurrection and made me the object of his grace and mercy. I no longer live a limousine-driven life, and I often care for those without fortune. Under the nonprofit organization Wheel of Grace Unlimited, I share my resources with the marginalized and needy. I have received many awards for my service to humankind, but the love of Jesus I feel daily enables me to take up my cross and follow him, and this is my saving grace.

If you feel abandoned as I did as a child and countless times as an adult in Hollywood's fast lane, give your heart to Jesus. He will heal you with his love and give you his joy and peace.

---

6. Eph 1:6: "To the praise of his glorious grace that he freely bestowed on us in the Beloved" (NRSV).

Jeremiah 29:11 gives us hope in God's promise: "'For I know the plans I have for you,' declares the Lord, 'plans to prosper you and not to harm you, plans to give you hope and a future'" (NIV).

RESOURCES

To purchase an autographed copy of Susan Stafford's book *Stop the Wheel, I Want to Get Off!*, please visit her website, SusanStafford.org. If you would like to have Susan speak at an event or order a copy of her book by email, write to Tammy Files at Believers2000@aol.com.

4

Hollywood's Circus of the Stars Stuntman

Bob Yerkes
Written by Jeanne DeFazio
as told to her by Bob Yerkes

LEFT TO RIGHT: BOB YERKES, DOROTHY YERKES, FAY AND ROSE ALEXANDER

PHYSICAL POWER AND MIGHT are paramount to success and excellence in the stunt and circus industries. Bob Yerkes understood that, to survive in this world, a person is expected to be tough, strong, and unbending, and Bob has received many awards for his prowess. One award was even created in his honor.

In 1970, the Circus Hall of Fame gave Bob the Award of Excellence of Flying Artons for his work in a trapeze act together with Reggie Armor. "Artons" is a neologism, a made-up name from these famous stunt performers combining "Ar" from Reggie Armor and "ton" from Brayton (Bob Yerkes's given name). Reggie and Bob both attended Palms Grammar School in Los Angeles and later became acquainted learning acrobatics at the original Santa Monica Muscle Beach. Bob is a member of the prestigious Stuntmen's Association of Motion Pictures and received the Stuntmen's "best high work" award in 1986 for hanging off the scaffolding surrounding the Statue of Liberty in the movie *Remo Williams*.[1] In 2004, Bob became a member of the World Acrobatic Gallery of Honor. He served on the board of Ted Baehr's Christian TV and Film Commission and received Ted Baehr's MOVIEGUIDE® Lifetime Achievement Award in 2004 "for helping entertainers understand God's love and grace." He received the award under his birth name: Brayton Yerkes. In 2008, Bob received the Paul Stader Stunt Award "for a lifetime of caring, giving, and providing a foundation of strength and passion for our dreams." The tribute to Bob stated: "Your door of love and guidance has always been open and has helped spring us into the people we are today. We love you and thank you. Your friends forever." In 2011, he received a Naperville Independent Film Festival Best Short Award for *Butterfly Circus*, a 2009 film he performed in and also associate produced.[2] Most recently, in 2013, Bob received the coveted Lifetime Achievement Award from the Stuntmen's Association.

Bob Yerkes had one more factor besides his strength, agility, and full command of his craft to account for his remarkably long and successful career. Throughout his career as a circus acrobat and through his legendary work as one of Hollywood's top stuntmen, as the Spirit of God brought him through various stunt accidents, he heard the Lord

---

1. Bob doubled in this action stunt for actor Fred Ward. There was no net or support underneath Bob while he performed this stunt. There was scaffolding around the Statue of Liberty while the monument was being refurbished.

2. *The Butterfly Circus* was written and produced by Joshua and Rebekah Weigel.

impress into his heart a Bible verse, Zechariah 4:6: "This is the word of the Lord unto Zerubbabel, saying, 'Not by might, nor by power, but by my spirit'" (KJV).

The purpose of this message from God to Zechariah was to encourage Joshua and Zerubabbel in their work of restoring the temple and the nation of Judah after the Babylonian captivity. They were shown that the true source of power was not merely by might, nor by human power, but by the Holy Spirit's anointing. This vision assured Israel that, despite the hindrance of the work on the temple, Zerubbabel would finish it (Zech 4:8–10).

Bob credits his spiritual and physical survival to his understanding of God's vision to Zechariah: "Not by force, nor by strength, but by my Spirit." Through his lifetime of professional achievements, Bob recognizes these key words from God's word were highlighted for him by God's Spirit. Bob has come to realize that it is only through God's Spirit that he has accomplished anything of lasting value. Zechariah 4:6 reminds Bob continually that he is on Jesus's side, and Bob has brought that message to many in the entertainment industry. As he lived for God, Bob was determined not to trust solely in his own strength or abilities, but rather to depend on God. Bob has moved in the power of God's Spirit, becoming a well-known witness for Jesus in the acrobatic, stunt, and entertainment industry.

In a *700 Club* interview, Bob is described as having led a life at the top of the stunt industry. After Bob came to the Lord, he kept all his capabilities, but aimed them in a different direction, bringing actors, actresses, and stunt performers to Jesus. The *700 Club* interview explained that Bob sponsored Centrum Ministry in Hollywood, a home that brings in runaways, exposing them to Christian values.

Bob invited M. R. DeHann of the *Daily Bread* and his family to the circus when touring Michigan. DeHann wrote the devotional "Witnessing on the Flying Trapeze" in January 14, 1971's *Daily Bread*.[3] That same year, Joe Stowell based a March 14, 1971, devotional on "The Catcher," as Bob had long been nicknamed.[4]

---

3. "Last night the phone rang and the voice said: 'My name is Bob Yerkes, I have been listening to you on the air all over the country.' I arranged to pick up the young man the next day so that he could meet the group at the office. This was unusual indeed, a radio Bible class listener, a flying trapeze acrobat with the circus." DeHann, "Witnessing on the Flying Trapeze."

4. "Life is indeed a risky business, if you put your faith in Jesus, the 'Catcher' is

In the summer of 2014, Bob Yerkes was interviewed by Gemma Wenger on her program *Beauty for Ashes*. Along with Bob, Gemma interviewed Media Fellowship International's founder, Bob Rieth, and myself, Jeanne DeFazio. In that interview, I summed up Bob Yerkes's gifting for relational evangelism. I described Bob as one of the most delightful human beings to walk God's earth. He ministers in the industry with great humor and love. Here is Bob Yerkes's story:

I was born February 11, 1932, in Santa Monica, California, to Bernice and Howard Yerkes. I grew up in the Culver City Palms area of Los Angeles, attending Palms Grammar School with actor Robert Blake, and was close friends with Robert's sister Giovanni Blake. I had one sister, Norma Lee, who was four years younger than I was. My dad was a mechanic who, during World War II, kept the trucks moving on the Alaska Highway in White Horse, Yukon Province. In 1943, our family moved from Los Angeles to White Horse, enduring weather 60 degrees below zero. After the war, we moved back to LA.

At fifteen, I actually did what many children have dreamt of doing: I ran away from home to join the circus (where I eventually found the love of Jesus). I had completed half of the ninth grade at Hamilton High School in Los Angeles before joining DeWayne Brothers' Circus when it toured LA in 1947. The circus came to town, and some of the people with whom I performed acrobatics on the original "muscle beach" in Santa Monica also performed in the circus.[5] Ted De Wayne of the DeWayne Brothers' Circus performed at the intersection of Lincoln and Washington Streets near what is now Marina Del Rey, California. At that time, it was a swamp, and the circus came into town and set up a tent there with live performers doing teeterboard[6] and risley[7] acts. They needed someone in the acrobatic act, so I did teeterboard, risley, and trampoline. This was at the end of 1947.

I traveled with DeWayne Circus up and down the west coast for a year. Dewayne joined the Clyde Beatty Circus in 1948, and I toured

---

waiting at the end to take you home." Stowell, "The Catcher."

5. I began performing acrobatics at eleven at Santa Monica's Muscle Beach.

6. Teeterboard is a teeter totter. You jump on one end and throw the person on the other end up in the air.

7. Risley is an acrobatic act where one performer lies down with his feet in the air and another performer jumps up and sits on his feet while he kicks him in somersaults.

with Clyde Beatty Circus all over the US between 1948 and 1951. At the Flamingo Hotel in Las Vegas in 1954, I performed with the DeWaynes at the same time Mickey Rooney did his standup comedy act. I have a photo of me holding up my stepson, Gerald Pina, with one hand, while Mickey Rooney spotted, making sure to catch Gerald if necessary. In 1958, MGM produced *The Big Circus* by Irwin Allen, starring Rhonda Fleming and David Nelson. I doubled for the actor David Nelson as the catcher in the film's trapeze act.

Gradually, I learned to perform a variety of acrobatic acts: trampoline, teeter board, and risley, eventually performing high wire and trapeze. As time went on, I began walking the high wire with no net for films. In 1956, I became Fay Alexander's partner in his troupe, the Flying Alexanders. A photo of the Flying Alexanders appeared in Bing Crosby's film *Say One for Me*.[8] I continued as an acrobatic performer in 1957 and 1958 with Ringling Brothers Circus, performing nationwide. Learning how to perform acrobatics worked out well, because I learned to teach acrobatics, and ultimately ended up teaching acrobatics for the *Circus of the Stars* television specials in the 1970s and 1980s. Most people still remember me from *Circus of the Stars*.

While with Ringling Brothers Circus, I decided to read the Bible. I grew up with a blind Christian aunt who possessed great spiritual insight, and her belief in Jesus impacted my early life, though I was reared in an unbelieving home. As a young adult, I have to confess I read the Bible planning to denounce the truth of it, but I realized that it had to be inspired by God.

Steve Terrell, the oldest son in the television series *Life with Father*, took me to the Village Church in Burbank, California. At 25 years old, I became a believer. I formed a group at Ringling Brothers Circus to read and study the Bible. I got my two friends, Reggie Armour and Bill Snyder, interested, and the first Bible study meeting was held in Little Rock, Arkansas. The group was nondenominational, including Roman Catholics as well as Protestants. My pastor, Reverend Phil Gibson, sent literature to help us in our worship. The original trio of the Bible reading group, Reggie Armour, Bill Snyder, and I, were in two acts with Ringling Brothers: the Flying Alexanders and the Glenhills

---

8. A picture of the Flying Alexanders was on a wall. Bing Crosby, portraying a priest, points to the picture and states that was he who was photographed with the trapeze artists.

Teeterboard Show. When Ringling Circus played LA, I became involved with a group of LA actors called the King's Stage. This group included Roy Rogers, Dale Evans, and Jimmy Dodd, one of the leaders in Walt Disney's Mouseketeers and part of the original *Mickey Mouse Club* television program. Jimmy came to speak to my Bible study group at Ringling Brothers. After he spoke, I decided to call the group at Ringling Brothers "The King's Ring."[9]

In 1967, I produced a film entitled *The Little People* with David Wilkerson, founder of Teen Challenge.[10] This film depicted the life of drug addiction and encouraged viewers to seek help in Wilkerson's Teen Challenge program. In the 1970s, I became involved with several Christian groups in Los Angeles, ministering on the streets of Hollywood and to members of the industry with Duane Pederson, a minister with the "Jesus People" of Hollywood. Duane mentored me as a Christian, keeping me in fellowship with strong praying Christians who trusted in the word of God. This group's close interpersonal relationships helped me grow spiritually.

In 1953, I married Dorothy Morales, a fifth-generation circus performer with the Clyde Beatty Circus. She had two sons by a former marriage, Gerald and Tony. We had one son together, Mark. Dorothy came from a Catholic background, and, during our early marriage, we grew together in our faith. Then, a devastating catastrophe happened. Our son Gerald, who was a strong Christian believer, was killed in Vietnam. After that, we decided not to travel full-time with the circus, but to spend more time at home, so I began to work more often as a stuntman in the entertainment industry.

Currently, I attend a Bible study at CBS Radford Studios in North Hollywood pastored by Reverend Robert Rieth of Media Fellowship International. In 1955, this was the home of GE Theatre. I recall rigging trapeze at an early GE Theatre program, narrated by Ronald Reagan, about a famous clown played by actor Henry Fonda. In a televised special, emceed by Merv Griffin, *Live at the Hippodrome* (London, England), the Flying Artons (Don Martinez,[11] Dorothy and Bob Yerkes)

---

9. Jimmy Dodd's group was called the King's Stage, so I decided to call my group The King's Ring, because we were Christians who worked in the circus ring.

10. Adult and Teen Challenge is a Bible-based recovery program for substance abusers.

11. I taught Don Martinez the three-and-a-half somersault on the trapeze, making

performed trapeze, executing three and a half somersaults in midair. We were the only trapeze act in the world to feature three and a half somersaults.

In 1973, I taught the "Share Ladies" aerial numbers for *The Share Benefit*, which starred, among others, Frank Sinatra, Gene Autry, Jack Benny, Marlon Brando, and Lucille Ball. *The Share Benefit*, dating from 1953 to the present day, benefits children and ministries that reach out to the needy.

In the 2006 winter edition of *Inside Stunts*, I am featured in an article written by Leigh Hennessey entitled, "A Life Stranger than Fiction."[12] Leigh refers to my backyard as the most famous place in the stunt world—a dusty one-acre lot in Northridge, California. I have amassed a historic collection of film stunt and circus equipment. My backyard has been the location for untold rehearsals, trainings, castings, media interviews, and even production shoots.[13] Cirque de Soleil performers came to my home in Northridge to work out. Stuntmen and -women in Hollywood work out to keep in shape on my backyard's aerial and acrobatic equipment. This week, as we are writing this chapter, Sony Studios' staff auditioned performers in my backyard for a live acrobatic show. My backyard is constantly filled with young stuntmen and -women working out and keeping in shape.

In spite of my acrobatic talent, I call myself a klutz, but I do not consider this a disadvantage. It made me a better teacher, because I had to experiment with learning methods to get the most out of my students. For many years, during the 1970s and '80s, I taught performers on the *Circus of the Stars* TV show. I taught aerial numbers to Mary Ann Mobley, the former Miss America, and her husband, actor Gary Collins, two strong Christians in the entertainment industry. I also appeared on *Circus of the Stars* as the catcher on the trapeze act with various stars, and I recall that one of the most talented and ablest stars to do aerial was actress Brooke Shields. Brooke performed different aerial numbers on *Circus of the Stars* for three different years. I enjoyed performing with Brooke in a TV special filmed in Las Vegas. I also remember with amazement that Todd Bridges, from the television show *Different Strokes*, performed a double somersault in the trapeze act on

---

Don the first flyer ever to feature the three-and-a-half in his act.

  12. Hennessey, *Inside Stunts*, 28–31.

  13. Ibid., 28.

Circus of the Stars. In the Fall/Winter 2004 edition of *ACRO Magazine*, I am featured on pages 22 and 23. This was the year I was inducted into the World Acrobatic Society.

Many of the stunts I am called to do are dangerous. I was in Paul Newman's first film, *The Silver Chalice*, portraying an acrobat entertaining the Roman emperor. I doubled for Eli Wallach in *Tough Guys*, where I got thrown off a moving train as it was going over a bridge and took a dangerous high fall into a stream of water. In 2009, I appeared as a cardinal in the Tom Hanks film *Angels and Demons*. This role called for me to be punished by being hung in the air and set on fire. I retain burn scars on my wrists from this stunt. I doubled for Arnold Schwarzenegger in the film *Commando*, doing one stunt: swinging through the air and landing on an elevator in Sherman Oaks Galleria Mall. In the *Back to the Future* films 1, 2, and 3, I doubled for actor Christopher Lloyd, sliding down from a clock. This is the same shot that is still shown repeatedly on commercials today. I fought Chuck Norris in *Forced Vengeance*. In *Psycho 2*, I doubled for actor Robert Loggia, falling down stairs after being stabbed. In *Towering Inferno*, I hung on the top of an outside elevator. In *Return of the Jedi*, I fell into a pit and did several other stunts. I was a stuntman on *Wonder Woman*, performing with Lynda Carter, who became my good friend. Once, I doubled for Gilligan on *Gilligan's Island*, swinging through the air on a rope. I doubled for Della Reese once in the *Touched by an Angel* series and was shot out of a cannon in a circus sequence. You can see why I depend on God's grace to get me through.

In summary, I began as a fifteen-year-old in the circus, trained countless people in trapeze acts all over the globe, and I am now in my sixty-ninth year in show business. Over the years, my faith has been nurtured by many strong Christians in the industry. For example, Ted Baehr got me involved with his organization, MOVIEGUIDE®. Ted stayed on my boat in Marina Del Rey during his early visits to LA. I also attended Bible studies in the West LA home of *Saved by the Bell* and *Last Comic Standing* producer Peter Engel in the 1980s. Today, I continue to attend Oscar award-winning composer Al Kasha's Bible studies in Beverly Hills, hosted by Al's wonderful wife, Ceil.

I first became involved with Media Fellowship International in the 1970s and am currently a director of MFI. At that time, Reverend Bob Rieth, MFI's founder, hosted events at the Marina City Club, often emceed by the multitalented Susan Stafford, former hostess for Merv Griffin's *Wheel of Fortune*. I also met philanthropist Michael P. Grace II at Reverend Rieth's MFI 1980s Bible studies in his Playa del Rey home. I also attended Michael P Grace II's World Alliance for Peace Hollywood outreaches in the 1980s and 1990s, hosted by Reverend Bob Rieth and MFI.[14]

Today, I minister with MFI's national and international outreach to the media during crises. I traveled with MFI on location to Virginia for outreach to the media during the Virginia Tech massacre, to New Orleans for MFI's Hurricane Katrina outreach to the media, and to Israel for MFI's outreach to the media during recent terrorist attacks. I also regularly attend MFI's CBS Studio monthly outreach to minister to entertainment industry members.

My motivation for ministry to the media could be summed up like this: I was mentored by the world's greatest stuntman who specialized in high work. His name was Jesus Christ. He stood in for everyone up on the cross. And he sustains me by His Spirit.

RESOURCES

The Butterfly Circus, Joshua Weigel film, written by Joshua and Rebekah Weigel, associate producer Bob Yerkes. Online at thebutterflycircus.com.

---

14. These events are chronicled in DeFazio and Lathrop, *Creative Ways*, 8. In that book, Bob Rieth's gifting is explained as outreach to the entertainment industry: "Encouragement, as Circus of the Stars Bob Yerkes explains, is one of Pastor Bob's great gifts: 'Pastor Bob Rieth is down to earth and kind. He listens and encourages us, sharing Scripture, praying with us and for us. Under his pastoral anointing, we bond and feel great joy in Christian community devoted to bringing others to Jesus.'"

5

The Hula Hoop Queen

Jozy Pollock
Written by Jeanne DeFazio
as told to her by Jozy Pollock

The Hula Hoop Queen

Jozy Pollock jokes that she gave up the hula hoop for the cross. She was Britain's hula hoop queen, but her career came to a halt when she married the famous magician Channing Pollock. She appeared on the *Ed Sullivan Show* and performed in Las Vegas as Channing's assistant. After accepting Jesus as Lord and Savior, Jozy gave up a life of glamour and volunteered with the prison chaplain services at East Lake Juvenile Hall in downtown Los Angeles. She became the first Protestant female chaplain at Los Angeles Men's Central Jail. Noelle Aimee Kozell directed a documentary about Jozy's twenty years in prison ministry entitled *On Faith Alone: The Jozy Pollock Story*. Throughout her life, she has met and befriended celebrities and understands from personal experience that many celebrities do not have the peace and love that comes from having a personal relationship with God. Here is her story:

I was born in the East End of London. While I was a little girl, World War II broke out. Many nights, we slept in an air-raid shelter with gas masks by our sides. My dad did night work, so my mum had to get my infant sister and me dressed and into the shelter. One night, I looked up into the sky and saw two planes in a fight with tracer bullets going back and forth. It scared me so much I took one step into the shelter instead of four. Providentially, I landed on the bed. We heard explosions as part of the air raids, and the worst explosions were from rockets. A rocket would make a loud whistle and, when the whistle stopped, you knew it was about to fall, and you just hoped it was not going to land on your house. There were casualties. My piano teacher got bombed out, which ended my future career as a pianist. When I first came to Hollywood and saw the searchlights they use for premiers and major events, it reminded me of the war. My World War II post-traumatic stress disorder would kick in. During World War II, searchlights were used to spot enemy planes over London. During the worst bombing, my family went to stay in the country. A lot of children were evacuated without their parents. I was blessed to have my mum, granny, aunt, cousin, and baby sister with me. It was food rationing time, and we only had so many stamps. Friday night was the best night, as we could get meat. My favorite time was going to a farm in the country. I made friends with the Land Army girls,[1] and I learned to milk a cow. I have

---

1. The Women's Land Army was a British civilian organization that recruited women to work in agriculture in the place of men who had been called up to the

always loved animals, and I experienced a traumatic incident when the calf I had seen born and had fed and petted each day was sent off to market. Its mother cried so much, and so did I.

When the war was over, I continued school in London and passed my scholarship, entering a high school in Epping Forest. During our time on the playground, we would look through the cracks in the fence and could see men standing behind the trees exposing themselves. My mother must have found out, as she had me transferred to a closer high school that was on a main road. I left high school at fourteen and went to commercial college for a year to learn shorthand and typing. I started work at fifteen.

I loved films and the bright lights, so I would go to the West End after work and started hanging out in a Soho café. There were several attractive older men who paid me a lot of attention and wanted me to be their girlfriend. One day, two policeman came in and asked me how old I was. They proceeded to put me in their squad car and drive me home. I was so embarrassed. They told my parents that I was hanging out in a place frequented by pimps and that I should stay away from there. I was furious to find out that these men who wanted to be my boyfriends were trying to groom me for prostitution. I did go back and gave them a piece of my mind.

I had befriended a young man from Cypress in that café, and he confided that he was being kept by one of the top girls in a Maltese gang's stable. He felt guilty, since his parents thought he was selling carpets. I told him to go home. Sometime later, I was in the ladies' room of a restaurant and I heard, "That's the [expletive] who's been messing with my old man." I looked up to see a tough-looking woman hanging out with several ladies of the night, and realized she was talking about me and the Cypriot boy. To this day, I cannot remember how I escaped those women, who carried razors. God put a shield around me and protected me from so many circumstances in my youth because there was a call on my life for ministry. I believe those women were blinded by the Holy Spirit, and I think I may have been translated just like Philip was when enemies were about to kill him (Acts 8:39–40).

A friend of mine was going on an audition and asked me to go with him. I did, and I was booked to be on a television show.[2] I enrolled

---

military.

2. Incidentally, my friend became the CEO of Jimmy Choo Shoes, which is now

in acting school, did some modeling, and worked in a nightclub as a receptionist and cigarette girl to pay the bills. There were girls working there as hostesses who also sold their bodies. I had many offers of big money to go home with customers. Richard Burton said he would get me fired if I would not leave with him. I was pursued by princes, sheiks, dukes, earls, lords, and movie stars. One society man tried to get a "madam" to put me on her books so he could get me.

In the club, I first saw the man I was to marry. He was six-foot-four and so handsome. When Channing came in the club, I told the girl I worked with, "This man just can't leave me alone. Here he is again." Talk about calling things that are not as though they are! Finally, I was introduced to him, and that was that. We sat up all night talking. He took me to the best restaurant for lunch, and we started dating. He was appearing at the London Palladium. We had been together about six months when my friend Diana Dors asked me to go on tour with her. I did not realize Channing could not be alone, and, during the time I was gone, he disappeared and went back to his ex-girlfriend in Paris. It was all over the papers that the magician disappeared, because Channing did not show up at the Pigalle supper club where he was working. Months later, he showed up drunk at my door with the girl I worked with at the club. His hand was bleeding. She said that she had mentioned me, and he broke a glass in his hand. I was just on my way to Royal Albert Hall where I was modeling swimsuits with the hula hoop. I had at that time become the "Hula Hoop Queen of Britain" and was featured on the cover of several magazines. Photos of me hula-hooping were published all over the world. My photograph was on the record cover of the *Hula Hoop Song*. Channing and the girl insisted on coming with me to Royal Albert Hall. After that night, Channing and I got back together. In 1961, we married, and I appeared on the *Ed Sullivan Show* and performed in Las Vegas as Channing's assistant. Channing and I toured in the United States as an opening act for Liberace. We worked the Tropicana, the Stardust, and the Sahara in Las Vegas and the Latin Quarter in Manhattan.

I always felt God's protection in my life, even before I came to the Lord. Channing and I divorced in 1968, and, in 1970, I was living in Los Angeles as a young divorcée mingling with the rich and celebrated. I intended to be at Roman Polanski's the night of the Sharon Tate mur-

---

his daughter's company.

der. I had a terrible migraine that prevented me from attending. The next morning, I prepared to drive over to Sharon Tate's house and was stunned by the news reports about the murders. Sharon and four others were slaughtered by cult figure Charles Manson's followers. God protected me. I now believe God spared my life for future ministry. A migraine saved my life. God protects us when he has a purpose for us.

The paparazzi headline in the "Good News" read, "Migraine Saved Super Groupie from Sharon Tate Murder." I was termed in the press a "super groupie," but this is inaccurate, as I never actually followed famous musicians. After divorcing my husband in 1968, I dated a number of famous men and was for a time involved with a famous British rocker named Nigel Olsson. He was a drummer in Elton John's band. To get out of a couple of relationships, one with a married man, I took up Nigel's offer to go on an Elton John tour. That lasted for five years and involved traveling the world, where I was always running into people I knew in different countries. Elton John and his manager John Reid were fascinated by the celebrities I knew and wanted to buy my phone book. One time we were out on a yacht in Marina Del Ray and a little speed boat pulled up alongside with two men yelling my name. "[Expletive] me!" cried John Reid, "She even knows people at sea!" It was actor Ian McShane and Wes Farrell, co-writer of many rock classics such as Jay and the Americans' "Come a Little Closer," working then as David Cassidy's producer. We were invited to Kensington Palace to have dinner with Princess Margaret. Elton's co-writer, Bernie Taupin, split his pants, so we went in to Margaret's office to pin him up. Her telephone was sitting on the desk with her number in full view. I recorded it in my mind, and, weeks later, Elton John offered to give me Princess Margaret's number in exchange for Elvis Presley's number. I laughed and said I already had her number.

In 1982, a relationship I had with a man I had found through a psychic's predictions brought me to the end of my rope. I called a friend named Mike who had accepted Jesus after years of drinking and drugging. I told him that I had had enough torment and I wanted peace. He told me that, if I prayed the sinner's prayer, I could have peace. I did not feel like a sinner, because I had always been a good friend and looked out for others. I was the unpaid psychiatrist to my friends who were going through traumas. I prayed the sinner's prayer, but pleaded with the Lord not to turn me into a Jesus freak. I went to a Chi Coltrane

Christian concert at the Vineyard.[3] She was talking about being "born again," explaining that it was a step of faith, and that salvation is assured even if you are not feeling it. This was exactly where I was in my walk. I found out she had a Bible study at her home, and I attended. I told her how I was feeling. She prayed with me and laid hands on me. I started speaking in tongues. Suddenly, I had a huge hunger and thirst for God. It took me a long time to submit to the Holy Spirit, but, after I gave up my will, I had peace. When I was water baptized in a home in Bel Air, I fell in love with Jesus and became invisible to men. I needed to build my relationship with Jesus. I have been celibate since being saved. This was God's shield.

After I got saved, I went to a couple of concerts wearing many crosses. Elton John joked, "Are you afraid of vampires?" Then, we went back to Bernie Taupin's house and ordered hamburgers. When I asked which one was mine, Elton John quipped, "The one with the cross on it." I did write Elton a letter, since he always wanted to contact the celebrities I knew well, and said I just met the most famous one they should get to know—his name is Jesus. They told me the letter went all round the office. My friends in the fast lane mocked my faith. They drifted away, and I stopped going to the parties and became drawn to Christian ministry. One by one, I sold the pieces of jewelry given to me by famous men.

I joined a drama team from church that performed Christian skits on the streets of Hollywood. Then, a woman who had just been released from prison said she wanted to start a prison ministry. I thought that taking the skits into lockup facilities would be a good idea, so I signed up. God had other ideas and turned me into a preacher. This was amazing, as I had once told him not to give me the gift of prophecy, as I was too shy to stand up in church and give a word. When I was first saved and still rebelling, I went to a Bible study where the teacher was discrediting other ministries. I asked God, "How can we save the world when we are so divided?" I had become angry with people who said the Lord told me this and that. Then, for the first time, God spoke to me. He said to listen to all my teachers and the Holy Spirit would give me the gift of discernment. Through the years, I have discovered that no one gets it all right.

---

3. Chi Coltrane had a notable hit with her song, "Thunder and Lightning," but was now singing for Jesus with songs such as "Go like Elijah."

So, I began to volunteer in prison ministry. I loved to exhort and encourage the inmates by sharing God's word and explaining that Bible heroes were imprisoned while continuing to fulfill God's call on their lives. I had married a famous magician and had had a lot of magical times. After I came to the Lord, the magical part of my life was introducing prisoners to Jesus, who supernaturally transforms the lives of those who receive him as Lord and Savior. The inmates were encouraged by this message of hope and many prayed the sinner's prayer. They claimed I had a direct line to God and sought me out for prayer at the Los Angeles County Jail. I never had children, and I loved the inmates as if they were my children. People in jail do not understand that God still loves them. They need Jesus's love.

I called a man up to my office at the Los Angeles County Jail to give him a death notice of one of his family members. He said, "It's been a bad year: first my wife, then my aunt, and now my mother."

"Oh you poor dear. How did your wife die?" I commiserated.

"I killed her," he said. Now, I could not change my expression and express my feelings, so I asked, "Have you asked God to forgive you?"

"Yes," he replied.

"Didn't you love your wife?" I inquired.

"Oh, I loved her very much," he responded emphatically.

"Were you fighting?" I asked.

"No, we never fought," he insisted.

"What happened?" I questioned.

"Well, we were smoking some weed and drinking champagne, and I heard voices, and next thing I was in the police station covered in blood," he answered.

"Lord, don't let him hear voices while he is in my office!" was my silent prayer.

Another inmate who wanted to change his life and clear his conscience confessed to me he had two bodies hidden on his property: One was his father, whom he had killed ten years before, and the other from a deal gone bad. He wanted me to advise the proper authorities. I asked him if he was sure. Priests cannot expose things said in confidence, and I thought the rule might apply to me too. Yes, he wanted this done. So, I went and informed the sheriff, letting his office know where the bodies were. This was Friday, and, on Monday morning, I received a call at my office job for Christian Chaplains' Services where

I worked part time. It was the Catholic volunteer berating me for betraying confidence and informing me the inmate was furious. I did not want him mad at me. He was scary. I told her there must be some misunderstanding, and we would talk to him together when I got to the jail. This was the first time I dreaded going to jail. I told her to call him up and, when I walked in, he gave me a big smile and thanked me for taking his burden off him. I told him I had carried his burden all weekend. He was not mad at me. The police had torn his house apart and showed him a picture. He was mad at them. Later that night, he was sitting in a front row at my service in the chapel. I thanked God I had confronted the problem. If he had been mad at me, he could have just jumped up and attacked me, because security was not that tight. But God was working a change in his life.

Although I felt quite comfortable walking the high-power rows alone, God gave me the desire to minister on the mental rows. I called Mel Novak, an actor who was a minister in prisons and on skid row. We had met on prison tour with Calvary Chapel.

I told him I could get him a chaplain badge if he would accompany me. I told him to watch out for anyone throwing feces or urine, as he was always dressed so well. Because a lot of mental issues are also demonic, we would hear growling as we entered in, and the Holy Spirit in us collided with the demon spirits. So, imagine my initial delight when I arrived at a cell and the occupant greeted me, "Hello, my sweet angel."

So I asked, "Do you know Jesus?"

"I am Jesus," came his reply.

I said, "Oh, I don't think so."

He replied, "So, f— off, you Limey twit." He ranted on a bit more (very un-Jesus-like) about how he had built that jail and I needed to leave.

I carried on down the row and, on my way back, I asked him, "If you are who you say you are, why don't you escape?"

He looked me straight in the eye and said, "Are you crazy? I have come in here for a rest. It's chaos out there." He got that right.

On the juvenile row, I met a young offender who had a tattoo around his neck that said, "F— the world." When he saw me look, he said, "You like my tattoo?"

I said, "No, do you really feel like that?"

He said, "Yes."

I asked him, "How old are you?"

He replied, "Seventeen."

I asked, "How did you get so bitter?"

He said, "What does that mean?"

I defined bitterness, adding, "You know, the Bible says, 'God will take a heart of stone and turn it into a heart of flesh.'"

He replied, "You don't believe all that stuff do you?"

I said, "Yes."

He asked, "Don't you ever doubt?"

I said, "Yes, I get doubts, and then God does something amazing and restores my faith." I prayed for him and walked the row.

On my way back, he called me over and said, "Chaplain, will you please pray for me?"

I said, "I just did."

He replied, "No, when you go home, will you pray that God changes my heart?"

I did that every night. I did not see him there the next week, but the Catholics told me he wanted his tattoo removed and was going to take communion. Prayer works.

In the 1990s, Prince Charles visited Los Angeles. He had recently written a book about his breakup with Princess Diana. Before he arrived, I wrote Buckingham Palace and invited him to tour the Los Angeles County Jail. I received a reply stating that the prince's itinerary was already set, but that I was invited to a reception to meet Prince Charles during his stay in Los Angeles. When we met, Charles asked me what I did in the jail. I told him that I counseled men in crisis, and I offered him my card. He replied, with good humor, "Does it work?" It worked for musician Billy Preston, who met me when, as he put it, "God was punishing [him] in the LA County Jail." One of the best times for my prison services was when Billy Preston was incarcerated. He was my worship leader. I gave him some lyrics and a salvation prayer that I always said. He put them to music and recorded them under the titles: "Thank You, Jesus," and "Father, Forgive Us."

God has blessed me by sending my testimony out through the media. Noelle Aimee Kozoll produced and directed a documentary about my twenty years as a chaplain in the Los Angeles County Jails: *By Faith Alone, The Story of Jozy Pollock*. On August 29, 2013, Sheri Pedigo's *Live from the Red Carpet* at the Hollywood premiere of *Baseball's Last*

Hero: 21 Clemente Stories was published on YouTube. Sheri featured me discussing the film, how I narrowly escaped being a Manson murder victim, and my work at LA County Jail. In this interview, I discussed my friendships with Hollywood celebrities and my marriage to Channing Pollock.[4] I have given my testimony on *Victory Road*, Lee Benton's show on The Cross TV. In that interview, I focused on my early life in show business, how I became born again and came to Jesus's victory road, and my subsequent chaplaincy in the Los Angeles County Jail.[5] Actress and singer Lee Benton leads a prayer meeting on a CBS studio lot, where, in January 2015, I had the privilege to testify about my chaplaincy in the jails transforming men's and women's lives by the power of the Holy Spirit.[6]

I believe that Hollywood needs missionaries more than Africa does! African Christianity is strong and thriving, but people in Los Angeles are very self-centered and so into money and fame and all the things that are really unimportant in the divine scheme of things. I continue to tell my story to bring anyone who can identify with me to find forgiveness, peace, and love by accepting Jesus as Lord and Savior. I now live in modest circumstances, removed from my former lifestyle with the rich and famous. I have been Britain's hula-hoop queen who became a glamour girl and journeyed through the fast lane, but I found no peace in any of it. I found true peace when I accepted the gracious gift of living my life in the Beloved—Jesus.[7] If you are reading this chapter and you need peace, open your heart to Jesus. His heart burns with love for you. Open your heart to him, and he will embrace you in his everlasting arms of love. His will give you his peace.

RESOURCES

I am available for speaking engagements. You can view my interviews online:

On Faith Alone: The Jozy Pollock Story, directed by Noelle Aimee Kozoll. youtube.com/watch?v=auNvGVfes5U.

---

4. Pedigo, "Jozy Pollock Interview."
5. Benton, "Studio Meetings."
6. Ibid.
7. Eph 1:6: "So we praise God for the wonderful kindness he has poured out on us because we belong to his dearly loved Son" (NIV).

Sheri Pedigo, "Jozy Pollock Interview on Clemente Movie, Manson, and Magic," *Live on the Red Carpet.* youtube.com/watch?v=8KhI2Yh3VrE.

"Lee Benton, producer of *Victory Road,* The Cross TV, interviews Jozy Pollock."
youtube.com/watch?v=ATHHLa86Akw.

Lee Benton's CBS studio meetings, guest speaker, Jozy Pollock. youtube.com/watch?v=EJHNBivDUTE.

Contact me by email for speaking engagements or interviews: *haleluiaholywood@aol.com.*

6

Heavenly Manna, Inc.

Mel Novak
Written by Jeanne DeFazio
as told to her by Mel Novak

Clockwise from left: Mel Novak in *Hard Way Heroes*, Mel and Bruce Lee in *Game of Death*, Mel in *Sword of Heaven*, Mel and Chuck Norris in *Eye For An Eye*, and Mel in *Giants*

Mel Novak is an award-winning character actor[1] who starred or costarred in twenty-five films. He is best known for villainous roles in

---

1. Among other awards, Mel has received the Bronze Halo Award from the

Black Belt Jones, Bruce Lee's *Game of Death*, Yul Brynner's *The Ultimate Warrior*, and Chuck Norris's *An Eye for an Eye*. He always performed his own stunts and fighting scenes. He acted in many independent features, such as *Lovely But Deadly* for director/producer David Sheldon, starring Lucinda Dooling. In the 1990s, he appeared in two films for director Garry Marshall: *Exit to Eden* (1994), based on the novel by Anne Rice, and *Dear God* (1996). In 2005, he starred in the action/horror film *Vampire Assassin*. Today, he hosts a weekly global radio program with Sherri Emily on WLOR.net and *The Omega Man* radio program two hours per week with Shannon Ray Davis. God is blessing these programs, which are flooding God's words of life all over our planet. Here is Mel's remarkable story:

I am Mel Novak, founder of Heavenly Manna, Inc. I am an ordained minister called by God to share the Good News of Jesus Christ, particularly God's message of salvation to the homeless on skid row and to inmates in prisons. Under the guidance of the Holy Spirit, Jack Hayford and Charles Stanley mentored me. Adversity is what made my faith strong.

I was blessed with a praying Christian mother. When I was a child, the medical prognosis was that my leg would have to be amputated. Through the prayers of my mother, God miraculously healed my leg. Her faith influenced my life deeply. My faith in God grew as I experienced a series of injuries that were miraculously healed. A native of Pittsburgh, Pennsylvania, I was an outstanding athlete in several sports who passed up sixty football scholarship offers to sign a pro baseball contract with the Pittsburgh Pirates. My career was cut short by a massive rotary cup tear. Through prayer and very challenging rehabilitation therapy, my rotary cup tear healed. I endured ten failed surgeries on my throat in ten years, and, once again, the example of my mother's deep faith and prayers encouraged mine, resulting in each miraculous healing. I look back now and realize that, through every infirmity, God gave me healing after healing that encouraged my faith in him. The Lord healed a serious injury to my eye, a torn cornea, only hours before surgery. On Easter 1983, I was spared from death after serious hemorrhaging from surgery. On March 14, 1998, I almost died from peritonitis caused by anti-inflammatory prescription medication. I had

---

Southern California Motion Picture Council.

prostate cancer for seven years until God healed me without chemo or radiation. My faith in Jesus is strong because my testimony about the healing power of God is sincere.

Due to injury, I never realized my childhood dream of playing baseball for the Pirates. Through networking, a series of divine appointments brought modeling and acting offers to me from Hollywood. Agents recognized my ability to look good in clothes. Directors and producers saw my acting potential. My injuries prepared me with the patience needed to pursue the acting profession long-term. When Jesus healed me, he gave everything he had to give me. When I act, I give everything I need to give the role.

My personal experience of physical brokenness also brought spiritual understanding. In ministry, I give everything I have to Jesus. I preach Christ crucified to the hurting and downtrodden who have lost all hope. My ministry succeeds with the prisoners and those on skid row because I speak to them where they live. I am able to demonstrate that Jesus is the way out of pain and suffering because my own physical pain and suffering brought me to Jesus. I teach directly from the word of God and preach that nobody in this world goes through life without trials, troubles, and tribulations. I know!

Paul in Romans 8:28 explains: "And we know that God causes everything to work together for the good of those who love God and are called according to his purpose for them" (NLT). God does not leave us in isolated incidences of misery, but works "everything together" for our good.

This does not mean that all that happens to us is good. Evil prevails in a fallen world, but God is able to turn every circumstance around for long-range good. God is working through trials and tribulations to fulfill his purpose. This is a promise claimed by those who love God and are called by him—that is to say, those whom the Holy Spirit convinces to receive Jesus. Christians have a new perspective: they trust in God. Their security is in heaven, not on earth. Their faith in God does not waver during pain and persecution because they know God is with them. I tell prisoners and those on skid row that, despite whatever they are going through, God can use what the devil meant for evil for good.

Each of us experiences the pain of brokenness. As we go down this broken road of mixed emotions, it is hard to realize that strength with blessings are to be the end result when pain is overwhelming—though it is not difficult to recognize that we are in the "furnace of affliction" (Isa 48:10)! I encourage those in prison and on skid row to run to the Lord like world-class athletes and to find him in the Bible, God's word. Matthew 6:33 promises, "But strive first for the kingdom of God and his righteousness, and all these things will be given to you as well" (NRSV). I encourage them to rest, trust, and lean on Jesus who brings the healing and restoration, to become reliant on the God who speeds up the healing process. I explain that Jesus himself was the epitome of reliance on God on earth, leading us by example to his Father. In John 14:10–11, he says, "Do you not believe that I am in the Father, and the Father is in me? The words that I say to you I do not speak on my own initiative, but the Father abiding in me does his works. Believe me that I am in the Father and the Father is in me; otherwise believe because of the works themselves" (NRSV). I identify the fact that God's purpose for allowing brokenness in our lives is to bring us to a place of wholeness and maturity. I equip inmates and those on Skid Row with what I call "the arsenal prayers for protection." Those who faithfully say these prayers leave prison and are not repeat offenders.

Creative Ways to Build Christian Community, edited by Jeanne DeFazio and John Lathrop, chronicled my ministry. In her chapter, "Building Christian Community through Meetings and Meals," Jeanne DeFazio identified the impact of my ministry and the arsenal prayers for protection on her life:

> Mel Novak's ministry, Heavenly Manna, Inc., has greatly impacted my life. He reaches out to those that many people do not want to have anything to do with. His ministry is unique in that it builds Christian community among the helpless and hopeless: those who have nothing and no one. Mel's deliverance and protection prayers build Christian community within the walls of penal institutions and among the homeless. Sixteen years ago, Mel gave me a copy of the arsenal prayers for protection. These prayers are the backbone of his ministry. Saying these prayers daily for the past sixteen years has changed my life. I have emailed these prayers to those in need and prayed for people in groups using the arsenal prayers. I believe that these scripturally based prayers are effective in providing protection and deliverance and also in building Christian community. Arsenal prayers have helped build Christian community in a unique way. Thousands of intercessors repeat these prayers daily. Members of national prayer chains use this miraculous arsenal of prayers

to begin their intercession for the lost. Many people bound by torment and despair within the penitentiary walls and in homeless camps in the inner city say these arsenal prayers and are released from isolation and come into community with Jesus and others. Mel's arsenal prayers have a breaker anointing that sets captives free and brings the lost to Jesus and into Christian community. Thousands have found Christ through his preaching and teaching. Mel says that he is not the one doing the work: "I give God the honor, worship, and glory. So I count it an honor and privilege to be able to share my faith and lead lost souls to Christ. The Lord truly blesses me as I serve him in whatever way he leads."[2]

My ministry, Heavenly Manna, Inc., succeeds in bringing those in entertainment to Jesus. On October 23, 2014, manager Joe Williamson and I flew to Dayton, Ohio, for the celebrity Epic-Con Geek Fest. Twenty thousand people attended. I was flown there, and they put me up in a local hotel. There were two independent films being shot there, and the directors asked me to do a special appearance role. I also did three TV interviews. I met Producer-Director Christopher Booth, who was writing his next film and who cast me in a costar role in his horror film. The greatest blessing of this event was that I was able to witness to fellow actors and attendees.

For the past thirty-three years, drawing strength from the Lord (John 15:5; Eph 6:10), I have ministered on the streets of Los Angeles, California. For thirty-two years, I have ministered in the chapel services at the Union Rescue Mission, Fred Jordan Mission, LA Mission, and the Long Beach Rescue Mission doing Bible studies on spiritual warfare, counseling and praying with and for the multitudes. I also have been distributing Bibles out of my car trunk for more than thirty years. I have conducted more than five thousand services in the past twenty-plus years.

For the past thirty years, in my prison ministry, I have preached Christ crucified at chapel services in prisons and penitentiaries around the US. I met Los Angeles County Jail Chaplain Jozy Pollock at Christian meetings in Hollywood for members of the entertainment industry. She recommended me as a chaplain to the Los Angeles County Jail. As my experience ministering to inmates grew, I had the opportunity to minister at Pelican Bay Penitentiary, Washington State County

---

2. DeFazio and Lathrop, *Creative Ways*, 13–14.

Rehabilitative Facilities, and many others. Many inmates I counsel are level 3 and level 4—the highest levels of security. There are times when I minister in the yard and one-on-one in the cells. In the prisons, they call me "machine gun" because I back up everything that I say with one, two, or three Scriptures.

My acting career has enhanced my prison ministry. I am typecast as a villain in many films. This gives me identity with those behind bars. They can understand my film work from personal experience and bond with me. I tell inmates that, when I portray a heavy in films, my characters always get what they deserve. Then I remind them that Jesus paid the price for their sins, and they can accept him as Lord and Savior, be set free of condemnation, and have a second chance.

Revivals are going on in prisons where I have preached. Since January 2013, 97 percent of those who attend my prison services say the sinner's prayer. To identify the way that my ministry, Heavenly Manna, Inc., works in bringing those in prison to Jesus, here are two sample monthly reports:

- In September 2014, I started off at a juvenile facility and ended up at the hardcore Pelican Bay Penitentiary, a super-max level four state prison, performing six services for the extremely high percentage of lifers. If I do not reach the youth in juvenile facilities, I get them later in the state penitentiary.[3]

- October was another month of harvesting souls. More than 500 prayed the sinner's prayer. At Taft Prison, two hundred and thirty came forward in two Holy Spirit–anointed services where inmates clapped nine or ten times when God's word touched their hearts. It blessed me when Chaplain Dale Scardron, a loving and compassionate brother, told me the inmates wanted me to return.

I was at the "war zone," the LA County jail, five times that month. The inmates responded to God's call, receiving the arsenal prayers for protection, Bibles, reading glasses, and devotionals. I counseled and walked the tiers to minister to the inmates housed on the high-security levels: those who were locked down and not permitted to attend services.

---

3. Novak, untitled document.

Here is a composite from letters I received recently, from an inmate telling me how personal involvement in prison makes a difference in the lives of inmates:

> I have a lot of love and respect for you, Mel, and already miss you. I miss looking out through my bars seeing you headed down the tier. . . . I want to thank you, Mel, from the bottom of my heart for your spiritual guidance, good words from God, and most of all, the friendship that you and I cultivated through the past year, a friendship that I hold dear and value very much. I had a rough ride this past year, but hearing you around made things better. You need a GPS tracker to locate me because of all the moving I did, my friend. God bless you, friend. If they transfer me to Wasco, it's way out there in the middle of the country near Bakersfield. I know that you don't believe in luck, so by God's grace, I landed in a cell with a friend of mine. He was my yard dog when we were in Corcoran together back in 2011. We both got out and came back, but to my surprise, he is walking with the Lord these days. And to his surprise, I am also walking with the Lord. In the morning we start out our day by reading the *Daily Bread*, then reading the Scripture aloud with a small prayer. I gave him the arsenal prayer as well. I still have the Bible you gave me and wrote on the inside. I will not allow the slick one as you call him to take control of me again. . . . I strive to turn it all around, brother, I honestly do. I send my utmost respect to you, Mr. Mel Novak, full blast.

My career in the movies where I pound on heroes and ultimately get beaten, and my present ministry where the Holy Spirit pounds on the "Slick One," have important parallels: My ministry success demonstrates that Jesus's shed blood on Calvary can turn a villain into a hero, a loser into a winner, a bad guy into a good guy, and a heavy into a champion for God's righteous search-and-rescue hit squad. God's word that I preach and my testimony have brought over one hundred thousand to know Jesus as Lord and Savior. Please visit my website, melnovak.com. Go to the warfare section and download my arsenal prayer. I have given out more than 124,000 copies. This powerful prayer dresses you for each day's battle.

RESOURCES

If you would like to have Mel speak at a conference or church event, contact him through his website, melnovak.com.

7

The Flight of a Butterfly

Sheri Pedigo
Written by Jeanne DeFazio
as told to her by Sheri Pedigo

Left to right: Rod Jackson, Joanne Cash Yates, Kimberly Jackson, and Sheri Pedigo at the Cowboy Church in Nashville, Tennessee

Sheri Pedigo and Jeanne DeFazio met through a mutual friend, famed Hollywood Stuntman Bob Yerkes. Sheri is a major horse activist who has also produced events dedicated to "saving K-9 lives." A prolific songwriter, she provided two songs, *Caravan* and *I Find You*, for James Kleinert's television documentary *Horse Medicine*. Sheri has written songs for the reality show *Blind Date*, and, in Europe, she had a hit single on the dance charts with *Caravan*, which was the theme song for Cannes Film Festival red carpet in 2010. Sheri was the opening act for country singer Randy Travis at William Shatner's Hollywood Charity Horse Show, held in Burbank, California. She has shared the stage with many musical icons, such as Toto's lead singer Bobby Kimball, Spencer Davis, Patti LaBelle, the Temptations, and Martha Reeves and the Vandellas, to name a few. Her duet with Eric Van Aro, *Born Again*, was up for a Grammy in the jazz category in 2014. Here is her story:

Second Corinthians 5:17 explains, "If anyone is in Christ, he is a new creation; the old has gone, the new has come!" (NIV). If anyone knows what the cocoon feels like, it is me. I have been through a lot of faith testing. When you are stuck in a cocoon and you know you are ready to fly, it is frustrating. My story identifies a few people who have tried to keep me in the cocoon and many people who have helped me break out of it. It describes my fight to keep my wings from being clipped and my deep understanding of God, who sees my heart's desire to soar for him and to spread his love throughout the world.

I grew up in Glasgow, Kentucky, a town of about twenty thousand. My parents had three children, and I am the middle child. My dad always had his own business as a mechanic working on race cars. He gave everyone who came along a job. He was a giving, wonderful man. No one could ever say a bad thing about my dad. Dad was not present in my life much because he was always working. I did not have the relationship with my dad that I wished for. I always wanted to hang out with my dad. I would go to his shop, go fishing with him, and try to find time to be with him any way I could. The feeling of disconnect with my father affected my life in many ways, especially in my dating relationships. Seems I was always seeking Daddy.

I started playing piano at eight. I taught myself harmonies from old hymnals, and I would make up songs with my own chords on the piano because I could not read music. I created my own melodies. I did all this by ear. I would be on that piano day and night, driving my family crazy. Since age ten, I sang in the choir and in the youth group of my church, Coral Hill Baptist Church in Glasgow.

I made my commitment to Jesus Christ in a KOA campground at a youth retreat. There was a speaker there from Dwight L. Moody Ministries. I was twelve years old, sitting in the back, flirting with the eighteen-year-old youth director I had a crush on. I was not paying attention to the message, but I remember hearing the speaker say he had the whole Bible memorized. I was impressed by that because, outside my bedroom door, we had a bookshelf of books from A to Z, and I was determined that I was going to learn all those books—so I started reading them from the beginning to the end. I had a thirst for knowledge. I started listening when the speaker said he memorized the Bible in its entirety. I recall finding myself at the foot of the altar, crying, not knowing what was happening to me, but my experience was so powerful that I looked back at my friends and thought, why am I here, and why are they back there? I wondered what was happening to me. I recall that the camp leaders lit candles, and everybody who got saved walked with a candle to a cross in a field, then stood and sang as a part of the youth festivities. I do recall feeling at that moment alone as far as my friends went, but I felt so full of peace, joy, and freedom, and such a love for the Lord. I had a love relationship starting in my heart with Jesus. My friends could not understand what was happening to me. I did not want my parents to know what was happening. My dad was not a Christian, and I recall feeling set apart and different from everyone else because the experience was so powerful. The next day, I went out in the field and read my Bible, and the word came alive to me. I went to be alone in the field because I did not want my parents to see me.

Pastor Larry Doyle showed up at our house that afternoon. I remember my mom saying to me, "Can you come out here?" I was nervous about what had happened because none of my friends had come up. I thought, What is my mom going to think? I had such a fear come over me that was trying to shut down my testimony before it had really begun, even to my own family. I did not know if my family had had this experience or not. My experience was so powerful and transformational that I did not know what was happening to me. My mom always recalls me praying for a kitten of ours that had gotten run over by a car. My mom said, "Your kitten got killed," and I prayed for this kitten, and to this day my mom still talks about this incident: Tiger the kitten got up and walked away like nothing had happened to him. My mom knew then that something was going on in my life for Tiger to be healed through my prayers. This realization is still within me now: fear is still trying to keep my testimony from being revealed, because it is empowered by the Holy Spirit. John in Revelation 12:11 explains, we overcome by the "blood of the Lamb and by the word of their testimony." I want our readers to know that their own testimonies can be powerful.

This reminds me of something T.L. Osborne said at his church in Tulsa, Oklahoma, about preaching amazing sermons in Africa. He said, "I would have sermons prepared to preach and God would tell me: 'Keep it simple: John 3:16: "For God so loved the world that he gave his only begotten Son, that whoever believes in him should not perish but have everlasting life"'" (NKJV). I connected with T.L. Osborne when I attended Oral Roberts University and studied music. I was on the worship team at T.L.'s church. One day, I twisted my foot and limped onto the stage. T.L.'s wife Daisy prayed for my foot, and it was immediately healed. I have seen many miracles and experienced the miracle-working power of prayer.

As a child, I had big dreams for myself. At seventeen, I went to Houston, Texas, to be in a big city and realize my dreams. My cousin Bill, who had visited for a family reunion, invited me to live with his family in Houston. Two months after that, I saved up for an airline ticket and left home for Texas. My parents let me go, although they were reluctant. After I had made my commitment to Jesus, I had always felt there was something big for me to do in my life. I could not understand how it could happen in Glasgow, Dry County, where all my peers were partying and smoking weed. At home, there had been no way to accomplish my dreams and no friends to share my vision, so I had begun smoking weed while at the same time preaching to everyone when I was high. Every time I drank or smoked marijuana, I would start preaching to everyone. I remember people sleeping around; I did not do any of that, but I did have a big crush on a preacher's son. I thought, I have to be like everyone else, so I planned to get drunk and have sex with him when I was sixteen. I started taking all my clothes off when I was drunk, but he said, "I can't do this to you. You are the best girl in school and beautiful, and don't ever change." I never forgot his words. He was sleeping around with other girls, and I thought I had to do the same thing to get him. He was so good-looking, with jet black hair and green eyes. I recall on graduation night he walked up to me at my graduation party and said, "Sheri, stay the way you are and don't change." I was shocked that he actually liked and respected me because I was not like all the other girls.

I was in Houston for three months when I was introduced to the late John Osteen's Lakewood Church through my cousin Bill's secretary. At that time, I had a contract with the Houston Rockettes cheerleading team, my first taste of stardom. God turned me around and I walked into John Osteen's church and into a worship experience where everyone was hugging one another. I found a family of believers who felt to me like they were my people. I took a trip home to see my family. To my surprise, my parents stopped me from going back to Houston. My cousin's home in Houston had been broken into, and my parents worried for my safety. I was not able to go back to Houston and would not have been able to continue with the Houston Rockettes even if I had wanted to do so.

After returning home from Houston, I went to a Bible study with my neighbors, and the speaker prophesied over me from Genesis that, as God had promised Abraham as many descendants as the stars in the sky, I would bring many to righteousness like the stars of heaven.[1] This prophecy has come true and has continually happened in my life.

A new opportunity began for me with a girl named Martha Jo who attended a Bible study on her way to school. Finally, I had a girlfriend who was on fire for God and who sang and played piano. She told me I should come to Bible College with her at Liberty Bible College in Pensacola, Florida. I attended Liberty for two years, studying the Bible in detail. I went there to study music, but ended up in two years of Bible classes. This set the foundation of my life, and I am grateful every day for that. Going to Bible college probably saved my life!

People from Oral Roberts University (ORU) came to Liberty and spoke, and I felt I wanted to transfer there and study music. I wanted to find a Christian man I could sing with; what better place to find one, right? Or so I thought. "Never go looking" is a lesson I'm still learning! God has a jealous love for me, to fulfill his call on my life, not my call on my life! And that has not been easy for me. I do believe that, in time, I

---

1. Gen 22:17: "I will surely bless you and make your descendants as numerous as the stars in the sky and as the sand on the seashore" (NIV).

will meet someone that loves the Lord as much as I do and has a passion to serve him with the gift of music.

I was a danceaholic, and Liberty Bible College was very strict. The rebel in me talked the guard into letting me into the dorm after hours until I was caught and reprimanded by the dean for my behavior. I decided I wanted to go to another school. I had been dating a solid Christian who wanted me to become the wife of a preacher, but I wanted to be on tour as a Christian rock artist. He was very controlling and had my life planned out, and I did not want to do music only in the church. I wanted to be singing to the world. My dad called and told me his cousin had bought a Christian radio station in Glasgow, and he told me I should come back home and get a job working at the radio station. What my dad did not know was that I was already on my way home!

I worked at the radio station three months and was fired by my dad's cousin Howard one Sunday morning for skipping out and leaving the station unattended to attend a Christian rock concert. While at the concert in Bowling Green, Kentucky, I met more students from ORU. They encouraged me to apply, and I was accepted.

I was at ORU for one and a half years and then left to go on tour with a Christian Group called Destiny. We performed the story of Joseph's dream all over the US for about five months. I ended up as a youth counselor at Harvest Ranch in Muncie, Indiana, where I met Johnny Cash's sister Joanne and her husband, Harry Yates, who founded the Cowboy Church in Nashville, Tennessee. They told me to come to their church in Nashville if I ever was there.

I had been attending Victory Christian Center while at ORU, and there I met a composer named Forrest who talked me into moving to Nashville. My dreams of being a Christian rock star came back and I took a temporary agency job working on Music Row for all the country music publishers' labels, both contemporary and Christian country. I became acquainted with everyone on Music Row. But, I became disillusioned by the Christian music world and started investigating the country music world. Still, I had a fear that, if I went into secular music, I would be sinning. I did not know where I fit in. But I started writing songs. I got a developmental deal with a major country music label that lasted only three months. This disillusioned me even more.

While I was in Nashville, I became involved in an unequally yoked relationship with a Jewish unbeliever. He loved Johnny Cash. He attended the Cowboy Church, and Johnny Cash's sister Joanne led him to the Lord. But his life was still out of control and syndicate-run, and he destroyed many relationships with friends. He was part of the reason I left Nashville. I was in my twenties, and he was my first serious relationship; this made it difficult for me to break it off. I had always felt I would marry each guy I was with.

Then, Johnny Cash went out to Hollywood to work on the television show *Dr. Quinn, Medicine Woman*. My photos were sent to Hollywood for a stand-in position for Jane Seymour. I moved out to California very disillusioned by the Nashville music industry. Little did I know that I was being sent by the Holy Spirit to be where God wanted me. Hollywood embraced me. I ended up working with Dyan Cannon's ministry, God's Party, at CBS studios. For five years, I was her lead singer in worship at God's Party events held at the CBS studio lot. One of the ladies in the ministry gave me the nickname "angel with soul." Larry King, Raquel Welch, Olivia Newton-John, TV producers, musicians, TV writers, and people who would not normally come to church attended this meeting. I found my calling. I did not want to be singing in church and did not want to be singing to drunken crowds, I wanted to be singing the gospel to those who would not ordinarily walk into a church.

Billy Davis and Marilyn McCoo, formerly of the Fifth Dimension supergroup, asked me to sing on the worship team for their ministry, Soldiers for the Second Coming, at the same time that I was ministering in song with Dyan Cannon's ministry. Attendees included Sammy Davis Jr's wife, Altovise, a member of the Temptations, and other members of the rhythm and blues crowd.

I concurrently sang with Leon Patillo's ministry (the former lead singer with Santana) in Long Beach and in some of his concerts. I realized that God was putting me with music artists who were on fire for God. He put me in with top-performing artists of their fields who were able to minister to the secular world without changing who they were. They had already been at the top of their trade and had realized the limitations of stardom and success. They loved me and accepted me for who I was, and they recognized my talent, the calling on my life, and helped birth me into where I was headed next.

All these people were at the height of their careers when they found the Lord and their spiritual transformation, but they still continued with their careers and witnessed to those around them. They founded ministries, people came to hear them, and they brought new believers to the Lord.

Since I first came to Jesus, I had loved people right where they were. I could befriend and love anybody. I could recognize where they were in life and could get on their level. I could never be satisfied just handing out a tract to someone. That felt so unreal to my style. My anointing is to get into the heart of an individual through my music ministry and my songwriting. This approach comes from my heart and my love of Jesus and my real life experience and true love for people of all walks of life. This is why I feel I can go anywhere in this world and bring the truth of Jesus's love, because, as John 3:16 explains, "For God so loved the world that he gave his only begotten Son, that whoever believes in him should not perish but have everlasting life."

I ended up meeting a promoter named Gingio at a songwriters' group in Los Angeles. I was sitting next to a candle and my hair had caught on fire. I ran to the bathroom and bumped into Gingio, who gave me his business card. I had a meeting with him. I was intrigued by the fact he was from a country I had always wanted to visit, Switzerland. I hired him to promote me as a recording artist so I could travel to Switzerland. Gingio was telling me about Leo Leoni, the lead guitar of the rock band Gotthard, which means "God's mountain." I might be able to sing at the opening of his restaurant. While visiting Bob Yerkes's home (I met Bob through Billy Davis and Marilyn McCoo's ministry), I met two stunt people from Switzerland. They played me a song called *Heaven*. I decided to learn this song on guitar and have it prepared just in case I did get to go to the opening of Leo Leoni's restaurant. I arrived in Tesserette, Switzerland, the night of the restaurant opening, I met Leo and thirty or forty other guests. There was a guitar on the wall, and one of the guests took it down. I started singing one of my songs that I had written for guitar. Leo heard me and asked me to come downstairs and perform for everybody. Leo got emotional and actually ended up playing the song *Heaven* with me on guitar as I sang. Everybody said I sounded like an angel. I ministered to people with my voice. Leo introduced me to Steve Lee, the lead singer of the band. I ended up cowriting with Steve on Gotthard's record *Need to Believe*. The song I cowrote with Steve was called *Break Away*. They called me "Priest" Sheri. I witnessed to Steve, telling him that Gotthard needed to give the world something to believe in. He was very receptive to me and, during that time, I do believe he received Jesus and wrote about his conversion with me in song. Sometimes you just never know why you are put in someone's life. I would have never thought that, a year later, he would die in a motorcycle accident on the Route 15 freeway in Nevada just outside of Las Vegas. He acknowledged me on the *Need to Believe* record that went triple platinum twice, and he thanked me many times for my contribution to the record.

In 2013, my mother became ill, and I went to Nashville to be closer to her. I started doing speaking and singing engagements, even singing and speaking at men's prayer breakfasts. I gave my testimony many times at the Cowboy Church in Nashville, which is broadcast live globally. Joanne, Johnny Cash's sister and founder of the Cowboy Church, as well as Harry Yates, are a spiritual foundation in my life, covering me in prayer. I have continued to be a part of that ministry for more than twenty years. This butterfly is still in flight, moving with the wind of God's Spirit.

In closing, the message of Paul in 2 Timothy 1:7 has become very meaningful in my life. It insists, "For God has not given us a spirit of fear, but of power and of love and of a sound mind" (NKJV). These words speak to me each day, and I want to leave these verses with readers. As 2 Corinthians 5:17 explains, "If anyone is in Christ, there is a new creation: everything old has passed away; see everything has become new!" (NRSV). My Christian experience is like the flight of a butterfly. I pray that my testimony will encourage you to ask God's Son, Jesus, to fly through life with him.

RESOURCES

My music is available on my website, reverbnation.com/angelwithsoul. For a video of LeaAnn Pendergrass, host of *Uniting the Nations,* interviewing me, visit youtube.com/watch?v=_-c7KwkKCRo. If you would like to have me speak or sing at an event, or consult, please contact me by email at sheripedigo@gmail.com.

8

Healing through Faith and Compassion

Martha Reyes

LEFT TO RIGHT, MARTHA REYES AND MOTHER TERESA

MARTHA REYES WAS BORN in Puerto Rico and has resided in California, ministering to Hispanics in the United States and internationally since 1978. She has traveled to more than twenty-two Latin American countries and many parts of Europe and the Middle East giving concerts and retreats on inner healing and participating as a guest speaker in national and international conventions on healing and restoration. From 1992 until the year 2000, she organized the acclaimed Hosanna Multi-festivals conventions, international events with representatives from thirty countries in music, theatre, and arts, held annually in Mexico, Florida, and Israel. Martha is the author of *Jesús y la Mujer Herida* (*Jesus and the Wounded Woman*) and *Jesucristo, Tu Psicólogo Personal* (*Jesus is Your Own Personal Psychologist*). She has also written articles for a number of Spanish language publications. Here is her story:

I was born in San Juan, Puerto Rico, in the mid-1950s to Hector and Amelia, a very young couple who married at seventeen years of age. By twenty-two, they were the parents of four children. With no formal schooling, skills, or rich parents to help them, they felt they were too poor and too immature for this task. Thirteen years later, my father passed away very young from a heart condition, leaving my mother as a young widow with four young children. Now, we were not just poor; we had absolutely no source of income. Fear and insecurity invaded our young hearts, and quickly we had to find a way of surviving. This pressing need awakened in all four of us the gift of music. In order to support ourselves at a very young age, my brothers, my sister, and I formed a family music group. Inexperienced and naïve, our first gigs were mostly the birthday parties of our compassionate relatives and church friends. After many years of practice and exposure, eventually we were able to earn a name and some degree of recognition in some circles in the pop music world.

In 1972, our mother decided to move to California where some of her relatives resided. Rearing four children by herself was no easy matter, and her relatives were willing to help. Puerto Rico, as part of the United States, is a bicultural and a bilingual country. It shares the best of both worlds: the opportunities and possibilities of being part of a developed nation and a deeply rooted sense of connectivity with third-world countries in Latin America. For this reason, I integrated rapidly with Hispanics in the United States and have been part of the United States Hispanic subculture from day one.

In California, while working as a lounge singer and musician, I was also a full-time student of psychology at California State University, thanks to the help of some large student loans. While finishing a master's degree in psychology, through the efforts of Campus Crusade for

Christ, I came to the Lord and immediately began searching for God's divine purpose in my life. Having felt my mother's burden, grief, poverty, and sense of abandonment prepared me for what later became my mission in life: helping wounded and hurting women around the world.

My polished singing skills took me to faraway places. This was God's way of opening doors and venues for me, but not as an international songwriter and singer as I originally dreamt and planned, but as a healer of broken hearts and souls. Healing poems and songs became healing teachings and books. Using the same microphone, I went from singing a three-minute song to sharing sixty-minute teachings and, later on, all-day retreats. My few lessons from Sunday school were not going to be enough for this new challenge. I went to Israel thirty-five times to take Bible courses and to learn from historians, archaeologists, and biblical experts. I also enrolled in additional postgraduate courses in psychology in other colleges in the US in order to feel better prepared for this calling. I hope the story I will share with you now will give you a window into my soul and my world.

Have you ever felt overexposed to pain and suffering? I suppose that, as world population grows, we can expect that every condition or ailment that can be measured will grow proportionately. But, we are also supposed to be in the advanced stages of medicine, technology, communications, transportation, and so forth. I guess I was hoping that by now we would have eradicated hunger, infant mortality, plagues, violence, illiteracy, and human misery in general. What has all of this advancement accomplished in general? Just more comfort, connectivity, and mobility for some. Just a way of prolonging by a few months the inevitable decay or death for others and, eventually, for all.

In 1987, I visited Calcutta, India, for the first time and met Mother Teresa. A group of missionaries and I took four tons of medicine, clothing, and other gifts to Mother Teresa's homes and also spent some time with the sick and the orphans. The experience was very intense, especially the day we visited the lepers. Leprosy in this day and age? At the end of the trip, when we were discussing when we would return, Mother Teresa told us that we did not have to come back to India. "Why not?" we asked. "Because human suffering is everywhere," she said. "Just look around in your family, neighborhood, and town: you will find brokenness everywhere you go."

Along with the memories of everything I saw in India, I brought back with me those words. Now, everywhere I go, I can identify three groups of people on earth: the ones who live broken lives, the ones who heal the broken, and the indifferent. But didn't Jesus expose these three groups already in the parable of the Good Samaritan (Luke 10:30–37)? We see the broken man who fell among the robbers who stripped him, beat him, and departed, leaving him half dead. Along come the indifferent priest and Levite who feel nothing and do nothing, and then comes a compassionate Samaritan who "went to him and bandaged his wounds, pouring on oil and wine; and he set him on his own animal, brought him to an inn, and took care of him. On the next day, when he departed, he took out two denarii, gave them to the innkeeper, and said to him, 'Take care of him; and whatever more you spend, when I come again, I will repay you'" (NKJV).

Regardless of all the state-of-the-art medical care available, there are many people in the world today who have very little or no access to it. When they are hurting, their only hope is to be noticed by a compassionate heart that will not only recognize the pain, but will also feel the burden. Only when he saw the pain did the Samaritan feel it was his responsibility. In this parable, God answers Cain's strange question, "Am I my brother's keeper?" (Gen 4:9 NRSV) In my own experience, my days in India were spent living the gospel, and they changed the purpose and direction of my life. I saw the pain. It deepened the commitment I already had to easing the pain of women who are hurting and expanded it to reach out to everyone in pain. I was an accomplished singer and songwriter who, all of a sudden, felt the *burden* of all the brokenhearted. I realized I could use my gifts to help heal them.

After India, I began to visit many missions in Latin America. The subjects of my songs changed and became prayers with music. My concert halls were now the churches or plazas of villages. The ticket sales of my concerts became fundraising events for the needs of the poor. My eight years of college and degree in psychology (I will soon complete a Ph.D. in general psychology) would only make sense now if I used them for the inner healing of others. From that point on, I have written books and recorded teachings, given retreats, opened up small counseling centers in different places, and helped train caregivers in this mission of compassionate healing. Through prayer and counseling, group sessions and workshops, thousands of victims of domestic violence, physical and sexual abuse, abandonment, depression, divorce, and addictions have found comfort and new life through these ministries that I have helped initiate.

Isaiah 61 spells out the healing mission of Jesus, beginning with the anointing of healing *the brokenhearted*. Sometimes, healing will require great efforts or miracles of restoration and liberation, and, at other times, sufferers resign themselves to understanding the true meaning of suffering, acquiring the gifts of patience, sacrifice, tolerance, offering, and unconditional praise and faith (2 Cor 6:4: "We show that we are true ministers of God. We patiently endure troubles and hardships and calamities of every kind" [NLT]).

Make no mistake: I have not only been one of the healers, I have also been broken and in need of healing myself. But I have also discovered the virtue of undeserved brokenness and the power of the wounded healer. That is the greatest gift of love: not giving leftovers for care, but *breaking our own bread and our own life* in smaller parts to share with those who have nothing (e.g., as Phil 1:13–14, Paul notes that, because of his chains, others have been encouraged and blessed).

I guess, during different stages in my life, I have played the role of every character in the Good Samaritan parable (except the bandits!) because, before I felt God's calling in my life, I was also disconnected and dissociated from other people's needs. Just like the indifferent ones in Jesus's parable and, as myself in the past, there are many today who feel overexposed to the world's pain, so they become disconnected, blind, and deaf. We are tempted to say that it is not our doing or responsibility, but someone else's. We have no time for it. Or, we react only when it hits home in our own lives. I guess I have answered my own question of why all these advanced human accomplishments have not taken care of the world's urgent needs: because they are not always managed by compassionate, burdened hearts. To make a difference, we need to share everything unconditionally and freely, to be willing to invest our own lives in the process of healing. Imagine the tremendous power and potential if together we could link the wealth of knowledge and resources of this day and age with the most compassionate givers and healers! Love and its fruit would find no limit.

Those three groups of characters in the parable of the Good Samaritan will one day become two. The broken will be healed and become healers. There is no doubt in my mind that everyone can also be made to see with opening eyes, hearts, and arms those who are still in the gutter where they themselves were once found. And, when the question is asked, "Who gave me to eat when I was hungry and to drink when I was thirsty, and who visited me while sick and in prison?" (Matt 25:35–36), don't you want to hear your name announced, as the Lord, smiling at you, beckons you forward, saying, "Come blessed of my Father"?

This is the one calling that we all share in common, because ultimately sharing God's love with compassion will be the only thing that matters.

RESOURCES

Martha Reyes's books, *Jesús y la Mujer Herida* (*Jesus and the Wounded Woman*) and *Jesucristo, Tu Psicólogo Personal* (*Jesus is Your Own Personal Psychologist*), Martha's music CDs, and DVDs of her performances and teachings are available for purchase via hosannafoundation.com and marthareyes.com.

9

Ambassador of Prayer Ministries
From Show Business to God's Business

April Shenandoah

LEFT TO RIGHT, DALE EVANS, APRIL SHENANDOAH, ROY ROGERS

APRIL SHENANDOAH HAS TRAVELED down the road of show business, through political activism, to now taking care of God's business. Currently, she speaks, teaches, and writes on faith, prayer, and the power of words. Her life is gloriously intense with the God of her salvation, the creator of the universe! April was born on April 17, in the baby boom generation, and adopted by her grandparents Lester and Mary Hilborn of Jersey Shore, Pennsylvania. While in high school, she was pegged as one of the youngest journalists in the country with her column, "In Tune with Teens," in the *Jersey Shore Herald*. Her love for entertainment took her to Hollywood to work in film and theatre and later to produce Christian productions. As the press contact for Pat Robertson's presidential campaign in 1988, April developed a passion for politics. She combined politics and religion on her television show, *The Bottom Line*, and wrote the column "Politics and Religion" for the *Tolucan Times* in Los Angeles. She is the author of *So Help Me God* and *Your Tongue Determines Your Destiny*. Presently, April Shenandoah ministers and speaks on the power of words and freedom for the body, soul, and spirit. As an ambassador of prayer, April says, "Whatever the question, prayer is the answer." Here is her story:

Before God's intervention, show business was my God. After seeing the film *Singing in the Rain* as a child, I filled my room with movie magazines and covered my wall with Debbie Reynolds's pictures. Many people told me that I would outgrow this "Hollywood phase"; however, it became stronger as I entered my adult life. Eventually, I allowed it to destroy my young marriage.

As I participated in the foolishness of this world, I was blinded to the fact that I was out of step with the God who breathed life into me— the God who created me for a definite purpose. I know now that we all were created by God for God: for his purposes. The only things that will ever matter in life and throughout eternity are those done in the name of Jesus Christ here and now! The Good News is that God saves us from our mess-ups, and he will use our lost, crazy lives for his glory when we call upon the name of the Lord (Rom 10:9–10, 13).[1] He does not leave us on our own to try and figure out the meaning of life. He gave us the Bible as an instruction manual. These instructions are for our benefit, not our detriment. The answer for every issue or question we will ever

---

1. Rom 10:9–10, 13: "If you confess with your lips that Jesus is Lord and believe in your heart that God raised him from the dead, you will be saved. For one believes with the heart and so is justified, and one confesses with the mouth and so is saved.... For, 'Everyone who calls on the name of the Lord shall be saved'" (NRSV).

have, including our protection, financial provision, and health, is enclosed in the sixty-six books of the Bible, the greatest book ever written! When we are obedient to these instructions, life works. No God, no peace; know God, know peace!

The summary of God's word hangs on two commandments: "'You shall love the Lord your God with all your heart, and with all your soul, and with all your mind.' This is the greatest and first commandment. And a second is like it: 'You shall love your neighbor as yourself'" (Matt 22:37–39 NRSV). How glorious life becomes when we seek truth, find it, and are finally able to take these commandments literally—not simply to know them, but to live them.

Since I did not know God's word, the road I traveled was long and winding before biblical truth[2] took root in my soul—before God zapped me and flipped me 180 degrees, setting me free. It all began on one of those winding roads that literally led to a ranch house in Chatsworth, California, the home of Roy Rogers and Dale Evans. When I came to California from Pennsylvania as a young bride to pursue an acting career, I found myself living just down the road from them. At this juncture, show business consumed my thoughts, and, though I had a wonderful husband, I became dissatisfied with being married. One night, in desperation, I jumped in the car and drove up the lane that led to the Double-R Ranch. It was pitch dark as I knocked. Dale opened the door and welcomed me in. She introduced me to her family and, before I left, she prayed with me. She took me under her wing and invited me to the Chapel in the Canyon.[3] She also put me in touch with the Hollywood Christian Group, a gathering of Christians in entertainment. Since Roy and Dale were special to me as a young child, my connection with them is always in the forefront of my memory. Every Saturday afternoon, Grandpap and I had looked forward to watching the Roy Rogers show together. When "Happy Trails" played at the end of the show, I would become teary-eyed. I still do. Later, I learned that Dale wrote that song in about three hours by the guidance of the Holy Spirit.

Though I did not know the Lord in a personal way at that time, I was always a believer, intellectually. Through the years, I attended many different Hollywood prayer groups, but was not living a life that God, or my parents, would have been proud of. Since my young life paral-

2. "Then you will know the truth, and the truth will set you free" (John 8:32 NIV).
3. For a history of the chapel, see Dart, "A Romantic Era Ends."

leled Dale's in so many ways, she tried to set me on the right path so that I would not have to experience the same difficulties she did. Her heart wanted me, and everybody she met, to know Jesus. However, the magnetic lure of show business got its hooks into my soul so deeply that I had tunnel vision.

Ironically, as a teenager, I had said that, if I did not want to be in show business, I would be a missionary. That statement reveals where the affections of my heart were. Providentially, my praying grandparents had adopted me and reared me in a Christian home since the age of two. Without a doubt, their prayers and the grace of God were covering my lost life. After being in California only a short time, I went forward at a Billy Graham Crusade in Los Angeles. Twenty years later, in 1989, I had the privilege of attending Billy Graham's Walk of Fame Star[4] ceremony in front of Mann's Theater and Mama Dale (as many called her) was still ministering to me. Yet, I continued living life according to me.

Though I still did not have a personal relationship with Jesus, I told others about God and handed out Billy Graham's books. Since then, I have learned that churches are full of folks that are far from God, as I was. Many churchgoers believe that their denomination will pave their way to heaven. Some go out of a sense of duty and, for others, church is a social event. Sorry to say that there are numerous pastors and leaders in the church today who no longer preach repentance or minister in the power of the Holy Spirit. Many have fallen away from God's word and have been subtly seduced by the agenda of "humanism," emphasizing a separation of church and state which is not in the Constitution of the United States. However, it is in Karl Marx's *Communist Manifesto*! Woe to those clergy who are leading their flock astray! This is one of the biggest reasons why the United States of America is becoming blatantly godless, and why God's hand of protection is being lifted off it. The urgency of the times should have us all on our knees before our Heavenly Father!

---

4. Rev. Billy Graham received the 1,900th star placed on the Hollywood Walk of Fame. Graham said sheepishly, "I'm not sure a clergyman belongs in that group of entertainers," noting that his star would be near to those of Wayne Newton, Buster Crabbe, John Travolta, Judy Holliday, Julie Andrews, Olivia Newton-John, and Greta Garbo. A star was offered to him thirty years earlier, but he had said no. He changed his views, saying, "Some parents walking along there someday in the future might be asked by their child, 'Who was Billy Graham?' And they could say, 'He preached the gospel.'" Chandler, "He preached the gospel."

After spending many years in Hollywood, I did make a few waves in the business; actually, they were more like a ripple. The work consisted of bit parts in films and television, such as *Starsky and Hutch* and *Switch* with Robert Wagner, plus acting and producing theater. My last commercial was for Pollo Loco Chicken for the Japanese market. In between times, dancing paid my bills. My experiences were varied, to say the least: from playing a clown on *The Jerry Lewis Telethon*, to performing the closed-circuit opening act for Evel Knievel's jump at Snake River Canyon in Idaho, to assisting escape artist The Great Manzini. And I won the Ms. Unknown Comic Contest at the Hacienda Hotel (now torn down) in Las Vegas, while singing and dancing with a bag on my head. That led to a part in *Night Patrol*, which had a great cast, but, after editing, only amounted to a crude comedy.

However, I was unstoppable. If I decided I wanted to do something, I did it. It never dawned on me that I could not, or that I did not have the money, or that it was not the wise and sensible thing to do—I just did it! My decision to move to New York was like that. I had $70 to my name and did not know anyone there. Many of life's lessons were learned in New York, some through potentially life-threatening experiences. Since I was brought up in an atmosphere of love and integrity, I thought the whole world was like that. What a shock when reality hit!

One night, while I was eating in my favorite pub, I fell in love at first sight with a handsome (professional) safe-cracker. However, I did not learn where my diamonds and furs were coming from until years later. This man was straight out of the movies. I dubbed him my Greek god! One fine day, I decided to visit one of the heads of the Genovese crime family, thinking he could jump-start my acting career. When my Greek god (who was actually German) found out that I had gone to see his friend Matthew Ianniello,[5] better known as Matty the Horse, he made me promise that I would never go back. I promised!

This is just an example of how naïve young women and men can end up in a heap of trouble—often dead! Satan knows everyone's vulnerable areas, and that is where he will seduce your soul, to kill, steal, and destroy. Since I was doing my own thing, I had no spiritual antenna or discernment to guide me. The secular world offered adventure and excitement. Little did I know how I was breaking the heart of God. I

---

5. Matthew Ianniello passed away August 15, 2012. Cosa Nostra News website, "Ianniello Was a Huge Earner."

did not know about surrendering to God or how to wait on the leading of the Holy Spirit—and I had gone to church all my life! All the sin in my life I justified by thinking, "I'm not hurting anybody. I'm a good person." Any one of us can rationalize anything to fit our own selfish purposes, but that is rationalizing ourselves right into the pit of hell.

In the mid-1970s, Frankie Avalon introduced me to Carlo Mennotti, a voice coach at Carnegie Hall. My voice lessons allowed me to carry a tune, though I was never a great singer. Then, one day I wiggled my way backstage at the Minskoff Theater to meet Debbie Reynolds, who was starring in *Irene*. She was very cordial. Soon into our conversation, she blurted out, "Would you like to audition for the show?"

"Yes!" I blurted back. So, a week later, accompanied by my vocal coach, I sang and tap-danced for my idol.[6]

Debbie said, "When a slot opens up, we will call you." However, soon after that, Jane Powell took over the show, and the phone never rang.

Eventually, I moved back to California. However, I commuted to New York from time to time to worship at the Times Square Church, where many of Broadway's singers and dancers make up the congregation. Founder David Wilkerson, best known for his book and film, *The Cross and the Switchblade*, has been a major influence in my life. In 2002, Pastor Wilkerson entrusted the senior pastorate to Carter Conlon, who had joined the pastoral staff in 1994. Of course, like many, I was saddened by Pastor Wilkerson's death in 2011.

When in New York, I attended the World Alliance for Peace Bible studies in the early 1990s. The founder, Michael P. Grace II, held Bible studies in New York and Los Angeles. The heartfelt outreach that he sponsored in Manhattan was originally held at a McDonald's restaurant in the theater district, but was eventually moved to the third floor of the McDonald's on 58th Street because the attendance had grown to overflowing. These meetings were culturally diverse, from executives of the business world to the homeless, opened to anyone who needed prayer or just a comfortable place to receive encouragement and a meal.

During one evening at a McDonald's meeting, a small elderly man stood up to share. I do not know if he was homeless or just down on his luck, but I do know that I will never forget him. As he reached into his

---

6. "You shall have no other gods before me" (Exod 20:3 NRSV).

pocket and pulled out a small Bible, he spoke words filled with faith and such conviction that my spirit leaped for joy. His soft-spoken passion raised my faith when he told us not to look to people for anything, but to trust God for every need. This man was rich in my eyes. That is what these meetings were all about: being inspired and led by the Holy Spirit.

There are many wonderful friends whom I know to this day who attended and supported the World Alliance for Peace as well as Media Fellowship International directed by Pastor Robert Rieth, who was extremely instrumental in Michael Grace's ministry. The intellect of this group, Robert E. Theodore "Ted" Baehr, is an American media critic, chairman of the Christian Film and Television Commission, and founder of MOVIEGUIDE®. Jeanne DeFazio, Mr. Grace's executive assistant, author, educator, and minister in her own right, has been a good friend and encourager for these many years—truly a blessing to me. In her book, *Creative Ways to Build Christian Community*, in chapter 1, "Building Christian Community through Meetings and Meals," Jeanne shares the memories of the many events of that time and the joy that this special company of godly men and women brought. It was an honor for me to add a few words to the book about the unique Mr. Grace.[7]

My precious grandmother always told me to put God first; however, I did not understand what she was telling me, since I already believed in God. Life's distractions tended to get in my way of living for God. I was living for myself during the week and giving an hour or two to God on Sunday. That is how I lived for years. Then, it seemed everywhere I went, I started hearing "Seek first the kingdom of God." While I was attending different prayer groups, someone would invariably say to me, "Seek first the kingdom of God." It didn't stop! One evening, while visiting my friend Rita Seiffert (founder of Women of the Valley in Las Vegas), I once again heard those words from Matthew 6:33. In the early 1980s, as I was watching the *700 Club* on CBN (Christian Broadcasting Network), I felt like lightening came through the roof and zapped me. I gasped a deep breath and started weeping, literally sobbing for what seemed like hours. When I stopped crying, my first thought was, "That's what Gramy meant." Put God first; seek the kingdom of God first! In that instant, I thought differently and saw myself from a brand new perspective. That was the beginning of the greatest adventure of my life. The biggest change came when I told God from my heart, "I don't

7. DeFazio and Lathrop, *Creative Ways*, 9.

want what I think I want anymore; I want what you want for my life. I surrender my life to you!" The second was when I was baptized in the Holy Spirit with the evidence of speaking in tongues in the late 1980s.

A woman named Louise French prayed every week at our prayer group that I would receive the gift of tongues. I did not know much about it, but said that I was open to it if God wanted me to have it. Week after week, she continued to pray with no results. Then one day, while I was driving home after she had prayed for me, up out of my belly and out of my mouth came a different language. I could not stop speaking for quite a while. It put me on a high like I had never known. With the gift of tongues came the hunger for God and his word. After that, my life took on new meaning: answered prayer, healing miracles, divine encounters. God's provision and great favor were occurring on a regular basis. God ever so gently started stripping things out of my life that did not belong there. Soon, I lost my passion for show business, though I did act in and produce a few Christian productions before stepping into what I call my "stealth ministry" in the political arena.

The catalyst that drew me into politics was being appointed the Los Angeles press contact for Pat Robertson's presidential campaign in 1988. Suddenly, I was hungry to know the history of the United States of America and the issues facing this country. In 1993, the year President William Jefferson Clinton was elected, I found myself sitting at a front row table at the National Prayer Breakfast. My first book, *So . . . Help Me God*, was birthed from Clinton's speech that day. He said he wanted to sound like a statesman and pronounce boldly at the end of his oath, "So help me God." However, he said he was thinking, "So . . . *help me*, God!" The book garnered me three invitations to the White House. It was an honor to have been asked to pray after hours on one of those visits. How surreal it seemed, standing in the doorway of the Oval Office praying. In a matter of days after arriving in Washington, I was walking through some very impressive doors. All in the same day, Congressman Phillip M. Crane of Illinois (who ran for president in 1980 and passed away November of 2014) phoned and wanted to meet and have pictures taken with me. From there, I met with Senator Fred Thompson (Tennessee) in his office to discuss the book, and, to top the afternoon off, I had a private lunch at the White House with Ann McCoy (President Clinton's executive assistant) and ate the best pumpkin pie I ever had.

In 2000, the opportunity to write my column "Politics and Religion" opened up at the *Tolucan Times* in Los Angeles, as well as many political Internet sites. God was in all I did and all I wrote. My faith was constantly growing, and politics became my new passion. I thought that I would be able to take God into that arena with me—and save the world! However, I soon had a reality check and discovered how the system truly operates. My thoughts of running for Congress soon fizzled. This was not God's calling for me, though I did continue commuting from California to Washington, DC, to pray for several elected officials. My Ambassador of Prayer Ministry was born after meeting Senator Sam Nunn. Senator Nunn encouraged me to send him a letter that he would then pass on to Jesse Helms's office, as Senator Helms was then designating ambassadorships. The letter was sent, and, soon after, I was invited to Senator Helms's office in Washington to discuss this matter. Senator Helms encouraged me to minister to politicians in Washington, DC, and tagged me "Ambassador of Prayer." When in Washington, I made it a point to visit my friend Jeanne DeFazio, who was volunteering in the executive offices of the White House. We would attend the Friday afternoon luncheon and Bible study for the Senate staff, conducted by the chaplain of the Senate, Pastor Lloyd Ogilvie. It was a treat for me, since I had attended Hollywood Presbyterian Church, where Pastor Ogilvie was senior pastor before he became chaplain of the Senate. (Pastor Ogilvie honored Media Focus with prayer when he sat on the dais with Roy Rogers and Dale Evans for my first fundraiser produced for Media Focus, honoring Leonard Eilers, the "Preaching Cowboy.")

Earlier, I mentioned that I would share my "lesson in faith." During a road trip to do research for *So . . . Help Me God*, the gift of faith that I did not even know existed was about to befall me. Everything I needed began to be handed to me by strangers. It was uncanny! When things flow like that, I truly believe that we are exactly where God wants us to be. Then, on the way home from my research, the unthinkable happened. As I was driving through Texas at two o'clock in the morning, my trusty Honda suddenly stopped dead! I couldn't believe that God had allowed me to be stranded in the middle of nowhere in the middle of the night.

I remember thinking, I must stay calm. After signaling a trucker and being towed by AAA, I remained in my car all night waiting for the mechanic to arrive in the morning. Here is where the "fun" started. It was discovered that my timing chain broke. What? I had just had the timing chain replaced so this would not happen! We soon learned that it had never been replaced! The mechanic of the present garage did not know how to work on Hondas and said that I would need to be towed 100 miles back to Amarillo. I only had enough money to get back to California and I had no credit cards back then.

As I sat and watched all the vehicles rush by on Interstate 40, I noticed a truck towing an empty flatbed behind it. Suddenly, I knew a flatbed was the answer. The mechanic had no interest in my predicament, so I said, "Lord I need a flatbed truck like the one I just saw." Within minutes, a yellow truck towing an empty flatbed pulled up to the garage. Immediately, I knew it was mine. It was driven by a Christian couple on the way to Amarillo. The condensed details are: I phoned around for a mechanic who would work on Saturday in Amarillo and located Son Van Do, a Vietnamese mechanic who said, "Bring it in." He worked on it all day! I remember sitting on an old sofa outside the garage with my arms folded, saying to God, "I can't wait to see how you are going to do this." As I stated, I had no extra money for this repair. It was after dark when he finished, and, when it was time to pay the bill, I told him he would have to trust me for it. Without blinking an eye he said, "Okay." Then, he started giving me things for my car, plus he even replaced a burned-out headlight. After arriving in California, I told a friend about the experience, and she put an envelope in my purse with the money for Son Van Do. How incredible that experience was. That entire ordeal was handled by the hand of God. He gave me the gift of faith that day. It has produced unshakable faith in me.[8]

Whatever the question, prayer is the answer. Back in the '90s, Rhonda Fleming invited me to attend Bonnie Green's prayer group in Beverly Hills, California. We met every Thursday afternoon. The group was made up of many celebrities' wives and others like me who were in the "business called show." Bonnie's husband, Johnny Green, was a well-known film and music composer who also conducted the orchestra for the Academy Awards for many years. It was always fun to view his many Oscars on the fireplace mantle in the room where we held prayer. That special family of women is where I learned the importance

---

8. As Jesus says in Mark 11:23, "Truly I tell you, if anyone says to this mountain, 'Go throw yourself into the sea,' and does not doubt in their heart and believes that what they say will happen, it will be done for them" (NIV).

of prayer. We witnessed so many answered prayers. I realized prayer is the missing ingredient among so many believers. What God wants most is fellowship with his children. Prayer is simply talking to God from our heart. If we are so busy working for God that we do not have quiet time with him, we are off track. We have all been there! However, when we realize that we cannot go to the next level in our lives, or in our ministries, without developing a personal relationship with him, we can change course and climb up on Daddy God's lap. He is waiting with open arms.

Ambassador of Prayer Ministries is bathed in prayer and led by the Holy Spirit. Prayer covers every decision of the ministry and my life. I am always waiting for that "still, small voice" to guide me. When I hear nothing, I do nothing. When I slip and get ahead of God, I am always sorry, because things do not work well without his guidance. When well-meaning people offer opinions about what they think we should be doing, while the Holy Spirit is clearly saying something else, beware! It is God we must please—not people. One old hymn reminds us, "O, what peace we often forfeit, O, what needless pain we bear, all because we do not carry everything to God in prayer!"[9]

As God has blessed me, my books have given me opportunities to share on a variety of radio and television programs, such as *The Good Life* and *The Home Keepers* on the Christian Television Network (CTN). Other appearances have been on Dove Broadcasting, Cornerstone Television, News in Washington, DC, and American Family Radio, to name a few.

Lately, I have been thinking about the words of Proverbs 18:21: "Death and life are in the power of the tongue, and those who love it will eat its fruits" (NRSV). Our lives mirror what we speak, producing fruit after their own kind—be it rotten or sweet. The words we speak today will produce the life we live tomorrow. May our words be uplifting to others. Words are power in action and will either bless or curse. This message, if taken literally and practiced with perseverance, will bring victory over chaotic living and the challenges we face. Wherever life takes you, be it in media or elsewhere, take every opportunity to be a mouthpiece for Jesus. Time is short! Seek first the kingdom of God and his righteousness; and all these things shall be added to you (Matt 6:33 NKJV).

---

9. Scriven, "What a Friend We Have in Jesus."

RESOURCES

To purchase April Shenandoah's books, *So . . . Help Me God* and *Your Tongue Determines Your Destiny,* visit aprilshenandoah.com.

10

Amazing Grace

Beulah "Bee" Beyer Wenger
Written by Jeanne DeFazio
as told to her by Beulah "Bee" Beyer Wenger

IN MEMORIAM

Amazing Grace 109

Beulah "Bee" Beyer went from being a Kansas farm girl out of a one-room country grade school to becoming a thriver and survivor in Hollywood. She produced and hosted the syndicated programs *Cooking around the World* and *The Bee Beyer Show*, which brought her celebrity and national attention. During her seven years on live television, Bee was a successful entrepreneur developing a world-famous food dehydrator and authoring her bestseller, *Food Drying at Home the Natural Way*. She went on to become the executive senior vice president of the Southern California Motion Picture Council, which encourages high morality in motion pictures, television, and the performing arts. In 1995, she became the editor of the highly popular trade paper *The Hollywood Times*. Bee was a devout Christian, and her networking and business skills enabled her to support many Christian ministries, including the highly successful television ministry of her daughter Gemma Wenger.

Bee died April 24, 2015. I interviewed Bee in her West Los Angeles home exactly a month before she went home to be with Jesus. She was a beautiful, wonderful Christian, and I thank God for this chapter, which honors her memory. Here is her story:

I was born Beulah Lucille Beyer to a loving God-fearing farm family. My father, Frank Benjamin, and my mother, Elizabeth Luthi, lived in a farm five and a half miles outside the small town of Gridley, Kansas (population 395). My father said grace before each meal and read the Scriptures to us. He led an a cappella choir in the local church and taught Sunday School. My parents were loving but strict Christians, and I was reared to reverence God in a religious tradition that forbade dancing, makeup, jewelry, and attending movies. I never doubted there was a God, but I never understood the legalism of the Apostolic Christian Church. To become a member of our church, the initiated had to go through a repentance period in which the penitent sought forgiveness from those he or she had previously wronged. There was no infant baptism, and adults were baptized after repenting.

I recall my family showing compassion to those less fortunate during the depression. My mother shared what we had with those who knew our home to be one where the down-and-out could get a free meal, a cheerful smile, and an encouraging prayer. My father and my three brothers harvested the crops of a neighboring widow free of charge. I grew up understanding the Golden Rule because my family loved God and loved others as themselves.

Higher education was not stressed in my family, but I struck out and worked my way through the Kansas State Teachers College in Emporia, Kansas. After graduation, I taught junior high school for one year in Kansas City and then moved to Chicago because I was offered a better teaching salary there teaching kindergarten through twelfth grade in the public school system. While teaching school, I met my husband, Ray Wenger. Ray and I were introduced by a mutual friend who was having a party and needed more women to attend. I obliged, and she sent Ray to give me a ride to the party. Ray turned out to be a devout Catholic who, before graduating from Harvard Law School, attended seminary in preparation for the priesthood. He was taking a course in accounting when we met. Our friendship blossomed, and soon we married in Arizona when Ray was negotiating contracts for Hughes Aircraft. We had two beautiful daughters, Lisa and Gemma.

After I married Ray, I got through the door of a local television station where my career in front of the camera began. Eventually, my syndicated television show, *Cooking around the World*, brought me national recognition. Our family made the move to California where Ray worked in Los Angeles with Hughes Aircraft. We purchased a home in a good neighborhood in Los Angeles, and Ray decided to invest in real estate. Regretfully, these investments did not prove profitable, and I began to shoulder much of the burden of financial support in the family.

The Holy Spirit one afternoon gave me a vision as I was driving along the 405 freeway in Los Angeles of just how to develop a food dehydrator. I developed Bee Beyer's Food Dehydrator, which I sold on television as well as in local stores through an opportunity to advertise in newspapers all over California and the western states. I traveled, selling the dehydrators, and authored a book, *How to Dry Food at Home the Natural Way*,[1] which explained the health benefits of using my food dehydrator to dry fruit, fresh fruit rolls, vegetables, and meat. The traveling to make sales exhausted me and left me with little time to care for my precious daughters, and the financial stress of raising my children without Ray's financial support took its toll on my marriage. Ray was a wonderful father, and his legal expertise helped me make wise in-

---

1. *How to Dry Food at Home the Natural Way* sold more than 100,000 copies and was written in two weeks.

vestment decisions, since I was the businessperson in the family. Very young, the girls took on a lot of responsibility in the home.

We had some tough times, but God brought us through. I recall in the mid-1970s, when gas was rationed, that, one day, to make it home from a day of selling dehydrators, I had to travel along the Grapevine, a winding road that is the major route between Central and Southern California. The gas gauge was low, and there was no station in sight. I prayed, and, that afternoon, I came upon a gas station that sold snacks. I got off, bought gas and a sandwich, and then the man behind the counter said he had already closed the cash register for the day and that I could catch him next time. As many times as I returned to pay him back, I never found that station again. I believe the Lord supernaturally provided angels to help me that night: a woman driving home alone along the Grapevine at sunset. I learned during these years of struggle how to rely on God's provision. He always has provided.

Ray was a Roman Catholic and I was Protestant, and we brought the girls up in the Catholic faith. Ray brought us to Mass as well as to charismatic Catholic prayer groups in Los Angeles churches. In these meetings, we heard about becoming born-again Catholics. These were Catholics who accepted Jesus as Lord and Savior and who received the baptism and the gifts of the Holy Spirit. At these meetings, we met Christians who also fellowshipped among Protestants, and we had the opportunity to experience the flow of the Holy Spirit as revival came to Los Angeles in the 1970s and 1980s.

At this point, my family went on a missionary tour to Israel, and we were all baptized in the Jordan River. Sadly, shortly after that, due to the financial struggles that had eroded me emotionally, psychologically, and spiritually, Ray and I separated, but we never divorced. I grew up in a culture where the husband provided for the family, and this was not Ray's strong point. Yet, the challenges in our marriage brought me close to the Lord. I had to pray to hold on to my mortgage and feed the girls. In retrospect, I regret that the immense responsibility I shouldered caused me at times not to be the best wife to my husband in word and action, but I always loved him and appreciated his finer points. One day, I came home from work and found that Ray had taken the girls. He left a note that he had moved to Atlanta with them. This distressed me beyond distraction. He thought that this would bring me back to him. I was in despair and called every praying Christian I knew to intercede with the Lord for me. I visited the girls in Atlanta, and, eventually, God answered my prayers: Ray and the girls returned to Los Angeles.

In the mid-1980s, my Christian friend Madame Etienne promoted me to coproduce the Easter sunrise service at the Hollywood Bowl with Jan and Paul Crouch of Trinity Broadcasting Network. My television program provided me wonderful contacts in the entertainment industry. Jean Durand brought me into the Southern California Motion Picture Council, where I eventually became and continued to serve as the executive senior vice president.[2] The Council meets several times per year to honor those in the media whose work is Christian and elevating to the human spirit.

In 1996, I became the editor of *The Hollywood Times*. I interviewed celebrities at various benefits, took their photos, and, because I was a Christian, I introduced Christianity into this trade newspaper. For each edition, my daughter Pastor Gemma Wenger wrote an editorial that encouraged Christian principles. The newspaper became a form of ministry to Gemma and me. Gemma has gone on to produce her own television programs: *Beauty for Ashes* and *Gemma Wenger's Hollywood*. Lately, I have lessened my responsibilities in the Motion Picture Council to support Gemma's ministry. Through a series of wise investments, I have been able to support her in her ministry financially. I pray for her and attend her ministry speaking engagements and as well attend the church she pastors, which meets in my home in West Los Angeles on Monday and Friday evenings.

I have had many memorable adventures in faith over the years. I recall experiencing a miraculous answer to prayer at the Full Gospel Businessman's Fellowship fiftieth anniversary meeting at Clifton Cafeteria in downtown Los Angeles on February 17, 1997. I arrived about an hour after the meeting had begun, and God guided me to the one vacant chair left at a table where I knew four people. I did not know the other five people at the table. From the head table, Richard Shakarian was ministering, speaking about miracles, when the woman to my right, a stranger to me, fell back, and died beside me. I got on my hands and knees pleading, "Come back in the name of Jesus." As I was kneeling over her, I felt God telling me she was dead and speaking through me for the second and third time: "Come back in the name of

---

2. Beulah "Bee" Beyer Wenger served as vice president of the Motion Picture Council right up until her death.

Jesus. Come back in the name of Jesus." Then, God told me to stand and ask Richard and the group to pray. Again, God spoke through me and, so all would know that she was dead, God added "Lazarus" to the call: "Come back, Lazarus, in the name of Jesus. Come back, Lazarus, in the name of Jesus. Come back, Lazarus, in the name of Jesus."

When I looked at the woman, she still looked very dead, but I was at peace. I then spoke to the woman who was on the other side of her, saying, "Can you do mouth-to-mouth resuscitation?" The woman on her right, holding her right arm and taking her pulse, did not say anything for what seemed to be an eternity. Then she said excitedly, "We don't need to. Her pulse just came back!" God had put me on her left and a practical nurse on her right. Since she had no pulse for four or five minutes, she could only have been dead. The woman who had died then sat up and opened her eyes, and the color and aspect of death went away as she began to breathe and come back to life. Paramedics were called, and she was taken to a hospital in Pasadena to be observed and checked over. This happened around 1:00 p.m. in the afternoon on a Saturday. The hospital kept her until Monday for observation and testing. When she was released, they had not found symptoms of her former heart trouble and high blood pressure. God not only brought her back, he also healed her. About six weeks later, she came to Gemma's evening ministry as she felt the devil was trying to take her again. Prayer healed her and kept her going. She was eighty-three at the time this all occurred, and she spent the rest of her life praying and traveling for the church. She was like an angel. I mention this experience because, in the midst of the challenges of my life, it greatly encouraged my faith. God used me to heal and raise a woman from the dead. I was not perfect, but God honored my prayers for this woman. I learned that he will answer intercessory prayer regardless of the struggles and imperfection in our lives.

At the end of Ray's life, he was injured in a car accident and moved back into our family home. Gemma had struck out on her own as a teacher, and Lisa had moved to the East Coast to practice medicine. For the first time in many years, Ray and I were back together in the family home. He needed care, never fully recovering from this catastrophic accident. The Lord did use the accident to redeem our marriage. We had never divorced, but, in the end, lived under the same roof until he passed in 2003. We were able to reconcile the past, forgive one another, and accept the Lord's love and mercy and amazing grace. Those years

I now cherish, because God brought redemption to our family. It had been difficult for the girls when they were young and we separated, but, at the end, they had two parents who had forgiven and loved each other. We both thanked God for that.

In closing, I want to encourage those who need forgiveness and reconciliation in relationships. When God forgives our sin and restores our fellowship with him, we want to reach out to others who need this forgiveness and reconciliation. The more I felt God's forgiveness, the more I desired to tell others about it. In Psalm 51:10–13, David cried out to the Lord: "Create in me a pure heart, O God, and renew a steadfast spirit within me. Do not cast me from your presence or take your Holy Spirit from me. Restore to me the joy of your salvation and grant me a willing spirit, to sustain me. Then I will teach transgressors your ways, and sinners will turn back to you" (TNIV).

RESOURCES

Contact Gemma Wenger at gemmawenger.com for a copy of *How to Dry Food at Home the Natural Way*.

11

Unity

Gemma Wenger

From ministering in prisons and on skid row, former child actress Gemma Wenger has expanded her ministry to churches, radio, books, newspapers, evangelical outreaches, and television ministry. She preached at the Hollywood Bowl Easter sunrise service produced by the Trinity Broadcasting Network (TBN) and televised worldwide, and has also made multiple guest appearances on various TBN shows. Currently,

Gemma can be heard every Thursday evening at 6:45 p.m. on KTYM 1460 AM or on the Internet on ktym.com, and via satellite on Cross TV Wednesdays at 5:30 p.m. or live streaming on thecrosstv.com. After numerous appearances on TBN, Gemma developed her own shows, *Gemma Wenger's Hollywood* and *Beauty for Ashes*, currently airing worldwide on Time Warner Cable, Isaac Television, The Way TV, Jadoo Television, and Roku. She also has held biweekly church meetings in the Los Angeles area for the past twenty-five years. Here is her story:

As I reflect on my life serving God, I think of all the people that God has strategically placed along my path to bring me to where I am today. I also mourn the loss of relationships that were instrumental in molding and strengthening my character. The losses have caused me to value and appreciate the people that God has currently put in my life, as well as made me understand that God has designed humans to interact with one another and to work together in unity. I have come to the realization that no one can achieve what God has envisioned for that person to accomplish without the support and encouragement of others. It is summarized so well in the following Scripture: "From him the whole body, joined and held together by every supporting ligament, grows and builds itself up in love, as each part does its work" (Eph 4:16).[1] Every person increases the body of Christ by using his or her gifts and talents to strengthen those around them through love. Each person's gifts are necessary to develop the church toward achieving its greatest potential. One person cannot be successful alone. God has designed us to thrive as a team, working together to achieve his goals.

I was born to Raymond John Wenger, Jr., a brilliant Harvard Law School graduate who had a heart to become a priest. When the priesthood did not materialize, he instead married a Protestant woman from Kansas, Beulah "Bee" Beyer. Beulah had left the Midwest for California to be with my father and eventually became a celebrity cooking show television host. Through various real estate investments, my parents were finally able to purchase a modest home in a nice neighborhood in Los Angeles.

From a young age, I was groomed by God. My father, being a godly man, led me to the Lord when I was three years old with the promise that "presents" would ensue. He encouraged my sister, Lisa, and me to

---

1. All Scriptures in this chapter are NIV unless otherwise noted.

pray for an hour a day, and he, being Catholic, faithfully took us to daily Mass. I remember my sister and me lying with my dad on the big king-sized master bed with the gigantic orange velvet comforter and him telling us all about Jesus. He said that, if we asked Jesus into our hearts, then we would get presents. I said, "Oh, yes, I want that." My father led me in the sinner's prayer, and I remember the feeling I had at such a young age when Jesus came into my heart. I specifically remember asking my dad, "Where are the presents?" My dad responded, "They are coming, you will see. They don't come all at one time, but they will be here." I remember having a feeling of disappointment at not having actual presents, but God gave me a vision of presents in my head. I saw them in the Spirit. I can still see that exact same vision in my mind today that I had many years ago. I have seen the gifts of God in my life, and I do praise God for all of his miraculous wonders that he has done throughout the years.

The Spirit of God brought my father squarely into the Catholic charismatic movement, where the laying on of hands, prophecy, and speaking in tongues were commonplace. It also introduced him to the Protestant movement that already possessed a strong historical foundation of supernatural manifestations of the presence of the Holy Spirit. It was at that time in my life, at the age of nine, that I was baptized in the Holy Spirit and encountered men and women mightily used of God to impact and change my life forever.

My father was a brilliant scholar. He skipped two grades in school, attended twelve years of college, and graduated from Harvard Law School. If you asked him what any vocabulary word meant, he knew its derivation, multiple meanings for the word, and how to put it in a sentence. As my sister and I were growing up, his favorite words seemed to be, "That word is generally not used like that!" He would then proceed to tell us how it should be used correctly, and he encouraged us to study Latin. He said it would help us better understand the meaning of English words.

My father also saw the value of having a strong religious educational foundation for his children, so, in fifth grade, I changed schools from the public school to the Catholic school, St. Paul the Apostle, down the street in Westwood. It was at this time my father, my sister, and I started attending Catholic charismatic prayer meetings as well as nondenominational Christian services. My father was so in love with the Lord and so passionately cared about the spiritual growth of his children that he wrote beautiful books for my sister and me, entitled *Hi, Lisa, Hi, Gemma: Stories of a Loving Father to His Little Daughters*. My father would illustrate complicated gospel truths through the telling of everyday stories and analogies that could be understood easily by children. My father was planting the seed of the word of God in our hearts at our very young ages through storytelling.

When I was baptized in the Holy Spirit at nine, I immediately started telling my friends about the Lord. That same year, I joined the children's charismatic Catholic prayer meeting led by a nun named Sister Mary and began praying and laying hands on other attendees. My hunger for God was infectious, and I wanted to share my faith. In fifth grade, I witnessed to my friends in school; in tenth grade, I witnessed on the streets with my church. When I was very young, my father first began inspiring me to minister to those who were imprisoned. As I was growing up, he often told me stories of how he ministered to incarcerated youth and how God transformed their lives when they received him into their hearts and asked for forgiveness for their sins. I could not wait to minister and to follow in my father's footprints. I cared so deeply for the lost and hurting. I knew I had the answer. It was as easy as asking Jesus into their hearts.

At seventeen, I was asked to sing at the Los Angeles Mission on Skid Row by Mel Novak, a prison minister whom I met at the Southern California Motion Picture Council (SCMPC), an organization that awards morally uplifting movies and television shows. My mom happened to be the president of the SCMPC, so I was a consistent award presenter, and God used me to be a light for the Lord in the movie and television industry. At twenty-one, I began ministering to the youths in juvenile hall. From the prisons and skid row, God increased my ministry to churches, radio, books, newspapers (*The Hollywood Times*), evangelical outreaches, and television ministry. At the age of twenty-six, I preached at the Hollywood Bowl Easter sunrise service produced by Trinity Broadcasting Network and televised worldwide as well as making multiple guest appearances on such TBN shows as *The Joy Program* with Jay Jones and *Calling Dr. Whittaker* and *Behind the Scenes* with Paul Crouch. Currently, I can be heard every Thursday evening at 6:45 p.m. on KTYM 1460 AM or on the Internet on ktym.com, and via satellite on Cross TV on Wednesdays at 5:30 p.m. or live streaming on thecrosstv.com. After numerous appearances on TBN, God gave me my own production company. My shows, *Gemma Wenger's Hollywood*, *Beauty for Ashes*, and *Beauty for Ashes: Revival on the Streets*, currently air worldwide on Time Warner Cable, Isaac Television, The Way TV, Jadoo Television, and Roku. I also have held biweekly church meetings in the Los Angeles area for the past twenty-five years where people can receive personal ministry, be encouraged by the word of God, and receive the gifts of the Spirit.

While all this was going on, my mother was producing and starring in her own celebrity cooking shows, *Cooking around the World* and the *Bee Beyer Show*, in the early 1970s. At the age of four, dressed in an African safari outfit, I "oohed" and "aahed" on camera over my mother's latest concoction. As a pioneer in her field and an entrepreneur, she also invented the Bee Beyer Food Dehydrator and wrote the book *Food Drying at Home the Natural Way*, which did not advocate the use of chemicals or preservatives in the food dehydration process. She had international exposure through her appearances on *The Home Shopping Network*, *QVC* with Joan Rivers, *The 700 Club* on CBN with Pat Robertson, as well as numerous appearances on TBN. I so appreciate her raising me on healthful nutritious foods so that my physical body could grow and develop as God had intended. As a child who struggled with overeating due to emotional trauma, I found that excessive amounts of healthy foods did not seem to cause me to gain weight and, although I possessed an eating disorder, I was not overweight. God eventually delivered me from this addiction to food through the power of prayer and fasting.

My mother also encouraged me to audition for acting roles, and I soon landed parts on shows such as *General Hospital* and *Crisis Counselor*, as well as doing commercials for McDonald's, 7 Up, and Nestle. I also made friends with other children in the business. Kim Richards from *The Real Housewives of Beverly Hills* lived down the street. It was fun going ice skating with her and her little sister Kyle when I was in second grade, and all Kim's fans would walk up to her and ask her for her autograph.

My mother was the businesswoman. From her, I learned my business sense. She taught me never to give up, to overlook faults, always forgive, keep moving forward, and not to over-think anything, but just do it. Interestingly enough, my mom was reared Protestant, thus exposing me to a religious belief system other than Catholicism. She dabbled in healing and managed to take my sister and me to a couple of Kathryn Kuhlman services at the Shrine Auditorium in Los Angeles, where I experienced firsthand the supernatural, marvelous healing power of God. This proved to be an invaluable experience, as God later gifted me with the flow of his healing power in my own ministry.

Eventually, my mother bought a secular quarterly newspaper, *The Hollywood Times*, for which I wrote a faith-based article to encourage the readers. This was a new avenue of ministry that God unexpectedly opened. I never anticipated that my Catholic-school literature and writing teacher, Ms. Dunne, would ever contribute something meaningful and worthwhile to my ministry. It just shows that, if people are open, God will use them in any way that they allow. He will utilize them in unexpected ways and in circumstances for which they do not even feel prepared. God will take them along unknown paths and uncharted territory if they surrender their will to God's will. Solomon says in Ecclesiastes 11:6, "In the morning sow your seed, and at evening do not let your hands be idle; for you do not know which will prosper, this or that, or whether both alike will be good" (NRSV). Sometimes, we just have to walk through the doors that are open, even though we may have had something else in mind. God sees the bigger picture, and obedience is the key. But, even as I was growing spiritually and professionally, I was always aware that these conflicting emphases had taken their toll on my family.

My parents were separated when I was a toddler. My father was a gentle, loving man, but we lived with our mother. From the early age of five, after all our young female cousins from Kansas had finished taking care of us, my sister and I washed all the dishes, did all the laundry, and cleaned the house. My mother worked out of her home, but did not give her family and household the attention it so desperately needed. I remember seeing my mother do the dishes one time when I was growing up, and I took careful notice of it since it was so highly unusual. We rarely arrived at school on time because my mom had to make all of her business calls to the East Coast before 8:00 a.m. in order to receive reduced long-distance telephone rates. Getting picked up from school was equally challenging due to my mom's business schedule.

My childhood was a struggle. Growing up, I walked around with holes in my shoes, socks, and underwear. When my dad offered to buy me new shoes, I remember telling him that I did not need new shoes because the ones I had did not have holes in them yet. He bought new shoes for me anyway. In the ninth grade, I ran the entire cross-country season in a pair of Jack Purcell tennis shoes while the other children had technologically advanced running shoes. In the end, though, by the grace of God, my Jack Purcells and I both came up with the most valuable player award for that varsity cross-country season. I worked hard to excel both in sports and academics.

Considering that all this time I was doing commercials and television shows, it may seem odd that my sister and I could be neglected. My dad possessed a strong paternal instinct, but was hindered by my mother's dominance and her focus on the business aspect of life and the desire for increased worldly gain. She always said, "A penny saved is a penny earned," yet she rarely thought to spend those pennies on the practical needs of her family.

Early on, I began to meet people who influenced me to progress in my faith, supplementing my father's example. Since the fifth grade, when I changed schools from the public school to the Catholic school and started attending Catholic charismatic prayer meetings and non-denominational Christian services, through my father, I began to meet people whom God used to open the door and lead the way, and I obediently followed. One of those religious pioneers was Michael Grace. I met Mr. Grace through my father at St. Paul the Apostle Church. He faithfully attended the Catholic charismatic prayer meetings while setting up numerous meetings on his own to usher people into a new move of the Spirit, an even mightier presence of God. Mr. Grace was a jovial man and extremely popular. He had five beautiful children, and I became quite close to some of them. I will never forget my outing with one of his sons. We took the family's Mercedes to get a bite to eat, and, to my surprise, it even had a built-in refrigerator. My father and Mr. Grace had connected immediately: both were Catholics hungry for God, both attended Harvard, and both were East Coast natives. Mr. Grace never stopped inviting my father, my sister, and me to churches, ministries, brunches, and dinners. He sponsored free meals and fellowship, and the word of God was indelibly planted in our hearts. Ironically, his personal assistant, Jeanne DeFazio, editor of *Creative Ways to Build Christian Community*, with whom I built a relationship many years ago, has now come back into my life to be a blessing to me and my ministry.

She even quoted both my mother and me in her book to help encourage the body of Christ.

During this same period of time, Rev. John Chapell from Christ Faith Tabernacle in Echo Park, California, laid hands on me to be baptized with the Holy Spirit with the evidence of speaking in tongues and prophecy. I was being trained at a very young age in my mission as a preacher, teacher, healer, deliverer, and prophet called to evangelize the nations.

From there, I began my radio and television shows, preached at Trinity Broadcasting Network's Hollywood Bowl Easter sunrise service, sang and ministered at their church, Trinity Christian Center (TCC) with Pastor Ed Smith, and ministered and sang at various other churches and events such as Full Gospel Businessmen's Fellowship with Demos and Richard Shakarian. I began producing my own faith-based television shows at age twenty-one.

Professionally, my theatrical training at the Beverly Hills playhouse under Milton Katselas, my commercial training, and my filmmaking and television production classes at the University of California at Los Angeles (UCLA) proved indispensable in my current role as an actor and filmmaker. My UCLA filmmaking experience, which stemmed from a strong attraction to theater arts, was invaluable, as today I produce *Beauty for Ashes*, *Beauty for Ashes: Revival on the Streets*, and *Gemma Wenger's Hollywood*. *Gemma Wenger's Hollywood* has become the perfect venue for me to witness for Jesus in the entertainment industry. On the set of my show, I have talked to numerous celebrities about being positive role models as well as about how their faith has influenced their lives, including Lou Gossett, Jr., Jon Voight, Lou Diamond Phillips, Brad Garrett, Dennis Haysbert, Ed Asner, James Caan, and Connie Stevens, just to name a few.

I studied hard, graduated from UCLA, and have a Master of Educational Administration. I am a survivor. I never gave up, and I am still persevering. God's grace, faith, and sheer hard work have brought me through. God healed me particularly of my mother's neglect in the past through the power of prayer and perseverance. My childhood was far from normal, but now I have compassion on children and adults who have been neglected or abused, and I know how to minister to them. God has since ministered to my mother, and the person who hurt me in the past has now become a blessing and help in my life.

Through the power of prayer and forgiveness, God has touched my heart and my family and made everything new. I do not accept excuses from anyone. I conquered and overcame an abusive past; therefore, I know that, through determination, prayer, and hard work, anyone can be successful.

It is summarized so well in the following Scripture verse. "And the fruit of righteousness is sown in peace of them that make peace" (Jas 3:18 KJV). Each person brings unity to the body by sowing seeds of peace and love. Every person's gifts are necessary to develop the church to achieve its greatest potential, but are only effective as individuals speak words and exhibit actions that promote harmony and cohesiveness. Peacemakers who sow in peace reap a harvest of righteousness. You receive the blessing back to you from the hand of the Lord when you extend kindness and love to those around you. What you show to other people is what they will give you in return!

From all these examples and experiences, I have learned that my personality easily lends itself to the building of relationships. I realize that I need a strong person with me to guide me and encourage me. I do well when someone else opens the door and then I walk through it and use my spiritual gifts. I embrace the presence of catalysts encouraging me to come with them and then push me forward to achieve greater heights. I thrive in situations where I am in relationship with people working together in unity. The disciples were in the upper room in one accord, praying, when they were baptized with the Holy Spirit and fire! God moves when the body of Christ is working together in harmony. He puts people together. Remember, Jesus sent the disciples out two by two to preach the word of the Lord. I am always amazed at the power of God to put just the right people in my life to complement the gifts that God has given me. When one person falls, the other is there to lift that one up. God has designed a spiritual body that works together with its various members to achieve a goal. God truly used the people around me, even from childhood, to develop and train me to discern the movement of the Spirit of God and to respond accordingly by opening ministry doors for me. The importance of unity in the ministry is reiterated in Ephesians 4:11–13: "It was he who gave some to be apostles, some to be prophets, some to be evangelists, and some to be pastors and teachers, to prepare God's people for works of service, so that the body of Christ may be built up until we all reach unity in the faith and in the knowledge of the Son of God and become mature, attaining to the whole measure of the fullness of Christ." God gives each one special gifts for the perfecting of God's people. We all need pastors and prophets and teachers and healers in our lives to come to the fullness of his grace. Without the talents of others, God has designed it that we will not achieve our full potential. Hebrews 11:40 says that only together with us would they be made perfect. We might say, in the supernatural realm there is an intermingling of the spirits of God's people. Past and present come together to achieve the purpose of God!

When family members dwell together in unity, the beauty and love that result is mellifluous, but, without unity, the opposite is true. When people are divided and at odds with one another, no one is edified, and the entire body is brought down. Nothing can be accomplished. Paul says in Romans 16:17: "Watch out for those who cause divisions and put obstacles in your way that are contrary to the teaching you have learned. Keep away from them." Paul says that people who are divisive and have a doctrine different from the one that the Romans had learned should be singled out and evaded. Their mere presence and negativity will bring down the entire body of Christ! The Spirit of God is so sensitive that it is easily quenched. The members of the body of Christ must be aware of the strategies of darkness and diligently protect themselves!

Third John 1:9 talks specifically about a man named Diotrephes who "loves to have the preeminence" (NKJV). Because of his own selfish desires, he did not receive the disciples. He was not going to allow anyone else to have the limelight. He had to be the center of attention just like the Pharisees and Sadducees. We see that same spirit of self-centeredness in our society today. That spirit of selfishness and carnal desire in the body of Christ hinders the work that God truly wants us to do. Third John 1:10 says, "So when I come, I will call attention to what he is doing, spreading malicious nonsense about us. Not satisfied with that, he refuses to welcome other believers. He also stops those who want to do so and puts them out of the church" (TNIV). Diotrephes was trying to stop those who were actually helping the disciples. He was casting them out of the church. Do not let anyone control you to such a degree that you are hindered from doing God's work. Really think about it. This man would excommunicate those Christians who received and helped the disciples. How ridiculous is that? We, as Christians today, can be persecuted for doing the right thing. We are bullied by those with contrary doctrines into thinking that we are wrong when we are really doing that which is right in the eyes of the Lord. In these last days, it is more and more difficult to stand firm in our Christian beliefs because of extreme opposition and persecution. Some Christians do fall away in the face of adversity, temptation, and trials. The attacks of evil are so great that some give in. Each one who leaves or compromises one's Christian principles weakens the body of Christ as a whole. When you are strong, I become stronger. When you are weak, I become weaker.

At the same time that we are avoiding chronic troublemakers, we should not make it our mission to cut off all who offend us. We must not forget about forgiveness.

A very prophetic woman of God, named Barbara Evans, who worked for Michael Grace for a season and nannied my sister and me over a four-year period, always quoted Colossians 2:2a to us: "That their hearts might be comforted, being knit together in love" (KJV). She talked about how everyone in the body of Christ should be knit together, intertwined to such a degree that they are supporting, encouraging, and loving one another. As an avid knitter, I know that one dropped stitch will destroy an entire garment. The whole piece has to be unraveled in order to pick up the lost stitch and then the garment must be reknit. It is the same way in the body of Christ. One member who is lost must be restored before the church can move forward. God does not allow any one of his people to be left behind. The Bible confirms this in Jeremiah 3:14, when God says he is married to the backslider. The church needs to be knit together in love to such a degree that it will do whatever it takes to restore a soul to soundness. The body is so intertwined with each saint that we become one. We are all members of his church together. It is our job to do our part to build up the body of Christ. We, as one body, grow and mature together.

My charge to you, the reader, is to use your gifts to help others. Let your life of service flow from a heart of true caring and selfless giving. Ephesians 4:32 admonishes, "Be kind and compassionate to one another, forgiving each other, just as in Christ God forgave you." Be kind to the other members of the body of Christ. Do not neglect them. Have a tender heart and, most of all, forgive. That person who has hurt you may be one that God has lined up next to bless you! My mother is now blessing me after causing me great hurt and pain in my childhood. If you do not forgive that person, you will miss out on the blessing for yourself! It is difficult to love, forgive, and be kind, especially when someone has offended you, but Jesus calls us to do this. It is God's will that we humble ourselves and mend past relationships in order for God to show us that same forgiveness. As Jesus stated in Matthew 6:14, "For if you forgive others when they sin against you, your heavenly Father will also forgive you" (TNIV). It is imperative that we forgive in order to be forgiven. As a body, we must pardon others in order to please God and fulfill his plan for us as individuals as well as his plan for humankind as a whole.

You are God's temple. You are God's building. The Spirit of God lives in you. First Peter 2:5 so beautifully paints a picture of each individual as one of the living stones built up into a spiritual house. We are built upon the foundation that another has supplied, so it is vital that we help, encourage, support, and bring unity to the body of Christ. In Psalm 133, David clearly tells the people: "How good and pleasant it is, when God's people live together in unity! It is like precious oil poured on the head, running down on the beard, running down on Aaron's beard, down on the collar of his robe." Working together in unity with other members of the body of Christ is key to experiencing all that God has to offer his children. The blessings come from God as his people work together to accomplish his will.

RESOURCES

To view Gemma Wenger's program, see thecrosstv.com, LA36.org, isaactelevision.tv, and ktym.com.

To contact Gemma to speak or minister, visit gemmawenger.com.

12

Caretakers of the Future

Charlene Eber
Written by Jeanne DeFazio
as told to her by Charlene Eber

As Jesus and the disciples were going to an official's home, a woman who had had a hemorrhage for twelve years came up behind him. "She touched the fringe of his robe, for she thought, 'If I can just touch his robe, I will be healed.' Jesus turned around and said to her, 'Daughter, be encouraged! Your faith has made you well.' And the woman was healed at that moment" (Matt 9:20–22 NLT).

Jesus knew that this woman's pull of faith was strong enough to attract the sensitive healing of the Holy Spirit. He discerned all diseases and the hearts of those who had them because he had all the gifts of the Holy Spirit. This woman knew that the blue in the tassel represented the word of God, and that Jesus was a true Israelite whose hem was not worn in hypocrisy. It stood for the covenant of healing and the Word who had healed all Israel. She acted upon her faith, and it worked.

In the early 1980s, veteran actress Joan Caulfield found an advertisement for Video Ventures in the Los Angeles telephone book. She contacted Hollywood director and producer Charlene Eber from that advertisement at the request of her longtime friend, Michael P. Grace II. Mr. Grace, a former Broadway producer and the chief executive officer of Grace Motion Pictures, asked Charlene to film a ministry event for Breath of the Spirit, the international Christian ministry of Michelle Corral and her mother, Joanne Petronella.

Charlene's husband, Ken, asked Joanne to pray for Charlene, who was dying of cancer. One night, Charlene had a life-changing experience. She knew at that moment that Jesus had healed her. After her medical reports evidenced the miraculous recovery, Charlene recalls walking through the University of Southern California (USC) Hospital wondering why people in the hallway were applauding. She thought perhaps there was a Hollywood movie star passing by, and then she realized that the staff was cheering her for a miraculous recovery that defied the understanding of modern science and medicine.

Charlene grew up in a Roman Catholic home where she knew and loved Jesus, but her life-changing and miraculous healing from terminal cancer gave her relationship with Jesus a new start. Her personal experience of Jesus's healing touch allowed her to understand at the depths of her heart and soul the extent of God's mercy and love. Her answered prayer opened up a way for her to live her life more completely for Jesus.

She testified before crowds at Breath of Spirit Ministry events. Like the woman in Matthew's gospel account, Charlene reached out to touch Jesus in faith, and he responded by healing her. Charlene explained in her testimony that anyone can simply reach out in faith, and Jesus will respond. Jesus's healing changed Charlene's life. She made her Hollywood studio available for Joanne Petronella to teach Bible studies to members of the entertainment industry. Charlene and her husband, Ken, filmed international ministry events for Breath of the Spirit Ministries, traveling with Joanne, Michelle, and Michael Grace to Singapore, China, and India. God healed Charlene from cancer, changing what seems unchangeable and giving her life new purpose and hope. Here is Charlene's story:

I was reared by a single mom, Agnes, who defied cultural taboo as a devout Irish Catholic, striking out on her own to rear me. My mother and I moved from New York City to Woodside, Queens, and I grew up in a walk-up apartment. Agnes worked long, hard hours as a photographer at some of New York City's top nightclubs, most notably the Copacabana.

As an only child and member of the baby-boom generation, I was taught by my mother to have a sense of responsibility. Since it was just the two of us, I had household chores. Mom and I would have breakfast together. When I came home from school, we had dinner together, and she would go to work. She was a very honest woman who loved me unconditionally and who told me, "You can do whatever you want in this world if you put your mind to it."

After a long courtship, my mother remarried when I was fourteen years old. My stepfather was a wonderful mentor who taught me a lot about the business world. He was a New York restaurant and nightclub owner who took my mom to wonderful restaurants, and his influence on my life culturally was great. If he wanted to date my mother on Sunday, I chaperoned, and, as a result, I became known as "La Petite Connoisseur" at New York's finest restaurants. My mother never missed a chance to educate me culturally in the cosmopolitan borough of Manhattan. On Sunday, our day, she took me to "high tea" at the Russian Tea Room and to Tavern on the Green.

Since I was brought up in an Irish Catholic family, I always loved Jesus. I had a deep sense of his love for all humankind because my mother insisted that we are all God's children. I attended St. Mary's Help of Christians School in Woodside and Mater Christi in Queens. In the Catholic schools I attended, there were always paintings of Jesus surrounded by the children of the world. I knew and felt deeply that Jesus loved everyone and was no respecter of persons.

My parents moved to Florida, when I was in my teens, and I attended Nova High School. Nova is a Rockefeller-funded research high school program. After a successful interview, Nova accepted me into its program despite two hundred people on a waiting list ahead of me. I realize in retrospect that Nova was one of the greatest educational opportunities of my life.

In the 1970s, I met and married Ken Eber and supported his passion for media by moving to Hollywood and jointly founding Video Ventures. I directed, produced, and hosted my own cable cooking program, *Chef Secrets* (transmitted nationally by satellite daily). Video Ventures held auditions for mega movies, television, and pioneering work in the infomercial industry. I provided media and image consultation for top personalities and some Fortune 500 featured companies. I had entrée to every A-list party in Hollywood via Diane Bennett, music critic for *Variety*, and I networked to keep my business going.

Ken is Jewish, so, after we married and I gave birth to Tara and Brandon, we decided that our household would embrace both Jewish and Christian traditions. My son Brandon was circumcised by a rabbi and one week later baptized in the Catholic Church. Before both children were born, I studied with a rabbi, embracing Judaism, keeping traditional Jewish holidays, and attending the synagogue. Our family celebrated Hanukkah and Christmas, Passover and Easter.

When I was carrying my daughter, Tara, I was diagnosed with kidney cancer. After Tara's birth, I was diagnosed with renal cell carcinoma. Because I had had undetected cancer for so long while I was pregnant, the cancer had spread from my lymph nodes into my blood and eventually landed in my breasts. At this time, Michael Grace came to my studio to edit a video for Breath of the Spirit Ministries with my husband, Ken. During that editing session, my husband told Michael that I had cancer, and Michael insisted that I go to Joanne Petronella's healing services, which were part of Breath of the Spirit Ministries. The moment she laid hands on my breasts and prayed, the lumps disappeared.

About a week later, I was sitting in my living room, and my entire living room from ceiling to floor was saturated with bright white light. My first reaction was to wonder if I should be afraid. In that moment, I felt very calm and loved and warm. Then, the cynic in my mind wondered if this was really happening. I moved over on my couch where I could see my reflection in a ceiling-to-floor mirror in my dining room, and there I was: Charlene Mary sitting in this room saturated with a bright white light. Then I felt I was not alone. A voice in my mind said to me, "Charlene, you are healed of cancer." That's the only part of the message I remember. Then, I went back to the chief of oncology at USC, Donald Skinner, and told him I had had a miracle and was healed of cancer. This was not within the grasp of scientific understanding.

The medical profession saw me as a dead woman walking. After four years, doctors still did not accept that I had been healed, but, after seven years, my doctor said it was okay for me to have another baby. My cancer was an extraordinary thing, and visiting doctors from various countries who saw my imaging were astounded because a person with cancer like I had would have been dead. I told everyone that I had a miracle: I was healed of cancer.

It turned out that healing from cancer would be the greatest opportunity of my life. My faith in Jesus grew as I was prayed over for healing, and I began to have prayer meetings in my Hollywood studio. I volunteered myself and my husband to film overseas ministry outreaches of Breath of the Spirit. I met many Christians, and the fellowship encouraged my faith. I read my Bible. God opened doors, and I ran through them. I was in the missionary field every opportunity I had. I volunteered for ministry producing and directing films overseas for Breath of the Spirit Ministries. The biggest spiritual awakening occurred in a cathedral in Singapore. More than four thousand people were singing in tongues, and I had to hold on to two lampstands to stay standing because something was knocking me over. I was on an ear set communicating with my husband and said, "Something is knocking me over, do you feel that?" Ken said "Yes, what is that?" I said, "I don't know." That was the first time I felt the anointing of the Holy Spirit and when I received the gift of tongues.

Subsequently, we went to a small village, and there were a lot of people gathered to receive prayer. Joanne Petronella pointed at me and asked me to pray for a whole group of women who were barren. I was surprised, because I was filming the missionary tour and was not a member of the ministry team. But I laid hands on these women, praying for them in tongues. A year and a half later, a member of that ministry team testified at the ministry's birthday banquet that there was a population explosion in the village after I had prayed over those women. I felt humbled that the Holy Spirit would impart the healing fire from my hands to heal women who miraculously were able to conceive. It was awesome to me to realize that little Charlene Mary from Woodside was enabled to participate in a miracle so profound.

I started to accept the fact that the Holy Spirit of God was everywhere and that, if we are willing and open to receive the anointing, it will come through us. At the same event, I laid hands on a woman who fell on the floor screaming and writhing. Joanne immediately came over, laid her hand on her chest, and prayed, and the woman became calm. This was my first exorcism. The translator explained that this woman had been mute since childhood and had now received the gift of speech. The first time I prayed over anyone, women who were barren were able to conceive. Now, a woman who was mute since childhood received the gift of speech and was exorcised. These events had a powerful effect on me. To this day, because of these faith-bolstering experiences, I pray with faith for healing for anything and everyone.

I traveled with Breath of the Spirit Ministries and smuggled five hundred Bibles into Communist China. The penalty for this crime at that time was very harsh. Joanne Petronella and Michelle Corral met with the customs officials who inspected their bags, which contained Bibles. They explained later that the man was "blinded in the Holy Spirit" and never saw the Bibles. I did not understand what "blinded in the Holy Spirit" meant at the time. We distributed Bibles to strangers on the street in Canton. Then, on a train ride headed to the next ministry point, Joanne said we had to get rid of the remaining Bibles because there would be an inspection at the next stop. I opened the door and started to throw Bibles off the train. There were people in the rice paddies running toward the train to receive the Bibles. There are no words to describe the experience of seeing these people in the water of the rice paddies coming to receive what they did not know was the word of God. People ran for miles to receive the Bibles. This experience was one of the most awesome in my life. At the next train stop, there were indeed many soldiers inspecting the train.

I had another profound spiritual experience that resulted in my founding the World Alliance for Peace (WAFP). A voice in the night woke me, and I heard it explain that this world does not belong to us, but to our children and our children's children. We are caretakers of the future and need to start making a difference. I shared this experience with Michael Grace, and his response was that we have to take action. Michael and I came up with the name World Alliance for Peace. WAFP's vision is that the whole world is a community. We are all God's children and responsible for each other. With Major General Uban in India, WAFP was able to help initiate peace talks between India and Pakistan, have medical equipment donated to the Okanarth Health Center and medical assistance supplies provided to Mother Teresa. WAFP helps grassroots organizations that need support.

In 1987, representing World Alliance for Peace, I traveled with Christ in You, the Hope of Glory Ministry to Mother Teresa in Calcutta. Along with Joanne Petronella, Michael Grace, and Jeanne DeFazio, I prayed for lepers and untouchables, encouraging the sick and the despairing, reaching out by faith, praying and healing in the power of the Holy Spirit just as Jesus had healed me. We encouraged sufferers with the Good News, telling them that problems do not keep us from God, because he is always there to help. Just as Jesus had healed me when I reached out to touch him, so for each of them genuine faith involves action and reaching out to touch Jesus.

Today, I continue to minister as the founder of Caretakers of the Future. My focus is that humans had faith in God when they were created, but doubt entered in at the fall (Gen 3:1–7). When faith is restored in new birth in Jesus, and exercised and maintained, it will grow to fullness and power. Just as faith in the blood of Jesus and in his name saved and healed me, it can save everyone and heal everyone's sickness of body, mind, and soul. What I learned from my own healing is that grace is the unmerited love and favor of God to each of us. When we receive Jesus, God shares an incredible journey of faith with us, extending a healing ministry to Christians who are caretakers of the future in every community. You, too, can make a difference if you step forward and accept Jesus's offer of new life. He will open doors for you, and you will be blessed to walk through them. If you are reading this testimony and you need a healing, do not give up. You are on the brink of a miracle.[1]

---

1. Baker, "Don't Give Up on the Brink of a Miracle."

RESOURCES

If you would like Charlene Eber to speak at your event, contact her at blissburger@gmail.com. If you need prayer for healing, email her and she will pray for you and encourage you to victory.

13

Christ in You the Hope of Glory International Ministry

Joanne Petronella
Written by Jeanne DeFazio
as told to her by Joanne Petronella

JOANNE PETRONELLA AND POPE JOHN PAUL II

JOANNE PETRONELLA IS THE founder of Christ in You the Hope of Glory International Ministry based in Anaheim, California. For thirty years, her international ministry has brought many to Jesus, reaching the poorest of the poor in India, doing intense ministry in the Middle East, and ministering to several heads of state. As a member of the Vatican Board of Charismatic Catholics, Joanne attended a private audience with Saint John Paul II and worked closely with Blessed Mother Teresa of Calcutta. Her early ministry training was under the anointing of famed televangelist Kathryn Kuhlman. Jan and Paul Crouch's Trinity Broadcasting Network featured her cooking show, *In the Kitchen with Mama Joanne*. She was also a guest of Paul Crouch on *Behind the Scenes*, discussing her ministry in the Middle East, as well as a guest on *Praise the Lord* with Dwight Thompson, sharing about her ministry in India. Harry John, Miller Brewery heir and founder of Heart of the Nation Catholic television network, endorsed her ministry. Michael P. Grace II of Grace Motion Pictures and Charlene Eber of Hollywood Video Ventures, board members of World Alliance for Peace, produced videos of her international ministry teams in India, Singapore, and the Philippines. Joanne received three Angel Awards from Excellence in Media for bringing Christ's message to the media.

Joanne holds a doctorate in theology and founded an institute of ministry. She has authored the following books: *Deliverance from Fear, How to Lead Someone to Jesus, Disappointments Transformed into Victory, Exceedingly Great and Precious Promises with Effectual Prayer, Touch the Hem of His Garment, Litany to the Divine Lamb of Love*, and *A Manual for Ministers*. She is currently writing a book entitled *Breaking the Bondages of Witchcraft*.

Joanne was the primary caregiver for her beloved son, Victor Petronella, who dedicated the last two decades of his life to ministry and, at forty-seven years of age, televised a deathbed testimony, inviting everyone to come to Jesus. Her daughter,. Michelle Corral, is the founder of the high-profile, worldwide Breath of the Spirit Ministries. Michelle was interviewed recently on Pastor Gemma Wenger's *Beauty for Ashes* program, and rightly stated, "My mother is one of the generals of God's End Time army. We need to listen to her." Here is Joanne's story:

I am the only child of Julia and Salvatore DiTavi. My father, Salvatore, came to America from Sicily in pursuit of the American Dream. He met and married my mother in Rochester, New York. My beloved mother was stricken with tuberculosis and placed in a sanitarium most of my early life. When I was thirteen, Jesus miraculously healed mama of tuberculosis. Thanksgiving of that year she had been put in the death ward of Olive View Sanatorium in Arcadia, California, as the nurses thought she was dying. But my mother had great faith in Jesus and proclaimed to the nurses that she would be home for Jesus's birthday. On December 22, she had a vision of Jesus walking into her room and touching her. She was instantly healed of tuberculosis and was able to come home to our family on December 24. Life without Mama had been difficult, so her healing greatly encouraged my faith.

I grew to love Jesus while attending Catholic schools. Twelve years of Catholic education increased my faith and understanding of Jesus as my Lord and Savior. After high school graduation, I interned as a dental hygienist before marrying my first husband, Michael Constantine. We had three beautiful children: George, Michael, and Michelle, but our marriage ended due to Michael's constant gambling. As a young, single, divorced mother, I struck out on my own to support three children. This was a difficult time in my life. I cried out to the Lord, and the Holy Spirit led me in the sinner's prayer; no human being was present, but God himself spoke to me, and I surrendered my life to Jesus. I told the Lord I did not feel I had anything to give him, but he told me there was a great calling on my life. Shortly after that, I received the baptism of the Holy Spirit at a prayer meeting where charismatic Catholics from Notre Dame University ministered to me.

Then I met Pete Petronella. Pete had two children, Lisa and Rick, from a previous marriage. I married Pete and reared his two children along with my three children, and we had a son, Victor, together. We lived in Brea, California, and operated a very successful Italian restaurant in that community for twenty-five years. All the children worked with us in the restaurant. I was busy working in the restaurant, caring for all our children, and holding weekly Bible studies and prayer meetings in my home. I was attending both Melodyland Christian Center services and my Catholic church. After attending Melodyland Christian Center for three years, I was asked by Pastor Ralph Wilkerson to participate in his healing service ministry as well as conduct my own weekly services in the Prayer and Share Fellowship Hall at Melodyland.

Catering was a big part of our business. My husband depended upon me to arrange the tables for catered events, because that was not his talent. I would ask the Holy Spirit how to arrange the tables. Immediately, I would get a vision and be able to arrange the tables quickly and get to my prayer meetings. Pete had not yet received the Lord and was jealous of my time spent with the Lord in prayer and the time I spent serving the Lord in ministry. He would at times become angry and, as a result, I was persecuted by my husband for serving Jesus. Thankfully, Pete did receive the Lord before he passed away at the early age of fifty-two.

I was mentored by Kathryn Kuhlman, the famous television evangelist who had a powerful healing and revival ministry. She taught me how to operate in the gifts of the Holy Spirit. I ministered extensively in India with Mother Teresa and the Sisters of Charity. Mother Teresa often called my home for prayer. In 1987 and 1989, Jeanne DeFazio joined my ministry team, which each year performed a play at Mother Teresa's leper colony. We vividly remember the lepers kissing the feet of the performers as an expression of gratitude, seeing miracles occurring during healing services, and the excitement of the Indian "untouchables" when the ministry team showered them with candy. This experience changed Jeanne's life.[1] By the grace of God, in the past thirty-five years, my ministry team has been used to transform lives because Jesus lives in our hearts. By the power of the Holy Spirit, I have journeyed from the experience of being a single, divorced mother who accepted Jesus to become the founder of an established and powerful worldwide ministry.

As a missionary, I have traveled to some fifty-three countries, teaching in worldwide healing services from Scripture to reveal the work and manifestation of the Holy Spirit, the third person of the Trinity. I have ministered to several heads of nations, including Egypt's Anwar Sadat, Palestinian leader Yasser Arafat and his wife Suha, and Ram Baran Yadav, president of the Federal Democratic Republic of Nepal.

At this writing, I have just returned from Croatia, Herzegovina, and Bosnia, where I had ministered in the Holy Spirit twenty-five years ago to the soldiers who were at war. On this last trip, we held huge miracle services, ministering to thousands of people. On Pentecost Sunday alone, we ministered to 1,350 people. Each service held from 270 to 800 people. Many miracles were performed by God the Holy Spirit, and hundreds dedicated their lives to Jesus and were filled with the Holy Spirit.

For thirty-five years, I have led a reenactment of Jesus's final steps to crucifixion on Good Friday on the Via Dolorosa, in the Old City

---

1. For a more detailed account, see DeFazio and Lathrop, *Creative Ways*, 14–15.

of Jerusalem. I directed and often acted in these dramas. Discovery Channel and *Time Magazine* documented my Good Friday pilgrimages along the Via Dolorosa. In 2008, Jaron Gilinsky filmed my Good Friday processional and Time.com featured the film.[2] As the ministry team walks the Way of Sorrows, reenacting Jesus's passion, we sing hymns as Jesus carries the cross, while cameras flash and onlookers react to the mystical reminder that Jesus's blood was poured out to redeem them. This is usually filmed by CNN, BBC, PBS, Jordanian TV, French TV, and other television stations, as well as international magazines from Germany and France. Onlookers bond as their hearts are touched by the message of Jesus's redemptive love. The passion play is a compelling and creative way that my ministry helps fulfill Jesus's Great Commission via media. In our global high-tech culture, media play a vital role in bringing Christ's message to the masses and fulfilling this prophecy: "The message has gone throughout the earth, and the words to all the world" (Rom 10:18 NLT). Many hearts have been touched for Jesus as my ministry's religious dramas have been performed around the world (including in Russia before the fall of communism).

I chose my ministry's mission statement from Paul's letter to the Colossian church: "To them God willed to make known what are the riches of the glory of this mystery among the Gentiles: which is Christ in you, the hope of glory" (Col 1:27 NKJV). I chose this Scripture because it corrected false teachers in the Colossian church who believed spiritual perfection was a secret and hidden plan meant to be exclusive for a privileged few. Paul combated this heresy by proclaiming the word of God in its fullness to the Colossians, explaining God's plan as a message kept secret for centuries and generations past (Col 1:26), not in the sense that only a few would understand, but because it was hidden until Jesus came. My ministry, Christ in You the Hope of Glory International Ministry, manifests the promise of Colossians 1:27 that Christ lives in us. Also, it is the end-time message for the church: as we move with Christ within us, we are walking in the victory and glory of God.

I also chose this mission statement from Colossians because I see this biblical letter as a book of connections that models relational evangelism. Writing from prison in Rome, Paul explained to the Colossians that only by being connected with Jesus through faith can anyone have eternal life, and only through a continuing connection with him can

---

2. Gilinsky, "Californians bring Passion."

anyone have the Holy Spirit. Jesus is God incarnate and, as God's only Son in human flesh, is the only way to forgiveness and peace with God the Father. Colossians 1:27 identifies believers' connections with each other as Christ's body on earth. It identifies the essence of lifestyle evangelism that my ministry embraces. In the book, *Creative Ways to Build Christian Community*, Christ in You the Hope of Glory International Ministry is identified as a model of relational evangelism sharing Jesus's redemptive love.[3]

My weekly television program on The Cross TV every Friday reaches the Middle East, Libya in North Africa, continental Europe, Canada, the United States, and Sweden. With an Arabic interpreter sharing the screen, I relay the message via satellite that Jesus is not hidden, because Christians accept him in their hearts as Lord and Savior, growing daily in his love and extending that love to others. I teach the truth of God's word via the media in fulfillment of the end-time prophecy for the gospel to reach the entire world before the imminent return of Jesus (Rom 10:18–20). This program also encourages the suffering church, including in the Middle East, where we receive calls from Dubai, Egypt, and Saudi Arabia.

My teachings, televised by satellite/dish, focus on the movement of the Holy Spirit through believers to create an end-time church. I quote Jesus's final promise to his disciples in John 14:26: "But when the Father sends the Counselor as my representative—and by the Counselor I mean the Holy Spirit—he will teach you all things and will remind you of everything I myself have told you" (NIV). I explain that the Greek word for "counselor" or "comforter" means "enabler," and that the end result of the Holy Spirit's work in each Christian's life is deep and lasting peace that provides a confident assurance in any circumstance. I warn against the spirit of fear, emphasizing that true believers have no need to fear the present or the future. I explain that, while contemporary life is full of stress, Christians must allow the Holy Spirit to fill them with Christ's peace by praying to and worshiping Jesus and by meditating on the word of God. My book *Deliverance from Fear* develops this theme, explaining that service to Jesus creates the opposite of fear, loss, uncertainty, and doubt within the human psyche. I remind everyone that Jesus promises to give peace to anyone who is willing to accept it from him. I constantly remind viewers that Jesus wants them in these end

---

3. DeFazio and Lathrop, *Creative Ways*, 14–15.

times to fulfill his Great Commission, and that victory is theirs through the blood of Jesus.

Recently, I had a hip operation and am temporarily using a wheelchair to maintain my ministry schedule. In a recent teaching on Gemma Wenger's *Beauty for Ashes* program, I spoke from my wheelchair, exhorting believers to continue to serve Jesus whatever their circumstances.[4] I announced, "Don't tell me you can't serve Jesus! Do you see this wheelchair? I ministered from this wheelchair in Pakistan. If I can serve Jesus in this wheelchair, you can serve him." Please keep me and my ministry in your prayers.

RESOURCES

Joanne Petronella's books *Deliverance from Fear: How to Lead Someone to Jesus, Disappointments Turned into Victory, Exceedingly Great and Precious Promises with Effectual Prayer, Touch the Hem of His Garment, Litany to the Divine Lamb of Love,* and *A Manual for Ministers* (these books are also translated into Croatian) can be purchased by emailing thegreenolivetree@yahoo.com. To view her television program, visit thecrosstv.com. To invite Joanne to minister or to speak at an event, please email thegreenolivetree@yahoo.com.

---

4. I still needed prayer to regain mobility after the hip operation.

14

Uniting the Nations through Media

LeaAnn Pendergrass

SHIRLEY BOONE (LEFT) AND LEAANN PENDERGRASS

P<small>ASTOR</small> L<small>EA</small>A<small>NN</small> P<small>ENDERGRASS WAS</small> born in Fort Payne, a small town in northeast Alabama with a population of approximately eight thousand people. LeaAnn was born to LaVan and Brenda Pendergrass. Brenda was a secretary, and LaVan was the vice president of a large company in Fort Payne. He prematurely lost his life in a car accident at the age of 32. LeaAnn was a student at Fort Payne High School and attended Bishop State College in Mobile, Alabama. In 2004, she attended Bible school at Creative Living Institute, which enhanced her leadership skills.

Growing up, LeaAnn loved music. She loved playing records as a child. The joy she experienced at an early age listening to great musicians' work motivated her to become involved in media.

Pastor LeaAnn promotes a five-fold ministry according to Ephesians 4:11–12.[1] She produces *Uniting the Nations*, a weekly program on The Cross TV Network, which is broadcast on seven satellites and viewed internationally in more than one hundred million homes. Pastor LeaAnn interviews actors, producers, authors, and professional singers as well as church leaders and politicians. The Lord inspired her to produce Uniting The Nations by putting Psalm 133:1 on her heart: "How good and pleasant it is when God's people live together in unity" (NIV). Uniting the Nations brings Jesus's message to the forefront of the media. LeaAnn believes that using television as a tool to reach the world with the gospel of the saving and healing power of Jesus is an idea directly from God. Here is her story:

I grew up in Fort Payne, Alabama, a town with a population at the time of approximately eight thousand. When I was eleven years old, the minister at the Lebanon Methodist Church in Fort Payne asked if anyone wanted to receive Jesus and join the church. I lifted my hand and made a decision to accept Jesus as my Lord and Savior and to join the Methodist Church. I became a believer whose salvation was secure and a faithful churchgoer. But, when I turned twenty-three, I realized that I needed to know the Lord better. I would wake up in the night to pray and seek God for my future.

In 1992, one morning at 2:00 a.m., on the steps of a church in Mobile, Alabama, I was seeking Jesus in prayer. I asked the Lord to speak to me through Scripture and was reminded of Jesus's words in

1. Eph 4:11–12: "The gifts he gave were that some would be apostles, some prophets, some evangelists, some pastors and teachers, to equip the saints for the work of ministry, for building up the body of Christ" (NRSV).

John 15:18-19: "If the world hates you, remember that it hated me first. The world would love you as one of its own if you belonged to it, but you are no longer part of the world. I chose you to come out of the world, so it hates you" (NLT).

I wept as I prayed, understanding that God had chosen me to come out of the world to serve him. Then, I was filled with the Holy Spirit and started to speak in a heavenly language, according to Acts 2:1-4. On the day of Pentecost, seven weeks after Jesus's resurrection, the believers were meeting together in Jerusalem. "Suddenly from heaven there came a sound like the rush of a violent wind, and it filled the entire house where they were sitting. Divided tongues, as of fire, appeared among them, and a tongue rested on each of them. All of them were filled with the Holy Spirit and began to speak in other languages, as the Spirit gave them ability" (NRSV). I started to receive greater revelation from the Word of God. The Lord gave me John 15:16: "You did not choose me, but I chose you. And I appointed you to go and bear fruit, fruit that will last, so that the Father will give you whatever you ask him in my name" (NRSV).

After God spoke to me, I packed up and moved from Alabama to West Virginia, where I lived for almost seven years. It was a big step of faith and, when I look back on it today, I see the grace, love, and mercy of our Heavenly Father as he led me first to Charleston, West Virginia, with a population at the time of approximately one hundred thousand people. The Lord taught me what faith is all about. I drove from Alabama to West Virginia with only $40 in my pocket and, later on, when I drove in faith to Charleston (which was a ten hour drive), I had no GPS and no MapQuest, just the Holy Spirit. This was a time of testing and listening. God said, "Get up and go now. Follow me." I followed a van with Virginia license plates all the way to West Virginia. The van driver went one way and I kept going north. It was an act of absolute dependency on the Lord. But that was what I wanted. I wanted total dependence on God, because, unless we rely on him and trust him completely, we will never know how to walk fully with him.

When I arrived in Charleston, it was pouring rain, so I parked under a bridge. I could not see my car hood in front of me, so I prayed, "God, if you don't help me, I'm stuck." Remember, I had only $40 to my name. Then I looked down the road and saw a Motel 6 with rooms for $29.95 a night. I pulled in, bought a room for the night, and then got a newspaper. I lay on my face and began to pray and cry. "God, where do you want me to live? What do you want me to do? I need a job." Then I got up off the ground and praised him and thanked him for what he was doing, guiding me into a life of faith.

The next day, I walked into the Temple of Grace Church, and the secretary asked me if I was "that lady from Alabama." I asked her how she knew, and she told me, "Your mom called and was concerned for you." I was grateful for this response, glad that I remembered to give my mother the contact information for the church and overjoyed that the church secretary took me over to the Mattie V. Lee Home for women in the heart of Charleston, where I was given a room to live in. To my surprise, there were prostitutes on the corner at night. Coming from Fort Payne, I had never seen anything like that before. My evangelistic call was put into action immediately as I arrived. God placed me in this community to love and minister to these women in the streets.

Three days later, I had a job. I was to do seasonal commission sales for Sears and made more money that Christmas than I had made my whole life. That was the beginning of my journey of faith and obedience.

I began to share the gospel on the streets by handing out tracts, because I was not strong enough or bold enough to speak a lot. So I just gave out the word of God in Scripture tracts and would pray for people on the streets of Charleston, West Virginia. Even on my lunch break from work, I would fast instead and go to witness on the streets in front of the mall where I worked in sales. I would share the love of Jesus. And there, on the streets, the Lord began to develop the gift in me for ministry. He put evangelism in my heart according to Mark 16:15: "Go into all the world and proclaim the good news to the whole creation," and Proverbs 11:30: "The one who is wise saves lives" (NIV). Years later, Oral Roberts would lay hands upon me and pray, saying: "Do not forget the souls. Win souls. It is all about soul winning."

During weekly intercessory prayer, the Lord began speaking words of encouragement and prophecy for me to share with individuals and the corporate church. I began to develop gifts of ministry that Paul described in 1 Corinthians 12:10–11: The Spirit "gives one person the power to perform miracles, and another the ability to prophesy. He gives someone else the ability to discern whether a message is from the Spirit of God or another spirit. Still another person is given the ability to speak in unknown languages, while another is given the ability to interpret what is being said. It is the one and only Spirit who distributes all these gifts. He alone decides which gift each person should have" (NLT).

I heard the Lord speak within my heart, "I will take you into your destiny." He said to me, "Obedience will take you into your destiny." As I obeyed him and followed him, many doors began to open. I went on the road, serving at church events, singing on the praise team at church, and, in 1998, preaching for my pastor before the whole congregation at New Life Church. I also volunteered in a worldwide ministry, driving many hours just to help serve, by ushering, or by singing in the choir. God taught me how to love and trust him. I trusted him to guide me. Trusting in God comes from spending time with him to develop a relationship. My relationship grew through meditation on the word of God. Isaiah 26:3 always reminded me: "You will keep in perfect peace those whose minds are steadfast, because they trust in you" (NIV). It is all about trusting God. It is all about having a relationship with him. Knowing when to act upon his still small voice in your heart and listening to his voice speak to you in your heart.

For all those who are reading this chapter, I want to encourage you. Don't quit! Never give up, because God's plans are so big for you! Maybe you can't see them right now, but years down the road they will all start to unfold. He truly orders your steps—where you are today and where you are going to be ten years down the road.

One thing he showed me is that living a holy life is powerful. If we give him our lives and cry out to him, he will bless us with holiness. "Holiness" is actually a word of consecration. In the Lord's Prayer, Jesus taught us that the Lord's name is to be hallowed: "Hallowed be thy name" (Matt 6:9). "Hallowed" means holy! So, if we look at him and keep our eyes on him, then we will see ourselves and what we are to become: holy, just like he is.

My journey brought me to California. The seed of faith and prompting of the Holy Spirit put California on my heart. I was in Los Angeles for the first time in April of 1997 at Eastertime. I stepped out in the leading of the Holy Spirit to come and work as a volunteer at a Good Friday event of a mega-televangelist's ministry. I heard the Lord say, "Drive to Hollywood and pray." I was staying with a friend named Pat who lived in Simi Valley, and I asked her to let me drive her car to Hollywood Easter night. She said "Now?" and I said, "Yes, the Lord wants me to go and pray." So we took off, and, for three and a half hours, we circled Sunset Boulevard and Hollywood Boulevard praying and worshiping with the windows down, decreeing revival over Hollywood and claiming souls saved by Jesus's shed blood on Calvary. After we prayed and worshiped, I sensed the Lord asking me to go and witness to one person, so I stopped and handed a tract to someone in Wendy's on Sunset Boulevard. I said, "Jesus loves you," and planted a seed. I believe it pleased our Lord.

The next day, when I was flying back to West Virginia, I sat in a row of seats that were all empty next to me. As we took off out of Los Angeles International Airport, I heard the Lord say, "You are leaving your home." I began to weep, actually sob, because it was so powerful and strong a message from heaven. This was the seed sown that I see today as part of the process of planting my present church, My Gathering Place International, which now holds services in an upper room on that same Sunset Boulevard in West Hollywood I circled in prayer in 1997. Jesus explains seed faith in Matthew 17:20: "If you have faith as small as a mustard seed, you can say to this mountain, 'Move from here to there' and it will move. Nothing will be impossible for you" (NIV). My testimony is proof of the Biblical conviction that the faith of a mustard seed can move mountains. Through obedience to God, in 1997, I prayed for a harvest. My Gathering Place International first met on Hollywood Boulevard on Saturday nights, spiritually thriving in that location, Evangelists Bill Henderson, Dana Roman, Susan Stafford, Florence La Rue from the Fifth Dimension musical group, Pastor Betty Green, and actress Lee Benton have all ministered to members of the entertainment industry there. In the fall of 2014, My Gathering Place International's anniversary celebration was filmed and posted on Shirley Boone's website, We Win Ministries.[2] Both Shirley and Pat Boone ministered at the event.

Each Sunday, My Gathering Place International's service is livestreamed via mygatheringplace.com, and its message of Jesus's love and mercy goes global.

Two years ago, I started a television broadcast called *Uniting the Nations*. For eighteen years, I was given this prophecy: "You need to be on TV." A precious Christian lady named Christine took me to The Cross TV in 2013 to meet the founder, Joseph Nassralla, who prophesied over me, saying, "You have been asked to be on several television broadcasts, but you turned them down. But today, you have been sent

---

2. wewinministries.com.

here to be with The Cross TV." His prophesy was true. I had been invited by several networks, but did not feel it was the Lord's time, and had declined the offers.

I want to stress in my testimony that the Lord opened this door by his Holy Spirit because of my obedience and faithfulness to him. So, I encourage readers to trust and obey the prompting of the Holy Spirit in their lives. *Uniting the Nations* in the past several years has been broadcasting the testimonies of many Christian leaders, including an exclusive ministry interview with actress Lee Benton, host of *Victory Road*,[3] on location in Japan on The Cross TV via seven satellites. Also featured have been famed Hollywood stuntman Bob Yerkes; chaplain, author, and former *Wheel of Fortune* hostess Susan Stafford; former political candidate Michelle Bachmann; actor and skid-row and prison minister Mel Novak; Joshua Mills of New Wine International Ministry;[4] musician and minister Tim Ehmann and his wife, Dana, who testified of Tim's amazing conversion; Howard Richardson of Gates of Glory Ministry; and Pastor Betty Green of Betty Green Ministries.[5] I have also cohosted on *LA Live Talk Radio* with Joel Ramirez.

One topic I especially want to address in my testimony is the way that media impact women's self-esteem and body image. Since I began my media ministry, I have become aware of the need to encourage women to embrace a healthy diet and exercise for weight control, but not to succumb to the pressure of the media to look like the Hollywood ideal. According to Psalm 139:14, we are "fearfully and wonderfully made" (NIV). Paul, in 1 Timothy 4:8, identifies the value of bodily training, but also explains that godliness holds promise for the present life and the life to come. I seek the balance represented in Paul's words in my daily life, doing my best to eat right and exercise for good health and a happy self-image. The media makes the average-sized woman feel she will never fit in if she does not have the ideal slim size or look, often making even those who are stick-thin feel that they are too big. It is a challenge to train our minds not to be affected by unrealistic body shapes. Despite the well-publicized fact that drastic measures are taken to alter images in advertisements, it is difficult for the average woman not to compare her own body with Photoshopped illusions of

3. leebentonministries.org.
4. joshuamills.com.
5. bettygreenministries.com.

Hollywood's view of perfection. I want to encourage the reader with my testimony by explaining that the images we see in the media are unrealistic and unhealthy, and that, as Christians, we must seek a true ideal of the human body.

I also want to share one more thought about health. Prior to beginning my own ministry, I was hired in California by a healing media ministry. I worked in the miracle follow-up department, documenting the miracles that occurred during each service. I also followed up by requesting medical documentation from those who claimed to receive physical healing. After years of documenting miraculous healings, I myself was diagnosed with breast cancer. Despite the many miraculous healings I documented, the prognosis filled me with fear. Each night, I anointed myself with oil, according to James 5:14, and I looked up and typed out healing scriptures,[6] praying over them for myself. During a healing service of evangelist Mother Ellen Parsley, I was healed. No malignancy has reappeared in my imaging. For five years, I have been cancer-free and praise God for his miracle of healing in my own life. I mention this to encourage anyone who needs physical healing. As Isaiah prophesied in his book in 53:5, "But he was wounded for our transgressions, crushed for our iniquities; upon him was the punishment that made us whole, and by his bruises we are healed" (NRSV). My testimony is that I am living proof that Jesus's shed blood on Calvary heals diseases. I am sharing this true account from my life to encourage anyone who needs healing to claim it in Jesus's name by virtue of Jesus's shed blood on Calvary. Don't neglect to work with doctors to get a proper diagnosis so you and your prayer partners can pray specifically for each step of your healing.

In closing, my testimony is one of experiencing the power of the living God. In 1992, God called me out of Fort Payne, Alabama. I was too timid to preach the gospel. Today, God has given me the boldness to preach the gospel globally! Mine is a living testimony of the fact that anyone can do anything for the Lord when Jesus Christ lays the foundation in our lives and we allow the Holy Spirit to build on that foundation. If God is the builder of our lives, it may take a while to lay his desired foundation of obedience before the building can go up properly. It was a major transition for me coming from a town as small as Fort Payne to the "wilderness" of West Virginia in prepara-

---

6. E.g., 1 Pet 2:24.

tion for my present ministry in Hollywood, California. In retrospect, I see that God favored me and blessed me with each breakthrough to prepare me for global media ministry. He called me, and, being true to his promises, God opened doors and provided Charleston as a training ground for me to learn to live by faith and walk in the Spirit. The Holy Spirit trained me to hear the voice of the Lord as I studied God's word daily, praying, worshiping God, and spending time serving in churches and at conferences. I had no one else to lean on, but the Lord continually showed me his love and intimacy and fellowship. And, in my daily prayer and reading of his word, he began to transform and renew my mind. He allowed me to see things through his eyes instead of my own, and he took away my insecurities.

Today, I speak live-streaming and by satellite to the ends of the earth from my experience, teaching that God's word is the best tool for inner healing and renewing our minds so that we can think like he thinks. I had fears of failure and speaking publicly, but God gave me boldness and confidence to trust in him so that my identity was in him. Part of my call is to do networking among church leaders to unite the nations according to Psalm 133. My April 17, 2015 event, "Outpouring in Palm Springs," gathered church leaders at the Oasis Fire Ministries, worshiping with Native American Pastor Ron Limon. The service was live-streamed and filmed to be aired on *Uniting the Nations* via The Cross TV. I filmed testimonies from Jensine Bard, whose radio ministry (Jensine Bard Ministries)[7] tells the truth of Jesus to change lives and give hope; Sklar's Ministry,[8] flowing under the anointing of Maurice and Devorah Sklar, sharing healing, the prophetic and the word of knowledge (Maurice ushers in the presence of the Lord as he worships on the violin); Franco Masada,[9] founder and leader of Masada, a Christian rock band, and the Capitol Records pop band Masada Jones;[10] Bill Henderson, author of *God's Radical Remnant,* who was on the original Power Team;[11] Pastor Daniel and Sharon Manriquez from My Father's

---

7. jensinebard.com.
8. mauricesklar.com.
9. masadaband.com.
10. masadajonesband.com.
11. "Bill Henderson was part of the original Power Team—the guys who blew up hot water bottles, ripped phone books in half, bent steel, broke stacks of concrete blocks all for the Glory of God." "Lance," Christian Forum website.

House[12] in Palm Springs, California; Tim and Dana Ehmann;[13] Linda Chapman author of the online *Prayer of the Morning*; Dana Roman; and many others.[14]

I praise God that years have passed since I first began this journey of faith and that I have learned so much about working in ministry. I learned the truth in Ecclesiastes 3:1: "To everything there is a season, and a time to every purpose under the heaven" (KJV). There is a process for each of us to walk through to prepare us for our dreams and visions to come to pass. God prepares us for his purpose. Jeremiah 29:11 promises, "'For surely I know the plans I have for you,' says the Lord, 'Plans for your welfare and not for harm, to give you a future with hope'" (NRSV). If I can serve God in ministry, so can you.

RESOURCES

If you need encouragement, contact my ministry at mygatheringplace.com, and I will pray for you. If you would like to have me speak or minister at an event, contact me at mygatheringplace.com. Visit thecrosstv.com to view *Uniting the Nations*. LeaAnn Pendergrass's *Uniting the Nations* interview of film critic Holly McClure[15] may be found at youtube.com/watch?v=QKgC2ptsW3o.

---

12. thefathershouse.org.

13. timehmannproductions.com/home.

14. To receive Linda Chapman's Prayer of the Morning, email her at HolySpiritOne2@aol.com.

15. Holly McClure reviews faith-based films: hollymcclure.com.

15

Media Fellowship International

Written by Jeanne DeFazio
as told to her by Bob Rieth

REVEREND BOB RIETH, FOUNDER of Media Fellowship International (MFI), has provided pastoral support, conducting prayer groups and counseling for Christians in the entertainment industry, for the past thirty years. The MFI ministry team goes on location to support the media during times of crisis: hurricanes, natural disasters, and crime waves such as school shootings and terrorist attacks. The MFI newsletter updates members about ministry outreach, prayer needs, and ministry events. MFI hosts a monthly meeting on a studio lot where Bob teaches from the Scriptures and prays for those in the media who attend. He meets monthly in Los Angeles with members of the media for one-on-one counseling. He respects the confidentiality of these public figures who need advice and support in crisis. Here is his story:

I was abandoned at birth and left in a garage to be found by a passerby. This birth circumstance turned out to be salvaged for good by the grace of God. A Christian couple, John and Ida Rieth, adopted me and I grew up on a small family farm near Valley City in eastern North Dakota. From an early age, my brother John and I helped with the milking and field work on the farm. John (who was also adopted by these godly people) and I both agree that the greatest blessing of our lives was being adopted into a loving Christian home. Daily, I counsel those who have made wrong choices because they were not reared with Christian values in a loving home environment.

John and I attended Green School, a consolidated country school with ten grades. When I was fifteen, I attended evangelistic services with my family in our country church, Zion Lutheran, and accepted Jesus Christ as my Lord. I think the congregation may have been disappointed that week because I was the only one who went forward to accept Christ, but it has made all the difference in my life. At that time, I felt called by God to preach the gospel and lead others to Jesus. After college, I taught for a year, but knew that was not where I needed to be, so I attended the Association of Free Lutherans Seminary in Minneapolis, Minnesota. I was called to start a mission church near Seattle, Washington. My wife, Marion, and I moved to Kirkland, Washington, where we reared our family and worked together to build a new congregation: Our Redeemer Lutheran Church.

In the 1970s, while serving Our Redeemer Church, I also ministered to the media in conjunction with Johnny Probst under the ministry name FCAME: Fellowship of Christians in the Arts, Media, and Entertainment. FCAME held monthly luncheons in the Marina City Club in Marina Del Rey, where members of the media were able to meet over an informal business lunch and hear testimonies of high-profile Christians. These events were often hosted by Susan Stafford, former *Wheel of Fortune* hostess, who is now part of the MFI chaplain team. Top Hollywood stuntman Bob Yerkes, a member of the MFI board of directors, brought many celebrities to these luncheons: former Miss America Mary Ann Mobley and her husband, Gary Collins, and former Miss America Lee Meriwether and other friends of Bob Yerkes from his *Circus of the Stars* days. Famed actor, professional football player, and political hero Rosey Grier testified at the early meetings. Dale Evans and Roy Rogers became a part of the FCAME family during the 1970s. Peer mentoring was key to the evangelistic success of FCAME, which provided a comfortable atmosphere for celebrities to hear about Jesus from Christian celebrities. Many celebrities who otherwise would not have met Jesus did so through FCAME.

I founded Media Fellowship International (MFI) in the mid-1980s. MFI is a publisher of "glad tidings" in the tradition of Philip the apostle (Acts 8:5, 26–40; 21:8).[1] In this account, Philip, one of the early church deacons, left Jerusalem and spread the gospel wherever he went, but, unlike most of his peers, he did not limit his audience to other Jews. He went directly to Samaria, the last place many Jews would go, due to age-old prejudice. The Samaritans responded in large numbers. When word got back to Jerusalem, Peter and John were sent to evaluate Philip's ministry. They quickly became involved themselves, seeing

---

1. Acts 8:26–35. "As for Philip, an angel of the Lord said to him, 'Go south down the desert road that runs from Jerusalem to Gaza.' So he started out, and he met the treasurer of Ethiopia, a eunuch of great authority under the Kandake, the queen of Ethiopia. The eunuch had gone to Jerusalem to worship, and he was now returning. Seated in his carriage, he was reading aloud from the book of the prophet Isaiah. The Holy Spirit said to Philip, 'Go over and walk along beside the carriage.' Philip ran over and heard the man reading from the prophet Isaiah. Philip asked, 'Do you understand what you are reading?' The man replied, 'How can I, unless someone instructs me?' And he urged Philip to come up into the carriage and sit with him. The passage of Scripture he had been reading was this: 'He was led like a sheep to the slaughter. As a lamb is silent before the shearers, he did not open his mouth. He was humiliated and received no justice. Who can speak of his descendants? For his life was taken from the earth.' The eunuch asked Philip, 'Tell me, was the prophet talking about himself or someone else?' So beginning with this same Scripture, Philip told him the Good News about Jesus" (NLT).

firsthand God's acceptance of those who previously were considered unacceptable. In the middle of all this success and excitement, God directed Philip out to the desert for an appointment with an Ethiopian eunuch, another foreigner, who had been in Jerusalem. Philip went immediately. His effectiveness in sharing the gospel with this man placed a Christian in a significant position in a distant country and may well have had an effect on an entire nation.

Like Philip's calling, MFI's special function is to carry the gospel to places in the media where it was previously unknown. Moving out of the traditional church into restaurants, hotel rooms, and studio lots provides a comfort zone for members of the media who are not comfortable in the traditional church. MFI takes advantage of every opportunity to explain the gospel. I reach out in taxicabs, planes, hotel concierge rooms, and over coffee in airport lounges. Metaphorically speaking, MFI puts sneakers on the gospel and takes it through the streets of Hollywood to its back lots, clubs, restaurants, and hotel meeting rooms. In the same way that Philip ran alongside a chariot to ask the Ethiopian if he understood a passage from Scripture, the MFI chaplain team follows the Spirit's leading, coming alongside people in the entertainment industry who are in need.

Michael P. Grace II, the grandson of New York Mayor W.R. Grace and an heir to the Grace trusts, sponsored several MFI meetings in Los Angeles and New York City. I spoke at Mr. Grace's Hollywood outreaches hosted in his home or in local hotels. I also preached at Mr. Grace's monthly meetings for the homeless in New York City from the late 1980s until Mr. Grace died in 1995. In the early 1990s, MFI hosted high-profile Christian testimonial luncheons sponsored by Michael Grace's organization, the World Alliance for Peace. Held quarterly at prominent New York locations, these luncheons highlighted powerful Christian testimonies from John Ashcroft (who later became the US Attorney General) and Martha Williamson, producer of *Touched by an Angel*, among others.

The celebrity Christian testimony is a key strategy of MFI's practical theology. People can argue theology, but they cannot argue with a testimony, because our stories are what they are. Mr. Grace's friends from high society, the business world, and members of his family attended the MFI luncheons. Mr. Grace's cousin Morgan Grace; Tony Duke, founder of Boys and Girls Harbor; Monsignor Avery Dulles (who later became Cardinal Dulles), and Ben Bradlee, editor of the *Washington Post,* attended MFI's New York City luncheons. Mr. Grace's sons Michael, Winston, and Zachary, and his daughters, Yvonne and Ginger, attended his Los Angeles meetings. His nephews William R. Grace and Joseph P. Grace attended MFI's Washington D.C. luncheons. These MFI meetings introduced people to Jesus because each meeting was conveniently located, and the testimonial speakers witnessed to the gospel in a language the attendees could understand. Each testimony focused on Jesus's love and redemption in a way that was meaningful to the attendees' lives.[2]

Currently, I host a monthly meeting on the CBS studio lots teaching from Scripture and praying for those in the media. Former CBS executive Charles Cappleman attends regularly. I meet with members of the media at a San Fernando Valley restaurant teaching from Scripture after dinner. Wink Martindale and his wife Sandy, as well as Marilyn McCoo and Billy Davis, dine with us often. I counsel high-profile members of the media confidentially and one-on-one each month in Los Angeles. Every year, MFI members attend the President's Prayer Breakfast in Washington DC. MFI hosts a luncheon for members of the Metro DC area media at the Mayflower Hotel during that week. Media Fellowship, International Emergency Response Team was called to Columbine and Virginia Tech to counsel survivors and families in the aftermath of the shootings. MFI went to New Orleans to pray and offer spiritual support in the aftermath of Hurricane Katrina.

In April 2015, the MFI media support ministry team traveled to Israel when media members were covering the crisis in the Gaza strip, using relational evangelism to bring Jesus's message of love and reconciliation to the media covering this global crisis. Members of the press

---

2. Jeanne DeFazio commented on the impact of MFI New York City events hosted by Michael Grace in the book *Creative Ways to Build Christian Community*: Grace "had a burning passion to bring the gospel of Jesus Christ to everyone, especially to those who were either 'up and out' or 'down and out.'" . . . Michael called on Media Fellowship International and Pastor Bob Rieth to help with this missionary effort. MFI is a ministry that reaches out to the secular media and entertainment community with the goal of introducing individuals to Jesus, nurturing them as they learn God's Word, and encouraging them as they walk with God in their professional and personal lives. It was a privilege and a blessing to be able to partner with him to preach and to teach the saving Word of the Lord to the people that Michael invited in from the highways and byways to come and sit at the table and be fed the Word." DeFazio and Lathrop, *Creative Ways*, 11–12.

often risk their lives to cover terrorist acts and natural disasters. In these life or death moments, MFI offers critical spiritual support.

At the time, there was a cease-fire in what was called the fifty-day war on the Gaza-Israel border. This trip was born out of prayer and deep concern for the people in the news crews in places of danger. We wanted to stand behind them and let them know they were being cared for. In light of the ISIS brutality, we realized we needed to pray urgently for them. Another purpose for this trip was to gather information on the possibilities for having a Media Support Team presence in the Middle East. We would be there to listen to them and talk to them individually, to pray with them, and to befriend them. I met a bureau chief for CBN in the Middle East, Chris Mitchell, who invited me and MFI to come at this time. We talked about what Media Fellowship could do to help and how we offered practical and spiritual support to be true to MFI's calling and purpose, expressing a willingness to pray for media members and to pass out New Testaments and grief materials. Chris referred me to a number of people.

This was a unique visit with so many opportunities. I felt the Lord was with me through the whole trip and led me to be able to talk personally with many individuals who asked if we would be willing, with no political agenda, to minister to Jewish, international, and Palestinian press representatives. I said yes. I would be open to reaching out to all the media there. We do not have a point of view politically. Our purpose is to be there for personal support and spiritual encouragement. We would be supportive of an international press in the country.

I went to Ramallah, which is a Palestinian city, to meet with the director of the BBC Media Action group. I met the director, who is Palestinian and was born in Ramallah. He has travelled to several countries because of his work. He is a very kind, patient, attentive host. He was trying to figure out who we were and what we would do in Ramallah. Because of his experiences, he believed we could be of help, especially in Gaza. The director said that all those I met felt a good vibe from me. Their office would always be open to me, and they would do anything they could to help. This was all so strange to me, because it was the first time I had been in an office of all Palestinians and I was treated so graciously. They were completely open to me as a Christian. They worked for a company that is funded by a nonprofit of the BBC. Their work was to provide help to the media people of this area.

I sensed the Lord's presence from beginning to end when we were in Israel. God opened one door after another. As I visited and prayed with people, I became so aware of the stress that they live under. Many are expecting war in the Middle East, not just skirmishes from Hamas. They are aware of the critical role in world history of the place in which they live. There is such a mix in Israel: Jewish, Christian, Muslim, and Palestinian. I was so thankful for the opportunity to minister to them.

In conclusion, I want to leave a word of encouragement with anyone reading this chapter. I was an infant abandoned in a garage. God fostered me through a wonderful Christian home and supernaturally called me at age fifteen to reach the lost for Jesus. I moved by the power of the Holy Spirit outside of the mainstream church, taking the message of Jesus's redemptive love to the fast lane of Hollywood and beyond. God has been faithful to provide for my ministry, which has led a great number of precious, vulnerable people from destruction in the grasp of the entertainment industry to freedom in salvation through the redeeming blood of Jesus Christ. If I can reach the lost for Jesus, so can you. God needs Christians to reach out and bring others to Jesus before his glorious return.

RESOURCES

If you read this chapter and need encouragement, contact my ministry team via mediafellowship.org. Please keep MFI in your prayers. Visit the MFI website at mfi.com to find out more about MFI.

16

The Cathedral of Love of the Seven Golden Candlesticks Church and World Outreach

Larry Abernathy
Written by Jeanne DeFazio
as told to her by Larry Abernathy

WHEN JOHN THE APOSTLE turned to see who was speaking to him, he saw "seven golden candlesticks," and in the midst of the seven candlesticks stood Jesus Christ (Rev 1:12–13). Larry Abernathy explains, "I chose 'Golden Candlestick' in the King James Version of the Holy Bible, because the description continues the word from the temple in Jerusalem and the Law of Moses. The Menorah held nine candlesticks prior to the use of 'lampstands,' which is the translation in the New International Version."

The Cathedral of Love of the Seven Golden Candlesticks Church (founded in 1976) has for forty years been a conduit for the oil of God's Holy Spirit pouring out the love, power, and light of Jesus.[1] As children, Larry Abernathy and his sister, Joan Jaggers Morton, were rooted in the Assemblies of God tradition, experiencing an outpouring of God's miraculous power and mercy in camp meetings throughout the Midwest and Southwest United States.

The only son of early televangelist O. L. Jaggers, Larry graduated from the O. L. Jaggers World Church's High School (1955) and Bible College (1959). He served as youth pastor at age fourteen and was elected pastor at nineteen. In 1970, the National Ecclesiastical University of London, England, conferred a Doctor of Divinity degree upon Larry for his many years of service, his authorship of many books and magazine articles, and his teaching of theology for seventeen years in the World Church's Bible School. Like his famous father, Larry is a powerful teacher of Scripture, gifted in prophecy, singing, and healing. Here is his story:

My name at birth was Larry Duane Jaggers. My parents were married early and soon divorced. I came under the care of my aunt and uncle. During the Great Depression, they were unable to provide for me and placed me as a young child in a Baptist orphanage. I was born during my father O. L. Jagger's profligate years. From the time I was a small child, I have recollections of my dad, O. L. Jaggers, as an amazing pianist and singer. He played guitar and several other instruments. As a young man, he traveled all over the United States preaching, singing, and playing instruments as well as his famous collection of antique glass goblets, which he also played as instruments. In his book, *How God Gave this Ministry to Me*, O. L. tells how his musical talents took him out of the

---

1. "God has given us some eight hundred churches in fellowship of the body of Christ, in the gospel of the Kingdom of our Lord Jesus Christ. We are in more than eighty nations. We are not a denomination, but rather a fellowship of men, women, boys and girls, preaching the gospel in the leading of The Lord." Abernathy, interview, 29 Dec. 2014.

church into the world of secular music. He formed a swing band, which led him to immense popularity at the age of eighteen. For five years, he reports, he turned to the beggarly elements of sin; he started to drink and eventually became discouraged with success. O. L. visited his parents, who had never stopped praying for him, and gave his life back to Jesus, knowing that he was called to preach and sing the gospel.

In 1942, when I was five, O. L. Jaggers came and took me out of the orphanage in Oklahoma City for a special weekend that changed my life. I heard him preach Scripture and heard each word of Acts 2:17 as if it were written directly to me: "And it shall come to pass in the last days, says God, that I will pour out of my Spirit on all flesh; your sons and your daughters shall prophesy, your young men shall see visions" (NKJV). I told my sister who was in the orphanage with me that this prophecy was about me. (This sister is the daughter of my adopted parents, not my biological sister, Joan Jaggers Morton.) On that day, I was filled with the Holy Spirit. At the age of eight, I was baptized in water and had a vision of Jesus calling me to ministry. I could not understand why everyone in the Baptist Home for Children could not understand this.

At the age of nine, I was adopted by my uncle and aunt, Ause and Omah Abernathy. This is why I use the name Larry Abernathy rather than Larry Jaggers. On August 23, 1946, my ninth birthday, I arrived at their little farm in Bernie, Missouri, where God's plan would begin. Our neighbors who owned a store next to our farm pitched a tent that held three hundred people. They asked me to pump the organ at the revival. A man wearing a black suit came to me and whispered in my ear that he wanted me to give my testimony and sing. I did so for two weeks, as the evangelist never came. More than a hundred people came to Jesus in the first week. Each night at closing, I prayed for the sick. Many adults were healed and received the Holy Ghost. On the first night, I prayed for a thirteen-year-old girl who was blind from birth. She received her sight. I was so jubilant that I stood to my feet and sang, "Hold the fort, for I am coming, Jesus signals still. Wave the answer back to heaven; by thy grace we will."[2]

A couple of weeks after this revival, in September 1946, I reconnected with my sister, Joan Jaggers (O. L. Jaggers's daughter by his first

---

2. "Hold the Fort" was inspired by a Georgia Civil War battle and written by P. B. Bliss in 1870. For complete lyrics, see www.hymnary.org/text/ho_my_comrades_see_the_signal_waving_in.

wife). Joan was four years older than I and had been taken to St. Elmo, Illinois to live with our grandparents. Joan and I have different mothers, being children of O. L. Jaggers by his two early marriages. In this visit, in an Assemblies of God Church, Joan played my theme song: *Hold the Fort*. My grandfather D. B. Jaggers and twenty other men began this Assemblies of God church in the Ozarks of Arkansas. D. B. built and pastored twenty-two Assemblies of God churches in three states. I helped D. B. build his last two churches, laying brick by day and singing and preaching at night.

In 1953, D. B. Jaggers and his wife moved to Los Angeles where his son (my father), O. L. Jaggers, founded the historic World Church, a church of four thousand members. I served in ministry for twenty-four years at my father's world-renowned church while my father traveled all over the world preaching revivals. I recall firsthand relationships with my father's peers, the highest ranking evangelists of the era, including the controversial William Branham, A. A. Allen, and Oral Roberts. I was present at the Clifton Cafeteria with Demos Shakarian breaking ground for the organization of the Full Gospel Businessmen's Fellowship. I recall many healings, release from bondage to demons, and even corpses returning to life. (Please watch for my autobiographical account of this era of church history.) I am among the last living of a generation that knows firsthand this era of great evangelists. Much is written of these great saints that is not accurate. For posterity and true church history, as much as possible, what we write should be accurate and honest—and much of it is not. When you are making church history, whatever is written about you should be honest; it will be on my part.

In the mid-1970s, the Lord put it on my heart to resign from the World Church, emphasize historic orthodoxy, and found the Cathedral of Love of the Seven Golden Candlesticks Church. By the mid-1980s, the church in Glendale, California, had hundreds of members. The call of God also brought me to minister in the desert in La Quinta, California. Currently, members of the Cathedral of Love of the Seven Golden Candlesticks Church's high-tech media congregation include former members of O. L. Jaggers's World Church. Cathedral of Love of the Seven Golden Candlesticks Church's live-stream video Sunday services in the past two years have reached more than 1.5 million globally via tcolm.org.

The three-hour-long Sunday service on tcolm.org offers the inspiring worship of my sister, Joan Jaggers Morton, who has faithfully accompanied my singing for more than sixty years. I often sing my own hymns (e.g., *You Are My Anchor*), the hymns of Rev. Carol Diane Weinberg (*Covered by the Blood*) and I read the poetry of Rev. Pamela Mechling (*A Bubble and White Cloud*). Rev. Linda Bair Smith teaches in each service. Guest speakers often include Jeanne DeFazio, author and editor; Charlene Eber, producer, director, and founder of World Alliance for Peace and Caretakers of the Future; Joanne Petronella, founder of Christ in You the Hope of Glory Ministry; Martha Reyes, psychologist, author, vocalist, and founder of Hosanna Foundation; and April Shenandoah, founder of Ambassador of Prayer Ministry and author of *Your Tongue Determines Your Destiny*. I have published and distributed over a hundred thousand copies of the book *Faith*, and I have authored a dozen books in a series called *The Light Bearer*. With my friend Eileen Jones in Tulsa, Oklahoma, I intend to recover O. L. Jaggers's books from collectors for the sake of posterity.

My website includes a popular blog, because I understand how the Holy Spirit is using social media to fulfill scriptural prophecy. Thumbs-up and thumbs-down symbols communicate to today's audience how the gospel is being revealed to all humankind before the return of the victorious Jesus: with a simple double click, right click, "The message has gone throughout the earth, and the words to all the world" (Rom 10:18 NLT).

In the midst of the vision of the golden candlesticks, John saw the glorified Jesus, whose countenance shone like the sun (Rev 1:12–16). The Book of Revelation was transmitted from God the Father to Jesus, to the angel, to his servant John (Rev 1:1, 11). In Revelation 1:11, the angel commands John to write. As Jesus's servant, I also write what I have seen and heard each week as I pray and pore over God's word. I seek the revelation of Jesus that unveils Jesus's multifaceted and full identity as well as his plan for this age. My messages focus on Jesus's victory over evil and the establishment of his kingdom. As I teach what I have studied from the word, I do not focus on the timetable of world events or the details of scriptural imagery, but instead I focus on Scripture's main message—the infinite love, power, and justice of Jesus.

In the Sunday service of Cathedral of Love of the Seven Golden Candlesticks Church, we seek a heavenly anointing that refreshes viewers with the divine fragrance and aroma of John's message in Revelation each Sunday, defining "revelation" from the Greek root word *apokalypsis,* translated "to unveil or uncover." I ask God to lift the curtain for viewers to understand the Holy Bible and the person of Jesus. In the tradition of John's Revelation, I ask God to reveal his truth as I interpret his word from a lifelong relationship with the Holy Spirit. My goal is to share the vision of the glorified Jesus from Revelation 1:12–20 to a postmodern world viewing our service via computers, tablets, and smartphones. I email follow-up with my global congregation, reporting on "the things which are" (Rev 2:1—3:22). Each week, online posts celebrate those who become born again, baptized in the Holy Spirit, miraculously healed, and experiencing God's supernatural provision. I also encourage viewers by prophesying "the things which shall be hereafter" (Rev 4:1–22:5).

I see Revelation 1:11–12's seven golden candlesticks representing the early church into today's postmodern church. Cathedral of Love of the Seven Golden Candlesticks Church continues a spiritual legacy from the early church to this millennial age, demonstrating via the World Wide Web that, through prevailing persecution, Jesus's open arms embrace each member in all-encompassing love and reassuring power. At Cathedral of Love of the Seven Golden Candlesticks Church, we believe through the Holy Spirit, in this era of tribulation, that Jesus abides in the church and calls each member to cling to his deep love and compassion.

RESOURCES

To receive Larry Abernathy's books, *Faith* and *The Light Bearer,* and to view his live-stream service, visit tcolm.org. To invite him to speak at a conference or event, email drlarry@gmail.com.

17

All Things Work Together for Good[1]

Linda Bair Smith

LINDA BAIR SMITH AND BILL HENDERSON

FOR THE PAST TWO years, Linda Bair Smith has taught Scripture each Sunday to Larry Abernathy's Cathedral of Love global live-stream

1. Rom 8:28 NRSV.

congregation, where her message of Jesus's redemptive love has reached 1.5 million people. A member of the baby boom generation, Linda is a mother, grandmother, and administrator who has contributed this chapter to encourage Christian women like herself in media ministry. Here is her story:

I was born in New Haven, Connecticut. My father earned a PhD at Yale University, and his academic career brought our family to the Midwest during the "Jesus Revolution" of the early 1970s. A paradigm shift occurred in my life when my culturally conservative and intellectual parents experienced an outpouring of the Holy Spirit at a Full Gospel Businessmen's Fellowship meeting. The forgiving and saving grace of Jesus's act of substitutionary atonement on the cross at Calvary flooded our lives (1 Cor 1:18, 23–30). We experienced great joy when the Holy Spirit imparted fire from heaven upon us and we understood firsthand the transformation that took place in Jesus's disciples' lives in the upper room on the historic feast of Pentecost. As my relationship with Jesus grew, I experienced being accepted in "the Beloved" (Eph 1:6), knowing that Jesus brought me into his grace, which became real to me: "What no eye has seen, nor ear heard, nor the human heart conceived, what God has prepared for those who love him—these things God has revealed to us through the Spirit; for the Spirit searches everything, even the depths of God." And God has actually given us his Spirit (not the world's spirit) "so that we may understand the gifts bestowed on us by God." How could the world understand? "'For who has known the mind of the Lord so as to instruct him?' But we have the mind of Christ" (1 Cor 2:9–10, 12, 16 NRSV).

I felt called by God to reach the lost for Jesus and became involved with InterVarsity Christian Fellowship while pursuing a B.A. in chemistry. While in a PhD program in nutrition at the University of California at Berkeley, California, I ministered to the radical counterculture via Jack Spark's highly publicized ministry, "The Christian World Liberation Front." I met my husband at Resurrection City, a small San Francisco Bay Area home fellowship. My husband and I attended Shiloh Temple's and Christ for the People's Bible schools in northern California, as well as Rhema Bible Training Center in Broken Arrow, Oklahoma. We started a church in Santa Rosa, California, and produced a television show as an offshoot of our church ministry. I spoke and taught at Women's

Aglow and Women's Agape meetings. In 1989, my family moved to the Coachella Valley, where I was introduced through Carol Diane Weinberg to Larry Abernathy, founder of the Cathedral of Love of the Seven Golden Candlesticks Church. Currently, I teach each Sunday to the Cathedral of Love's global live-stream congregation.

Reflecting on my life—where I am now, where I am going, and where I have come from—I see a picture like a puzzle being put together with "all things working together for good," as Romans 8:28 describes. Every person, every place, everything fits together and leads to the next, accomplishing the plan and purpose of God for my life. As Psalm 37:23 explains, the steps of the righteous are ordered by the Lord.

Growing up in an academic family, I did well in school, but I did not think of myself as intelligent in any sense. I lacked self-confidence. We were a normal, average, middle-class family. I am the oldest of five, four girls and one boy. My father taught at the University of Illinois; my mother was a stay-at-home mom. I remember feeling very happy to have her at home whenever I came back from school or other activities. She taught me to cook and to sew. My brother did not come along until I was eleven. Since I was the eldest child, I became my father's helper. We were members of the Presbyterian Church, and I gladly went to church every Sunday. It made me feel good. My favorite holiday was Easter, but I did not know why. In high school, I became very active with our church's youth group, but I did not realize that I could actually know Jesus—not just know about him.

When I went away to college, I stopped going to church, but was still involved in campus youth groups. The emphasis was mostly on social interaction and social service. During my senior year, my mother started attending a Bible Study. At the same time, our church started an adult Sunday school class on the "Jesus Movement," which both my parents attended. By the time I came home for spring break, my mother was very excited about this newfound interest. I thought it was great for her, but did not think it had anything to do with me. She invited me to attend a Full Gospel Businessmen's Fellowship meeting, where a Presbyterian chaplain was speaking. I went just to keep her company. Little did I know that attending that meeting would change my life forever. I felt Jesus's love and presence, and I experienced the manifestation of the Holy Spirit through messages in tongues with interpretation. This encounter made me realize that God was not only real, but that he was in that room and he was speaking to me. He said, "Trust me and follow me." I said yes in my heart, and went forward for the altar call. Afterward, I went with my mother to the prayer room where we prayed to receive the Holy Ghost. My life was instantly changed. The Bible now made sense, and I wanted to learn more. I now had a sense of purpose for my life. I knew God had something for me to do.

Returning to Carleton College to finish my BA in chemistry, I found that revival was happening. I became involved with InterVarsity Christian Fellowship, a group that was once very small and was now very large. I attended a leadership camp in Colorado and continued to grow in the Lord. Because I had already applied to graduate school and been accepted to the University of California at Berkeley's nutritional science PhD program before my salvation experience, I went there and enrolled, continuing my involvement with InterVarsity. This was during the Jesus Movement, and there was a developing sense of Christian community, the various groups often intermingling. My experience expanded to include Christian World Liberation Front (in which present editor Jeanne DeFazio was also involved), and Resurrection City (a small home fellowship meeting in the San Francisco Bay area where I met my husband). We both knew there was a calling of God on our lives for ministry, so, over the next few years, we attended Bible schools at Shiloh Temple in Oakland and Christ for the People (an offshoot of Christ for the Nations) in the Concord area. During this time, we were also ministered to by television ministries such as Pat Robertson's program on the Christian Broadcasting Network (CBN) and Jim and Tammy Bakker's *Praise the Lord* program (*PTL Club*), which were pioneering media ministries.

Continuously hungry for more of God's word, we eventually applied to Rhema Bible Training Center in Broken Arrow, Oklahoma, where we studied pastoral and teaching ministries. During this time, between our first and second years at Rhema, I was praying about whether I was to continue through the second year. Originally, we had planned to attend only one year. We had graduated in May of 1980 in the last class that could graduate after only one year. My husband had decided to attend the second year program, and, to fill in the summer, he was attending Norval Hayes summer school in Tennessee. Our third son had been born in February, and we had decided that I would take care of the boys and he would go to school. But I had a hunger and desire in my heart to follow the Lord's will. As I prayed, the Holy Spirit led me to 1 Corinthians 1 and 2. He spoke to me about my calling and ministry. I knew that, even though I had never had self-confidence, God could use me. God had a plan for my life. I knew he was preparing a ministry for me—a ministry of reconciliation as an ambassador for Christ.

> For the love of Christ urges us on, because we are convinced that one has died for all; therefore all have died. And he died for all, so that those who live might live no longer for themselves, but for him who died and was raised for them. From now on, therefore, we regard no one from a human point of view; even though we once knew Christ from a human point of view, we know him no longer in that way. So if anyone is in Christ, there is a new creation: everything old has passed away; see, everything has become new! All this is from God, who reconciled us to himself through Christ, and has given us the ministry of reconciliation; that is, in Christ God was reconciling the world to himself, not counting their trespasses against them, and entrusting the message of reconciliation to us. So we are ambassadors for Christ, since God is making his appeal through us; we entreat you on behalf of Christ, be reconciled to God. For our sake he made him to be sin who knew no sin, so that in him we might become the righteousness of God. (2 Cor 5:14-21 NRSV)

Upon graduation, my husband and I went to Georgia to pastor a church for one year. From there, we went to Santa Rosa, California, and started a church. It was here that one of the businessmen in the church thought we should have a television program, which he paid for. This was my first direct experience with media ministry. The programs were recorded in a small studio and broadcast on a local TV station. We interviewed each other, interviewed guests, and took turns teaching the word. During this time, besides ministering at church, I also spoke at women's fellowship meetings, such as Women's Aglow and Women's Agape. Our church purchased a satellite dish, and we held revival meetings (on the receiving end of media ministry). We prayed for the sick and saw many miracles, including deaf ears healed and cancerous growths eradicated.

Eventually, we turned the church over to another pastor and went into evangelistic and teaching ministry. By 1989, we relocated from northern California to the Palm Springs/Coachella Valley area of southern California. In 1991, we met a woman at a restaurant who was from

Palm Springs. She asked us to come do a Bible study in her home. At this Bible study, we met another woman, who subsequently introduced us to Carol Weinberg, gospel song writer, who attended the Cathedral of Love of the Seven Golden Candlesticks Church. Even though I did not attend that church, she stayed in touch with me, and we developed a friendship over the next few years.

Carol told us she was born again in 1977, baptized in the Holy Ghost in 1978, and met Larry Abernathy in 1983 at Toluca Lake Trinity Church, where he was teaching a class on the gifts of the Spirit. She had a great desire to sing and had already written several songs. So, in spite of the fact of being told she could never learn to sing, she joined the choir and learned to sing. When the Cathedral of Love moved from Glendale to Palm Springs, so did Carol. She continues to minister today, playing the piano and singing her songs of praise (over 350), continually developing her singing talent. She calls her ministry Covered by the Blood Ministries, and it is part of the Cathedral of Love's ministry.

Because Carol was so faithful to stay in touch with me at a critical time in my life, I reached out to her. By 1995, I found myself a single mother with five sons and no income. These were challenging years. I was evicted from three houses in one year. I had no idea how I was going to survive, but I was confident that God was able to make a way. I called Carol, and she invited me to the Cathedral of Love Church, where I met Larry Abernathy and was greatly ministered to through the word. The Lord opened the door for a part-time job at a travel agency, which led to a full-time job at a different travel agency. From the travel agency, I began working as housekeeper and caregiver in several homes. I found that, as I was faithful in seemingly little things, God opened the door to me more and more, until I was working seven days a week, with no time for church and little time now for my sons. Providentially, my sons continued going to church without me. Their pastor gave me some advice that helped turn me from trying to take care of everything by myself. He said, "Don't try to be both mother and father to your sons. Just be the best mother you can, and God will take care of the rest." It was not long until the boys told me that I needed to have Sundays off so I could go to church with them. I remembered that the Cathedral of Love services were recorded, so I called my good friend Carol and asked her to get me the tapes of the services. I received one set of tapes and, within one week, I was let go from my weekend caregiver job. (The family had decided to let all four caregivers go.) The boys' prayers were answered.

I began attending Cathedral of Love regularly. At first, I needed to receive and was blessed with a refreshing of my spirit from the presence of the Lord (Acts 3:19). I began to gain confidence in who I am in the Lord. I had previously seen myself as an extension of my husband's ministry. It was hard to see myself separate from him, but I grew to realize that I am called and chosen and ordained myself. Gradually, I began to share, only a little at first. I appreciated (and still do) the fact that Pastor Larry is accepting of anyone to minister what God puts in his or her heart. One Sunday, he announced that, in two weeks, everyone was going to read a poem that they had written. At first I started to panic. I did not think I could write, but then I prayed, and the Lord gave me the poem, which I entitled *A Poem from the Heart for the Heart*.[2]

Another remarkable woman who has inspired me is Pam Mechling. In spite of being diagnosed with cerebral palsy as an infant, Pam has never viewed herself as disabled, but has gone forward with determination to accomplish the desires of her heart. She had been born again and filled with the Spirit in the early 1980s, and began spending time in prayer with the Lord, developing a powerful intercessory prayer ministry. As a result, the Lord started speaking poems into her heart, words of encouragement and exhortation, which she has compiled into a book called *Expressions of Love*. Those who watch our church service will notice that the Lord often impresses her to share one or more of her poems that express a message that goes with the theme of the service.

When the opportunity first opened to be able to broadcast a regular Sunday service over the Internet on live-stream, I knew this was part

---

2. *A Poem from the Heart for the Heart* by Linda Smith, 2000: The heart is a marvelous thing, / for from it you worship and sing. / Out of the heart flow the issues of life, / so don't let in fear, doubt, or strife. / Cast your cares on the Lord, for He is here, / And a heart of peace will calm all fear. / A carefree heart is a heart that is free, / a believing heart that bears fruit like a tree. / We look on the outside; God looks in. / He is looking for hearts that are totally His. / He is looking for those to greatly reward. / So seek first His Kingdom and pick up your sword. / Your sword is His Word, placed in your heart, / When spoken with power, comes out like a dart. / That Word will accomplish things great and mighty. / So open your heart and shine forth His glory. / Keep your eyes on the Lord, undistracted, on Him, / And hear with your heart what will come from within. / For out of the heart comes abundance and praise; / His glory, His power, His honor to raise. / Yes, truly the heart is a marvelous thing, / for from it you worship and sing.

of God's plan to reach the world. Preaching in a church or at a meeting reaches the people in front of you. Ministering on television can reach those who are able to get the channel you are on. But ministering using the Internet reaches an unlimited number of people throughout the world. And this is not just a prerecorded program, although it is recorded and can be viewed at any time. It is a live church service. The viewers not only hear sound teaching, they also can experience the anointing and moving of the Holy Spirit as they receive wisdom and revelation from the Father. I am honored to be part of the ministry of the Cathedral of Love, teaching what the Lord gives during the last hour of our service. As Jesus said in Matthew 24:14, "This gospel of the kingdom will be preached in the whole world as a testimony to all nations, and then the end will come" (NIV). It is exciting to know that the Lord is reaching people all over the world. It is exciting to be part of what God is doing. As Larry Abernathy likes to say, "The Lord has me where he wants me, when he wants me."[3] And the Lord wants every believer to know for himself, receive for himself, and then go spread the gospel too.

As a word of encouragement, Carol did not let being told she could not sing stop her from writing songs and singing. Pam did not let a negative diagnosis get her down. She saw herself as an overcomer and kept walking through. And here I am with seemingly no time, five sons, ten grandchildren, and working full-time as office manager of a small construction company. I have a bachelor's degree in chemistry, a graduate degree in nutritional sciences, and am a graduate of a Bible college. I am an ordained minister and associate pastor of the Cathedral of Love, ministering to the world through a live-stream Internet program. I was able to endure all obstacles and hardships because God empowered me to do so. God made a way where there seemed to be no way as I adapt and declare Paul's words from Philippians 4:13 for you: You can do all things through Christ who strengthens you.

I am testifying to the love of God, which brought me out of underconfidence and abandonment. I do not harbor regret or unforgiveness. My former husband and I are friends for the sake of our children and grandchildren. This is by the grace of God. When I teach each Sunday, I thank God for what he carries me through to serve him. My gratitude for the opportunity to show others the way to salvation through live-

---

3. Abernathy, *Faith*, 28.

stream services is great. I conclude with these words of encouragement from Larry Abernathy's book *Revelation Knowledge*: "Don't let what you don't know keep you from doing what you do know. God does not require of you to know everything. Sometimes the greatest things he does in the greater works are because you do not ask about the things you don't know, but you're willing to love him and stand in faith. When you don't understand, just believe!"[4]

RESOURCES

To view Linda Bair Smith's teachings on the Cathedral of Love livestream, visit tcolm.org. If you would like to have Linda speak at a conference or an event, contact her through the tcolm.org website.

---

4. Abernathy, *Revelation Knowledge*, 22.

18

Following Our Rebel Lord

William David Spencer

Left to Right, The Spheres c. 1971: Rick Burton,
Bob Boenig, Aída Besançon, Bill Spencer
(Bruce McDaniel is taking the picture)

WILLIAM DAVID SPENCER is Distinguished Adjunct Professor of Theology and the Arts at Gordon-Conwell Theological Seminary Boston's Center for Urban Ministerial Education (CUME). He is the author or co-editor of fourteen books, two of which are universally accepted by critics as the definitive works in their fields: *Mysterium and Mystery: The Clerical Crime Novel* and *Chanting Down Babylon: The Rastafari Reader*. He has won twenty one awards for books and articles he has written; for a song he co-wrote; and for his work as editor of *Priscilla Papers*, the academic voice of Christians for Biblical Equality, which he edited for ten years, and *Africanus Journal*, which he founded together with his wife, Aída Besançon Spencer, professor of New Testament at Gordon-Conwell's Hamilton, Massachusetts, campus. Bill is listed in *Contemporary Authors: the New Revision Series*, *Who's Who in Religion*, and many similar publications. He earned his bachelor's degree in English education from Rutgers, New Brunswick, Master of Divinity and Master of Theology degrees from Princeton Theological Seminary, and the Doctor of Theology degree (specializing in the interrelationship of theology and literature) from Boston University School of Theology. But, beyond his academic credentials, Bill has been an active city minister since 1966 and an ordained Presbyterian minister since 1973, when he and Aída were ordained together in one great gala two-and-a-half-hour service that featured choirs and performers singing a number of songs he wrote in Spanish and English, including one co-authored with Aída. Interested in everything and dedicated to taking the message of redemption in Jesus Christ's love to everyone, Bill has ministered as a volunteer in four prisons in New Jersey and Massachusetts; done street ministry in Plainfield, New Jersey; helped organize block meetings to bring black and white neighbors together in Philadelphia; co-founded and taught in an accredited college level education program in storefront churches in Newark and Jersey City, NJ, and on Fulton Street in Bedford-Stuyvesant in New York City; co-organized and helped run two evangelistic coffeehouse ministries in Newark and Dunellen, NJ; served as teaching coordinator for an adult literacy program under the Board of Education of Jefferson County, Kentucky, setting up and supervising eight literacy and high-school equivalency training centers in Louisville and neighboring cities; co-led a Jesus band under the auspices of opera star Jerome Hines in Newark and his own band, the Spheres, for six years before and during the Jesus Movement; ministered as a protestant college chaplain to four colleges, and lived in community with seminarians, helping mentor them in city ministry in Newark. Since 1974, he has taught seminary classes in New York; Kingston, Jamaica; and now Massachusetts. His first novel, *Name in the Papers,* was given an award by the Southern California Motion Picture Council, and current creative projects, including a novel, *Cave of Little Faces*, written together with Aída , keep pushing him forward in the arts. Here is Bill's story:

I am the only surviving child of working parents brought to faith in Jesus in a separatist fundamentalist church in 1940s–1950s New Jersey. That experience from the cradle roll on through my formative years gave me several important gifts for which I am truly grateful, though these, I realized later, as with all good things in this fallen world, were tainted. It taught me to rely on the Bible, and I learned that lesson well, even if some of the teaching I received had bizarre interpretations—like the Sermon on the Mount not being applicable to today, but only to the time when Jesus rules in the Millennium. Even as a child, I felt this was impossible, because Jesus in his own example practiced neighborly kindness of this type. (I guess I was, unknowingly, a budding theology professor from the git-go, as they say, or more likely a pain in the neck for my Sunday school teachers). A second great gift my upbringing gave me was a sense of the power of community (after all, it was "us against them," "them" being nearly everybody else, churched or unchurched). That particular definition of community, however, I recall from my earliest years, excluded devout Christians of people groups who showed up at church but were not Anglo-American—a deacon quietly inviting such visitors of more melanin to consider attending "their" church downtown and thereby sending us children the message that, though we might be friends with others at school, there was no bringing those friends to church. Even as a child, I knew in my heart this was very wrong. And my birth church also assumed women were not to lead (a blatant manifest contradiction, since women ruled this church through their pliant husbands, and any pastor who offended any of these key women on Sunday was out on his ear, as we used to put it in those days, on Monday.)

I never imagined myself being called to teach seminary (over forty years now, since my wife and I were invited to help train seminarians, while living in community with them in Newark, New Jersey, when we ourselves were still in our twenties) or to experience the adventures I have had in nearly fifty years of urban ministry before and since that seminal entry into teaching. But I always knew I loved the process of creating things through words, and I loved books, so I started early on using that gift to forge a way through the trauma of childhood.

Two years after my sister drowned in a still-unexplained accident on a playground trip to a pool in the mountains, when I was six, my dad was hurt in a devastating work accident from which he valiantly struggled for years to recover. Reeling from two major blows in such a short span of time, my devastated family of three now pulled back into itself. My parents allowed me to do very little in school: no class trips or school events, certainly no dances, along with no movies, no sleepovers, no dating, no much of anything. All I was permitted to attend was school sports events as I entered what was then junior high and, afterward, high school, and these events were a blessing. I chose participating in wrestling, which matched my small size and my solitary temperament. It was all up to me. And I was allowed to go to church and Boys Brigade.

No rock 'n' roll was allowed in our house. Instead, I was reared on classic opera and thereby introduced to strong melodies with incomprehensible lyrics. This was a great formative gift, and I still love the old RCA Victor Red Seals' music of Amelita Galli-Curci, which I collected as a child and still have today. Eventually, I was also allowed to listen to folk and country music (mainly, though not exclusively, on older 78 RPM records) and to read incessantly with no limits, which was probably not such a good idea, since I read widely, and it gave me a lot of ideas. All in all, it was a very scary time for a small, single, surviving child. The specters of death and injury seemed to hover over us. But my family was strong and tightly knitted together.

I was much alone as my parents struggled to recover financially. My elderly grandparents lived on the floor above us and were always available, but, mainly, I took my solace in books and poetry and began writing early on. I wrote the first story I can remember in second grade about a town that hated magic, and the first song whose theme I can recall about a year or two before that time. I had always been fascinated by poetry and, particularly, by the tight structures of lyrics and how music enhanced the power of words by providing a setting and, thereby, increasing their effectiveness. I also deeply appreciated the discipline involved in sharing what one wanted to share within the discipline of a musical line. I remember serenading my grandmother, in her window two stories above me, as I was playing with my little Western action figures in the dirt. As I finished one particularly long improvised piece about birds of a feather flocking together, a phrase I had just learned, out of her window came sailing a nickel—a heady amount in 1952! I was astonished. This could pay off? I think it was the last time I ever earned anything decent from songwriting—but I have still written countless songs over the years. I can see now, the story I wrote was really about repression, the song about community. I was in an ideal situation to experience the first and create the second.

Imprisoned in a separatist church and a withdrawn family, I was ready to escape when I began commuting to Rutgers, at the time the local all-men's college. I had started a month late due to developing a duodenal ulcer in the summer between high school and college, mainly as fallout from all the weight I cut in wrestling (there were no limits then), so first semester was a case of hunker down like a hermit and study to survive. But, even without stalling at the starting line, commuting is not the ideal way to cruise in and meet anybody—not to mention any girls! At my mother's persistent insistence, I tried out InterVarsity Christian Fellowship (IVCF), though I had by now become an intellectual agnostic, the gap between my church and real life being so painfully large that I saw them separating completely. IVCF called me back to faith. I met Episcopalians and Lutherans who were actually Christians! Can such animals exist? My birth church had warned me only independents, some Baptists, and a few Presbyterians had any chance to negotiate the narrow tightrope over hell to heaven. But, in IVCF Rutgers, faith in Jesus came into sync with experience. In a few short weeks, I gave my life to Jesus once more, and this time for good—and, suddenly, I wanted to tell all the world about it.

My vehicle for sharing the gospel, after I finally became serious about serving Jesus in 1966, was this gift of creativity to me from God. I formed a folk band with college friends (something my fundamentalist church upbringing would allow), and we played for one of my dad's mineral show evangelistic presentations and at IVCF and college events and on college radio and at a few local churches and other colleges. At that point, I could not play anything myself, but my parents bought me an old $25 Wabash guitar on a family trip through Kalamazoo, Michigan, and a Christian friend at school who had become the lead singer of our group taught me a few chords.

I now had a car with which to commute, and in it was a radio, so I came up to date on music. There was no Christian rock vehicle for recording that we knew of at the time, Larry Norman's *Upon this Rock* not appearing for three more years. I had worked during my last year in high school in a Christian bookstore, and I knew all the records then available in the store's ample selection. Ralph Carmichael was doing the most exciting music of which I was aware with his "Theme for the Restless Ones." My church decided he was a "liberal," the worst category possible into which anyone could be banished, and many decided that went double for Billy Graham, with whom Ralph worked, since Billy allowed "liberals" up on his stage. That presaged a bad future for me. Three years later, I made two fatal "mistakes." First, I began to write more challenging songs, including one called *Our Rebel Lord*. I wrote it on a bass ukulele I had picked up at a thrift shop, and then transferred it to an electric bass we'd bought at a discount music store. Its words began, "Christ was beaten all the way to the cross, then killed by religious and political bosses, who feared his every word against their lies, treachery, hypocrisy, and blasphemy; he died—our Rebel Lord." That song, I did not realize, was my ticking bomb.

Our one brush with a wider venue was winning a spot as one of ten finalists in "Cousin" Bruce Morrow's WABC Big Break Contest, playing at the New York Hilton, before five thousand literally screaming fans, the draw being Steppenwolf, the band renowned for "Born to Be Wild," "Magic Carpet Ride," and "Rock Me, Baby." It was a terrifying experience. Bruce Morrow was a very gracious person. We went to the WABC studio in New York City, where he warmly welcomed us, put us all at our ease, and recorded us each separately, having the studio mix the tape. The song we did I wrote with Bob Boenig, a dear Christian brother and wonderfully creative friend, who has gone on to distinguish himself as a medievalist, a professor of English, a well-published poet, author, and, most recently, producer of a masterpiece on C. S. Lewis, *C. S. Lewis and the Middle Ages*, which completely opened my eyes and changed my understanding of Lewis's great contribution. Bob is a genius. In his youth, he was also a superb songwriter himself and wrote beautiful songs I still play today. Anyway, when we stepped offstage after our sound check, Bruce Morrow rushed up to me and warned me that our laidback conversational performing style was what was happening on college campuses, but the Big Break was still about over-the-top flamboyance, and we needed to liven up our performance of the song. This, as all of us were currently products of fundamentalist churches, was not in our vocabulary. We were clueless as to how to respond.

That night, we stole onto the stage before a wall of speakers into which I had no idea where to plug the bass I was playing, and the audience respectfully quieted down. Our excellent lead singer, Dave Rowe, who went on to become a university chaplain, told them we were going to give their ears a rest, which was just the right thing to say. Dave Howe, another fabulous composer of unforgettable melodies and today a long term pastor in Kentucky, with Bob, both marvelous guitarists, went into the lilting introduction to the song, and we put it across. Aída , who was then my girlfriend, but not yet performing with us as our eventual superb percussionist, reported to us afterward that people around her said it was a "good song."

For me, the introspective child, stepping reluctantly into the early no-man's-land of adulthood, it was one of the most upsetting events of my young life, scarier than any wrestling match I had ever done, including my epic battle beating the local district champ by one point, which had been number-one scariest event up to this point. Me, who had never even attended a school dance, quaking in front of five thousand restless fans, all of whom with one mind wanted "Cousin Brucie" to get the rest of us offstage as soon as possible and display the band they had come to support and get that done promptly, so, instantly afterward, they could all see Steppenwolf, the headliner. I realized performing was probably not my forte. My father, who never stinted on criticism, was furious. He snapped at me that we looked like four guys looking for the bathroom who happened to stumble out onto the stage. My dad was bald and, when he was angry, which was often, his whole head would go red and glow as he glowered at me. I thought about that comment for years. I'm sure he was right. But, finally, thinking about it as an adult, I realized, that, since my sister had died on a school-related summer event, and I had become an only kid who had been forbidden to attend virtually anything in all those formative years right through the end of high school, were the odds really in favor of me suddenly transmogrifying into John Kay, polished lead singer of Steppenwolf, writhing about on the stage like a boa constrictor, belting out "Born to Be Wild" at such a level of cacophony that he was deep into the second verse before I recognized the song? I was trained to be the inverse. And that was the end of our brush with big performance, such as it was. But the fallout was not over.

My old Brigade leader, a saintly man (whom we later learned provided the scholarship for Aída to attend the IVCF retreat that helped her move along significantly in her faith), invited my band to play at my birth church for the youth group and the evening service. I had misgivings. It felt like a bad idea, and I tried to worm out of it. But, he insisted that everyone had read about our exploit in a feature in the local newspaper and wanted to hear us. So, we did it just because he was the one who asked.

For the church's evening service, I selected two of our tamest and prettiest pieces, one an altar called I had written and the other a beautiful four-part harmony piece whose words I wrote to a lovely melody created by Dave Howe. Each of these featured a single acoustic guitar. However, this was now 1969, and the Jesus Movement was just beginning to kick off in our area, so, for the youth group down in the fellowship hall, we decided to play our more lively stuff.

Aída, who was in the audience, heard my bass resounding off the concrete walls as we thundered out *Our Rebel Lord* and, while loving the sound herself, wondered if it might cause trouble. It did. Deacons, who were hiding behind a curtain in the back, checking us out, kicked us out at the end of that presentation. They replaced us in the service with a musical saw. I still have vivid memories of standing out in the church parking lot, as a patina of snow softly graced the area, arguing that we had non-Christian guests coming and the deacons should at least listen to what we had intended to play for the service to see if it was appropriate or not. But they had heard enough. In fact, they did not even show themselves to kick us out personally. They dumped the job on my former Brigade commander and, while he commiserated with us with real sincerity, he could do nothing but deliver the orders. All we could do was pack up and slip away, or line up, march in, and listen to the saw. We slipped away.

My dad was an enigma. He could be so wonderfully calm and kind in a crisis, a great guy to have around, so gentle at such times that my maternal grandmother allowed only him to carry her from place to place when she was frail and dying. However, normal day-to-day living with him was tough. The word "dialogue" he had not allowed into his verbal skill set. One asked a question; he gave the answer: the conversation was done. He was what was called the strong silent type. He was strong; everyone else was silent. But, in a real crisis, Dad could change completely and become attentive and supportive. When I told him what had happened, he became furious, of course, but in a completely opposite direction than before—this time, he aimed his anger at the church. As I knew he would, he took my part. He was so outraged that he pulled his membership out of the church and never went back.

My second fatal "error" was enrolling in Conwell School of Theology, which, that summer of 1969, became a progenitor of Gordon-Conwell Theological Seminary. Billy Graham had brought Conwell together with Gordon Divinity School and agreed to sign on as the first chairman of the united board. Gordon-Conwell in Philadelphia was a delightful and exciting place to study. I loved it. At the end of that school year, however, the Philadelphia campus was gone. All the students were invited to move up to the new united campus in Massachusetts, but we wanted to stay with our new home church, the Presbyterian church in neighboring Dunellen, and all the ministries we now had going there, and so Elizabeth (NJ) Presbytery, under whose care our pastor, "Rev. Al" Ruscito, had placed Bob, Aída, and me, told us, "You picked your seminary and it closed on you. Now try ours." So we transferred to nearby Princeton Theological Seminary, where I had the blessing of having the late, great Bruce Metzger as my advisor. Thirteen years later, in 1982, after having done several ministries and then completing her PhD in New Testament at Southern Baptist Theological Seminary in Louisville, Aída was invited back to Gordon-Conwell to teach, and has now taught for thirty-three years in this wonderful school. The next year, I was invited to teach adjunctively, and I have done that now for thirty-two years, splitting each one in two: half the year writing and half the year teaching. So, we ended up anyway with Gordon-Conwell in Massachusetts, later not sooner.

Gordon-Conwell has an inerrancy pledge, meaning all of us on faculty and administration affirm the Bible is free of error in its original autographs and completely historically accurate, a position both Aída and I have held onto firmly since the days of our conversion. But my decision to attend this newly uniting seminary had thrown up the final wall between me and my birth church and made any real reconciliation impossible, since Conwell and Gordon were brought together by Billy Graham, whom I admired thoroughly, but some leaders in my birth church still ruled out. When my old Sunday School superintendent met me at the local Christian bookstore, as I clutched a copy of *The Sons of Thunder* record album that Zondervan had bravely released (and which I wish I still had, but it's lost), he looked at me over the great gap of ignorance and misunderstanding and asked sadly, "Billy, are you still a Christian?" "What would I be doing here, if I wasn't?" I exclaimed—the only thing I could think of to say.

Since then, I have realized that hyper-conservative fundamentalism such as that of the church in which I was reared is driven by fear (even if these days it can sometimes simulate a contemporary emerging church glaze). It fears women not knowing what it sees as "their place" and taking power over men, preferring to keep women the contemporary equivalent of barefoot and pregnant, so as to say, while still expecting them to do much of the volunteer work that every church demands, but without ordained credit. It fears minorities or even refugees sweeping across nations' borders and taking jobs away from all of us immigrants already here and holding on to our jobs with a death grip, climbing the ladder to safety and prosperity ourselves and then kicking in the head those beneath us trying to follow us up. It fears health care for everybody for which I (and all the undefined I's like me) will have to pay, even while many of the individuals who comprise these churches practice often generous if sporadic personal charity. In short, fundamentalism fears a lot of stuff.

What I have come to realize over the years, however, is that there actually *is* a lot of legitimate stuff to fear. According to the tapes released on the net at this time of writing, the abortion industry is just as scary, cruel, and mercenary as every one of us feared. Terrorists have proven to be just as terrifying and lethal as any apocalyptic preacher ever swore they would be. Pluralism weakens the gospel and eviscerates the faith once delivered to the saints just as truly as the Bible warned it would (Col 2:8). The loss of trust in biblical authority does indeed cause believers to cease to preach with the certainty of Jesus and begin to treat the Bible text with the equivocation of those who parade themselves as experts, but whose approach to the Scriptures Jesus deplored (see Mark 1:22). Loss of faith in Jesus's name as the only one by which we are reconciled with God (Acts 4:12) does indeed ultimately still evangelism and the spreading of God's reign by convincing us that everybody is already saved and worshiping the same God in many different (even if competing) faces, which is both biblically false and an insult to the integrity of other religions. Things like these *are* worth guarding against. While every fundamentalist concern may not be correctly aimed or even right, every one may not necessarily be wrong either. And the same is true for neo-evangelical and liberal Christian concerns. They are not all necessarily smoking with brimstone from the devil itself. We Christians of every stripe may simply be naïve as to what really goes on behind the social and political banner-waving of lobbies trying to enlist and manipulate the religious vote. We all need to keep our eyes open and not just vote straight down some party line, but be picking and choosing from all the social and political agendas the kinds of initiatives we think will actually serve the Lord's expressed interests in the Bible and move God's rule forward, giving life, and that more abundantly, to those who share this planet with us.

At the same time, "God did not give us a spirit of fear, but of power and love and sound judgment" (2 Tim 1:7). The gospel of Jesus Christ blesses us with a spirit that promotes reliance on the One who loves us and has created us for a loving relationship with our Creator and then intends us to extend that caring love to others. The problem with living in fear is that it barricades the door of the heart against love, choosing instead to be driven by prejudices or emotions rather than being guided by Jesus's counsel to be "wise" and "pure" (Matt 10:16) in our treatment of one another.

In an image, if hyper-conservatism is caricatured as the white blood cell of the body of Christ, overprotecting by killing everything in its path like the dysfunction of leukemia, then hyper–theological liberalism is like an overzealous red blood cell infected with AIDS, attempting to nourish the body, but unable to protect it and falling victim to every heterodox or cultic disease that attacks it. There is a moderation to which the Bible calls us, in which we learn to speak God's biblical truth in a spirit of love (Eph 4:25). That is what we all should be praying to adopt: a discerning attitude that lifts Jesus higher, even as it draws others to his love through our reflecting love.

In my case, my topic of contention was artistic, and the Presbyterian Church in the next town, graciously, did not think I had fallen from grace by attending a secular college and playing what was no longer exclusively folk music (though I have never stopped considering myself an urban folk singer) and welcomed me and the band in with open arms. I was now by present invitation—and prior de-invitation—a Presbyterian.

After that, our band suffered a serious case of graduation. Soon afterward, Jackson Browne, James Taylor, the Grateful Dead, and all the other non-flamboyant, relaxed performance artists came to prominence and took over the popular music scene, and our style was now in vogue.

Bob and I on guitars re-formed the group, and Aída joined us on percussion, helping us expand our sound with Caribbean rhythms. We were also joined by a decorated war hero medic, returning Vietnam veteran Bruce McDaniel on bass, who has gone on to a long-term career writing legal journals and editing a veterans' newsletter, and drummer Rich Burton, then a high school student, far mature beyond his years, an excellent musician and wonderful to work with, but the only long-term member with whom I have sadly lost contact at this writing.

The Jesus Movement had set in fully by now, and we went on for three more years playing Jesus festivals, coffeehouses (including one we now ran ourselves in our new home church), as well as college fellowships, youth events, and churches all around the New York, New Jersey, Connecticut, Pennsylvania area. And these activities extended throughout our seminary training.

By 1972, we were pretty polished with our drummer, electric guitars, and all our own songs, but most of us were marrying and graduating from seminary, and the band was wrapping up. A health issue had also activated and began curtailing my activist approach to ministry. After several hospitalizations for it, I was advised to change my lifestyle or else. I realized I was again primarily a writer.

All during that time, we were also doing urban ministry. In 1974, Aída and I were invited by New York Theological Seminary to help train seminarians in urban ministry by an evangelist with whom I had worked in Newark, and, after this program ran its course, sensing this was God's calling, we went on to earn doctorates, and continue teaching today. We have also been helping volunteer-pastor a storefront church, Pilgrim Church of Beverly, Massachusetts, that we planted with friends in 1986, along with pursuing all of our writing and editing projects.

As for my music, despite the wise, early-on advice of Roger Palms, then an excellent and caring local pastor in a town next to Rutgers and, eventually, the editor of Billy Graham's *Decision Magazine*, that I should simply write the songs and distribute them to as many performers as possible, and a very cordial, post-Big Break telephone invitation to meet with the manager of the band Blades of Grass, which was then riding on an East Coast hit version of "Happy" on Jubilee records, an opportunity which Aída urged me to do ("Don't you at least want to talk with him?" she implored), but which I ignored, I remained still locked into my fundamentalist mindset, distanced from everybody. I hoarded all my songs in the protective way in which I had been trained, turning down requests to use them by other bands (even ones led by former members of my own band!), fully convinced God had some special plan for me to present them all as a package. Honestly, what sort of attitude was that for one who valued community and thought he was seeking it? But, as stupid as that sounds now, that's how I thought then. Still, without my cooperation, some of them managed to sneak out of my grasp and travel all over. Years later, when I was asked to sing one of my songs at one of the churches in Newark related to our educational program, a student from California said, "Oh, you know that song too? We sing that in our youth group." It had wandered across the continent from coast to coast. Missionaries told me they had taken another one back to Thailand, and the head chaplain of the Navy used one in worship services on battleships, so a few of the songs managed to serve the Lord, even when I had no vision that they should do so outside my control. As I said earlier, one imbibes some wonderful benefits of a hyper-fundamentalist upbringing, like knowing one's Bible thoroughly, but there are debilitating debits like this siege mentality.

While I still write new songs and sing and play guitar on the praise team at our church, where we work in some of my original songs for worship, today I am primarily a writer, artistically speaking. In addition to a dozen authored or edited nonfiction books listed in the front of this one, my first urban adventure novel, *Name in the Papers,* is in print. My own life is very exciting too. Most of the final editing of this present book I did while traveling in various parts of southern Spain, where my wife had been invited to speak, and, before that, I edited the earlier drafts in the Dominican Republic, where Aída and I were double-checking details as we were completing our sweeping adventure novel, *Cave of Little Faces,* a story set among the Caribbean's First Nations people today. Aída is Dominican by birth, and I have Leni Lenape First

Nation heritage through my father, so we work in those connections as something we have known since birth.

The result of my brushes with performance is a profound respect I have brought with me to my work on this book for these talented performers and producers who stick it out despite adversity, take good advice from others, and have a career in the arts that they can lay before the Lord when the Holy Spirit calls them. Their true accounts rival anything we can imagine. They are living stories created in the remarkable lives of real people who went to Hollywood to live bigger-than-life lives and discovered instead a bigger-than-any-of-our-lives God who calls us to discover Jesus's true life and that more abundantly.

And as for the verses that mean the most to me now, I would have to start with 1 John 5:13, "These things I am writing to you in order that you may know that you have life eternal, to those believing in the name of the Son of God." This was the verse that convinced me to make a lasting commitment to Jesus, because it assumed I would be a frail and doubting creature (I have only to *believe*, which implies doubt), while God assured me that I could *know* I had life eternal from our gracious Creator God: doubt never being on God's side. This promise has comforted me all these years of negotiating a controlled disease. First John 5:13 has also supplemented the life verse I chose in childhood, Philippians 4:13, after my mother brought me to my first commitment (subsequent multiple commitments were common in my birth church). Philippians 4:13 told me I could do "all things" through the strength imparted to me by Christ. I was picturing I would be Superman. I did not realize the verse was talking about enduring suffering. So, the final verse that has been my operating ministry mandate since pastoring in Pilgrim Church of Beverly, Massachusetts, is Proverbs 14:10a, "The heart knows its own sorrow." It tells me that everyone I encounter has a heartache, no matter how together each person looks, so I must be gentle with everyone. I realize that all of us in this fallen world are in some kind of pain. That's why we translate the Holy Spirit's title as the "Comforter" as well as the "Exhorter." We all certainly need exhortation to inspire us to fulfill Christ's Great Commission, but we also need the comfort that true repentance and redemption brings us. The Holy Spirit does them both—and so much more for us!

The lesson I take out of my own life and my own mistakes as I try to help the others I teach and pastor is that, while some of the trauma we experience is unavoidable (like death of loved ones, accident, and disease), much of the rest of what we undergo is actually unnecessary. We ourselves are the cause so many of our own problems and so many problems for others. All we really need to do is live Christlike lives of grateful obedience to God (check out Micah 6:8), and a lot of stuff falls into place. We should definitely receive any gifts God gives us with thanksgiving, realizing that they are *gifts*, given to us to enrich others' lives of faith, by illustrating new vistas on life in general and the fruits of the Spirit in particular (see Gal 5:22). Specifically, artistic gifts are not supposed to be hoarded; they are to be shared as generously as God did when giving them to us in the first place. That's why God calls them "gifts."

RESOURCES

God through the Looking Glass, the book Bill and Aida edited on encountering God in the arts, *Mysterium and Mystery*, Bill's study of religious detective stories, *Dread Jesus*, his analysis of reggae music and the Rastafari Movement behind it, are all available both on the net as well as at aandwspencer@gmail.com, along with their other titles. Please check out our blog at aandwspencer.com

Conclusion

William David Spencer

IN THE WEE HOURS of a rainy March 15, 2015, a police cruiser with all its lights flashing stood sentinel next to a detour sign warning all travelers that the Route 28 bridge in East Falmouth on Cape Cod was out of commission. Suddenly, at 1:45 a.m., a twenty-two-year-old woman, roaring down the road, barreled past all the barriers and slammed her car into the cruiser. Shaken but basically unhurt, she staggered from the wreck, clutching her smartphone and checking it for injury. The police took this in and demanded to know how she had missed or ignored all the signs, all the lights, all the previous warnings, and managed to demolish both cars: her own and theirs. At first, she blamed her windshield wipers for obscuring her view, but, finally, she admitted she was texting a friend. The police charged her with "reading or sending an electronic message while driving, negligent operation of a motor vehicle and speeding." Of course, she pleaded "not guilty." Who goes to court for doing an activity as natural as breathing?[1] This young trans-millennial woman had become a "victim of the media," as the perceptive Olga Soler puts it so well in her chapter in this book.

Paul the Apostle enlightened the scholars of Athens that God our Creator "is giving to all life and breath and all things" (Acts 17:25),[2] but, these days, media seem to be invading our contemporary consciousness "as the air we are breathing," and it is not the message of God we often "breathe in" from the influence of the media. Paul explained that in our Creator we "live" and "move around" and "exist," but it seems we are all in danger of trading our orientation toward our sustaining Creator to a complete dependence on our own creation: the media.

This is why the astute Ted Baehr warns us all in his chapter, "When Christians abandon the mass media, they abandon their culture and their compatriots." The media is a tool, like any tool we use to help us negotiate our lives, our work, our consciousness-raising activities. And here, Ted summarizes the elements of all the references that just preceded: a warning sign (we need to heed it and not self-absorb our attention or we are in for a nasty cultural car wreck from which we may not walk away unscathed), a proper orientation (Christians, as exemplified by Paul, need to be actively enlightening our compatriots about the true source of our sustaining wisdom—forming the way we live our lives and the opinions we promote on the Bible's expressed desires of our Creator, and not simply on the variety of whims expressed in our own creation, the media), and we need to be intentional about not ignoring the great search-and-rescue command of Jesus Christ in Matthew 28:19–20 (not abandoning the global cultures that all the diverse views being pumped out by the entertainment industry seek to influence around the world, for, when those influences are not healthy, they create more "media victims").

1. Rennan, "Police: Woman texting."
2. All Scripture translations in this chapter are translated by its author.

Perhaps as you worked through the preceding chapters you too were struck with how particularly proactive they were. So were we. So we decided to start out with the nuts-and-bolts presentation that is Ted's opening chapter. Here is someone who lives by his own advice and is daily influencing the media to adopt Christian values. Of course, that is hardly surprising, coming as it does from the author of the definitive hands-on, how-to manual for Christians in the entertainment industry: *How to Succeed in Hollywood (Without Losing Your Soul)*.[3]

What struck me, particularly, as proactive in the approach of all the authors in this present book, *Redeeming the Screens*, is their clear devotion to God and goodness, the energy they invest in coordinating their desire to promote this devotion into action together, and the messy lives from which they emerged, most of them having plunged into their art headfirst, not really gauging the depth of that sea, and many of them spiritually drowning, until they were rescued by the Great Lifeguard and became rescuers themselves. Any one of these writers will admit they could have remained a victim. Instead, through God's grace, they have all become victors.

So this is what this book was about, as I see it: these are accounts of how a number of disparate artists came to a faith in Jesus Christ that healed their lives, bonded them into a community, and spurred them to work together to include others in their healthy new orientation. My co-editor, Jeanne, once helped long-term caregiver and poet Teresa Flowers record prayers she prayed for the orphans she tended through years of nights in their book, *How to Have an Attitude of Gratitude on the Night Shift*. Waxing poetic ourselves, Jeanne and I summarized that book as, "God enters our messy lives and makes the plain of despera-

---

3. This by no means suggests that the only events worth noticing are those in Hollywood. As I was writing this conclusion, I had the privilege to see *Woodlawn*, the excellent movie by Pure Flix. This was followed by *God's Not Dead 2*, *Risen*, *The Young Messiah*, all well made, gripping productions, along with the astonishing *Do You Believe?* which followed 12 different lives and managed to stay not only coherent but compelling. That suggested to me that independent Christian movies are really coming into their own. Similarly, *Woodlawn's* sensitive portrayal of the interaction between an Anglo-American coach and his African-American player in a high school football team in the context of the painful and prolonged working out of the mandate of the US government that all its children be integrated in education (while other lives, as in need of adjustment as our protagonists', swirl around them) is wonderfully uplifting in a way, as my wife put it as we left the AMC multiplex where we saw it, that is actually "inspiring and not simply sentimental."

tion blossom with the sweet fruit of salvation and the mountains of adversity scalable with the power of spiritual strength." That may describe this book as well.

To me, these chapters also showed a remarkable unity of perspective among the participants across the media art forms represented that is reminiscent of the unity of message among the biblical writers, as diverse in time and culture as so many of them were. What I am suggesting is an analogy, true at one parallel point, namely, that in this book we see a diversity of theatrical activities from flipping a game show card to kicking the stand-in of a famous actor in a simulated karate fight to demonstrating the hula hoop to dangling fifty stories up, revealing that these performers all hail from various areas of the entertainment industry. Other contributors to this book are producers, directors, musicians, preachers, but, as April Shenandoah, a model of perseverance in her own right, put it in her chapter, what all of them have in common is that they have discovered "God's business" in the midst of "show business." And this book flows along accordingly.

Performing, directing, producing, creating is tough work. It is often thankless work. The arts seem to me to be a lot like term insurance: they have the potential to pay off for a while, and then their earning days for you are over. When would-be authors contact me and tell me they want to write, I always advise them to write only if they can't not write. Any artistic endeavor is a lonely, arduous ordeal and, if you are looking for a financial payoff for your family, it is rarely worth all the effort you are going to put into it. Stick with a steady paycheck. "Starving artist" has become a cliché for a reason. Instead, you do the work because the gift inside demands that you do it, or you will be miserable, beset by a deep sense of loss, if you don't do it. So, if the only time you feel fulfilled is when you are using your gift, as time-consuming and exhausting as it is, then you do it—and you do it to God's glory with all the effort you have to give.

These artists we have recorded in this book are those who responded to the demands of their gift and then, despite actual success, turned to the Giver of their gift and discovered a whole new dimension to what their gifting was all about—and that is when they found the spiritual riches that make living and creating worthwhile.

So, as I read their stories, what are some of the facets I noticed about their lives now as artists and followers of Jesus? These are what struck me the most.

First, above all, the remarkable sense of community here. It is no small coincidence that so many of the participants appear in each other's chapters, helping each other find Jesus, assisting each other to start ministries, supporting those ministries, attending each other's events and churches. Hollywood had always struck me as a collection of superstars or would-be superstars and not a community. But these individuals have become aware of themselves as brothers and sisters now in the family of Christ, and they have bonded up together. These Christians in the entertainment industry have networked and are now looking out for each other, and we can see how often they meet and appear on each other's programs and travel together to do ministry. Many of them, of course, met each other in the events created by Jeanne DeFazio for the late Michael P. Grace II, to whom Jeanne dedicates the book. He was a kingdom builder of prodigious skill, and his events changed lives. Though he is no longer with us, the legacy of ministry he left still impacts these artists' own vision. Christian community in Hollywood, of course, is nothing new, as the exemplary lives of Dale Evans and Roy Rogers substantiate. But, in the case of these present writers, Michael Grace first brought, not all, but many of them together in community, and they have since brought in many more who never met Michael Grace, but are blessed by the legacy of his ministry. It is a wonderful legacy of God's continuing grace.

Also, it is imperative to mention that Jeanne herself is the sparkplug that got much of this going as the event planner for Michael Grace. Later, I met Jeanne when she enrolled as my student back in 2002. Very soon, she distinguished herself, earning an A+ in Systematic Theology 2 (a very rare and difficult grade to achieve), and she followed that achievement with a series of remarkable, directed studies in which she produced documentary films of high quality on theological and social issues. I try to keep track of my best graduates and invite them back to teach with me, and eight years ago I invited Jeanne back to work as an Athanasian Teaching Scholar in Theology, helping at-risk students negotiate the rigors of theological training. She had developed a specialty in second-language learning and took on our students most challenged in studying in English. As the years went by, Jeanne kept returning from her base in California to help in Boston, eventually creating a template for learning that helped every student with whom she worked to succeed. A common comment I see on student evaluations, including this year's, is "Jeanne is an angel." Actually, Jeanne is a disciplined, hardworking artist who applies herself (and everybody else she can recruit into her vision) to get her vision done. As a valued member of the editorial team of the House of Prisca and Aquila Series, Jeanne regularly creates spots to promote everyone's books, not just her own. And this is the kind of energy she invested years before in helping Michael P. Grace II create his vision of expanding the Christian community in Hollywood.

I suggested the topic of this book and its eventual title and agreed to work on it with her as a direct thank-you to her for all she has done over these seven years for students who might have given up without her mentoring. All the participants in this present book were recruited by her (I suppose myself included) and she helped with their chapters, since many of them were too busy to find the space and time to write and polish their work. In the truest sense, there would be no book without Jeanne. While it was quite a challenge for me to edit, coming as it did from her in bits and pieces, I could see that every one of those she recruited was a seriously godly, creative person who was making a contribution to the extending of God's reign, and so our task was to get down a cohesive, reflective report from each of them.

I suggested we ask all of them to tell us about their art form (in most cases their performance or production expertise and venue), their own lives, how they met the Lord, their resulting ministry, and the Bible verse or truth that centers their lives now.

To a pastor and a seminary prof like myself, one of the most fascinating aspects that I noticed as the book shaped up was in the patterns emerging as each author described the Bible verses that had become most important in the maturing of each life of faith and the developing of each ministry.

An early theme that emerged in Ted Baehr's chapter came when he cited Mark 18:6 to warn us all to consider the impact of the entertainment industry on our children, pointing out that Proverbs 25:26 makes every one of us, entertainment industry participant or not, ultimately responsible for what happens to the children, because compliance with less than God's desire equals pollution.

The theme of community, of course, was a major one. How could it not be central, given the way so many of the participants were introduced to faith in Jesus by their peers in the entertainment industry? Jeanne highlighted this theme early on, as she cited Exodus 23:20, wherein God sends an angel to guard the way of God's people. She coupled that verse with 1 Corinthians 12:13, where building a community to travel together is emphasized, becoming for her a strong aspect of God's strategy for guarding God's followers. Olga Soler added Deuteronomy 8:2–3 to God's leading, resonating herself with the humbling and testing God provides to help a community learn to keep God's commandments. All of this nurturing is based on God's gracious forgiveness, Bee Beyer Wenger reminded us, citing Psalm 51:10–13. So, Christ is now among us, Joanne Petronella explained, and out of that presence comes our hope of glory (Col 1: 26–27). Individuals are, thus, enabled by the Holy Spirit to mature in grace and become powerful witnesses for Christ (John 14:26), forgiven and forgiving. And, Gemma Wenger assured us, out of this forgiveness, God builds unity, joining Christ's community together (Eph 4:16, Col 2:2a). God is distributing a variety of gifts among us so that everyone can contribute (Eph 4:11–13, Eccl 11:6) and move forward in our spiritual lives together (Heb 11:40; Eph 4:32; Matt 6:14; 1Pet 2:5; Ps 133), so we must all be on guard to protect that godly community (Rom 16:17; 3 John 1:9–10, Jer 3:14). And LeaAnn Pendergrass reminded us that the Christian community's goal is no less extensive than uniting all nations under Christ (Psalm 133:1) and producing a multicultural church that serves with a full "fivefold ministry" (Eph 4:11–12; 1 Cor 12:10–11; Matt 17:20), so its task is a holy one. The church will face opposition (John 15:18–19), but must steadfastly bear its united witness across the world (Mark 16:15; Prov 11:30), maintaining confidence in the One who sends us forth (Is 26:3) to achieve God's goal of creating global unity under Christ.

Into this communal vision, Susan Stafford introduced the theme of discipleship, giving our lives daily to God to find them again, but this time refined (Matt 16:24–26), for these renewed lives are retooled graciously by God's kindness and mercy (Eph 1:6), being shaped by God's good plans for us (Jer 29:11). Jozy Pollock highlighted Ephesians 1:6 as well, wherein God's wonderful, divine kindness, centering as it does in Jesus, evokes praise of God from our grateful hearts, because, as Sheri Pedigo reminded us, citing 2 Corinthians 5:17, we are now new creations, our old spirit of fear is gone (2 Tim 1:7). We have become overcomers (Rev 12:11). Martha Reyes pointed out that the result of all this grace bestowed upon us is that we work for the benefit of others (Luke 10:30–37; Gen 4:9; Matt 25:35–36), even at great sacrifice to ourselves (2 Cor 6:4, Phil 1:13–14). April Shenandoah also developed this theme of sacrifice for others, underscoring it as a natural activity of our maturing in Christ (Rom 10:9–10, 13), which inspires devotion to God and service to others (Matt 22:37–39), as we become more like Jesus.

A third theme, sounded by Bob Yerkes, is the effect of our faith on our craft. He noted that strength for the craftsperson is drawn directly from God, and he held up the biblical artist Zerubbabel to highlight this truth: that God empowers the faithful to do their craft to God's glory by the power of God's Spirit (Zech 4:6–10). Mel Novak also assured us that this strength extends as well from one's work to one's ministry, since Romans 8:28 confirms that God is the One causing everything to work together for good, so Jesus, the Life-giver (John 15:5), will carry us through duress (Isa 48:10) if we put a priority on bringing in God's Rule (Matt 6:33). Since Jesus is centered in God (John 14:10–11), Mel showed that we can draw strength from our Lord in passages like Ephesians 6:10 and fire these promises back at evil in his "arsenal prayers." We can also draw healing from God's power, Charlene Eber explained, citing Matthew 9:20–22 and sharing her own personal story of healing as an antidote to the ravages of doubt, which are a ramification of the great fall of humanity (Gen 3:1–7). Healing is also featured in several other chapters, including LeaAnn Pendergrass's (Jas 5:14; Isa 53:5), while Bob Rieth pointed out that this healing includes bringing the message of salvation in Jesus through an evangelism that awakens and restores as it goes out across the nations (Acts 8:5, 26–40; 21:8). This is an active mission he does, as do others in this book, centering his own specific focus on those in the media who are placed in harm's way when they are dispatched to cover events in the trouble spots of the world. The promises of Acts, particularly in 2:17, to empower the gifts of the Spirit to evangelize for Jesus, also inspire Larry Abernathy to raise up the glorified Jesus (Rev 1:1, 11–20, 2:1—3:22, 4:1–22:5) and send Christ's good news around the world (Rom 10:18). This is a vision shared by his co-pastor Linda Bair Smith, who summed up this activist approach by reminding all believers that we are God's "beloved" (Eph 1:6), reunited with God by Jesus's sacrifice for us (1 Cor 1:18, 23–30) and given access to God's wisdom (1 Cor 2:9–10, 12, 16), so we can fit into God's plans for the world (Rom 8:28; Ps 37:23). This calling is a high one, nothing less than assisting God in reconciling the world to Godself (2 Cor 5:14–21; Matt 24:14). I closed this third theme of God's empowerment in our ministries with the assurance that our doubts do not annul God's faithfulness (1 John 5:13), nor our weaknesses God's ability to carry us through whatever we face (Phil 4:13), so we can, through our community, our talents, and the strength that God provides to empower each of us, reach out together and heal the broken (Prov 14:10a) with the good news we have all discovered: an unsurpassable comfort made available in Jesus's sacrifice for humanity and in the resulting reconciliation with God and empowerment drawn from the power of the One who created our world and even now is graciously recreating it through our united efforts for good.

These themes of children, community, and crafting summarize what we all value. We realize only too well that not one of us in this book is perfect. Each of us, including the editors, has made plenty of mistakes and disappointed the Lord and has much to regret. But this is not ultimately a book about mistakes, no matter how many of our errors we have recounted in it. This is a book about the graciousness of the God who forgives our mistakes, buries them in the deepest part of the sea, and then helps us repentant sinners heal from them, move on, avoid making such mistakes again, and, instead, do something worthwhile with our lives on the other side of forgiveness.

And how does the future look to us? Well, clearly we realize we now live in a world of screens, from the microcosmic universe of that smartphone clutched by our poor trans-millennial staggering out of her car, to the imposing vigil of the multiplex giants, looming over us in Imax and 3-D—more "real" than real—and to all the screens in between, from computers to iPads to silenced, high definition flat-screens pouring out images in homes, restaurants, banks, businesses, schools, doctors' offices, and hospitals and on and on everywhere we turn. We cannot change this reality, so what these Christians and so many like them are doing is trying to find ways to redeem what we put on these screens: what message we are sending out in word and image to the watching world.

So, clearly, our task, whether we have been called to create or not, is to join these artists as "screen redeemers," assisting the Holy Spirit in reconciling the world to God (2 Cor 5:18–19) through helping the pervasively influential means of the media adjust its goals to the mission of Jesus Christ.

Bibliography

Abernathy, Larry. *Faith*. Palm Springs: Cathedral of Love of the Seven Golden Candlesticks Church and Cathedral of Love Ministries, 1992.

———. *The Light Bearer*. Palm Springs: Cathedral of Love of the Seven Golden Candlesticks Church and Cathedral of Love Ministries, 1992.

———. *Revelation Knowledge*. Palm Springs: Cathedral of Love of the Seven Golden Candlesticks Church and Cathedral of Love Ministries, 1992.

———. Interview with Jeanne DeFazio. LaQuinta, California, 14 Dec 2014.

"The Alternative Jesus: Psychedelic Christ." *Time Magazine*. 21 June 1971. Online: content.time.com/time/covers/0,16641,19710621,00.html.

Baker, Tammy. "Don't Give Up on the Brink of a Miracle." Christian World, Inc., 2011.

Benton, Lee. "Lee Benton's CBS Studio Meetings, Guest Speaker, Jozy Pollock." 15 Jan 2015. Online:youtube.com/watch?v=EJHNBivDUTE.

———."Lee Benton Producer of *Victory Road*, The Cross TV, Interview of Jozy Pollock." 28 July 2014. Online: youtube.com/watch?v=ATHHLa86Akw.

Beyer, Bee. *How to Dry Food at Home the Natural Way*. Boston: Houghton Mifflin, 1970.

Bliss, Philip B. "Hold the Fort." 1870. Online: hymntime.com/tch/htm/h/o/l/holdfort.htm.

Chandler, Robert. "He Preached the Gospel." *Los Angeles Times*, 14 Oct 1989. Online: http://articles.latimes.com/print/1989-10-14/local/me-319_1_billy-graham.

Cosa Nostra News. "Ianniello Was a Huge Earner; with Son's Eulogy." 20 Aug 2012. Online: cosanostranews.com/2012/08/matthew-matty-horse-ianniello-dies-at-92.html.

Dart, John. "A Romantic Era Ends for Chapel in the Canyon." *Los Angeles Times*, 31 Aug 1996. Online: articles.latimes.com/1996-08-31/local/me-39310_1_christian-church.

DeFazio, Jeanne C., and John P. Lathrop, eds. *Creative Ways to Build Christian Community*. House of Prisca and Aquila Series. Eugene, OR: Wipf and Stock, 2013.

DeHann, M. R. "Witnessing on the Flying Trapeze." *Daily Bread*. 14 Jan 1971.

Gilinsky, Jaron. "Californians bring Passion to Jerusalem's Old City." Time.com, 2008. Online: content.time.com/time/video/player/0,32068,75560426001_1977063,00.html.

Hennessey, Leigh. "Bob Yerkes, A Life Stranger than Fiction." *Inside Stunts*. Winter 2006.

Kozoll, Noelle Aimee. *On Faith Alone: The Jozy Pollock Story*. 25 Feb. 2010. Online: youtube.com/watch?v=auNvGVfes5U. Accessed 12 Aug 2015.

"Lance." Christian Forum website comment, 21 June 2008. Online: christian-forum.net/index.php?showtopic=20473.

Lewis, C. S. *That Hideous Strength*. New York: Simon and Shuster, 1996.

———. *Surprised by Joy*. New York: Harcourt Brace, 1995.

Morris, James. *The Overreach of O. L. Jaggers: The Preachers*. London: St. Martin's, 1973.

Novak, Mel. "God's Arsenal of Protection." Online: melnovak.com/arsenal.htm.

———. Untitled document, 2014. http://www.melnovak.com/new/wp-content/uploads/2014/10/SEPT14-FULL.pdf.

Pedigo, Sheri. "Jozy Pollock Interview on Clemente Movie, Manson, & Magic." 29 Aug 2013. Online: youtube.com/watch?v=8KhI2Yh3VrE.

Pendergrass, LeaAnn. *Uniting the Nations*. 25 Mar 2015. Online: youtube.com/watch?v=nSFMoAJuPRk.

———. *Uniting the Nations*. 28 Apr 2015. Online: youtube.com/watch?v=_-c7KwkKCR0.

Rennan, George. "Police: Woman texting when she hit cruiser." *Cape Cod Times*. 13 May, 2015, A2.

Reyes, Martha. *Jesucristo: Tu Psicólogo Personal*. Corona, CA: self-publication, 2014.

———. *Jesús y la Mujer Herida*. Corona, CA: self-publication, 2012.

Scriven, Joseph M. "What a Friend We Have in Jesus." Online: hymnal.net/en/hymn/h/789.

Shenandoah, April. *So, Help Me God*. Beverly Hills: Eden Street Productions, 2004.

———. *Your Tongue Determines Your Destiny*. Tulsa, OK: Harrison, 2012.

Stowell, Joe. "The Catcher." *Daily Bread*. 14 March 1971.

Wenger, Gemma. *Beauty for Ashes*. "Jeanne DeFazio re: *Creative Ways to Build Christian Community*." Segment 613, 26 Oct 2015. Online: youtube.com/watch?v=78JbTZEzZc8.

www.ingramcontent.com/pod-product-compliance
Lightning Source LLC
Chambersburg PA
CBHW070318230426
43663CB00011B/2173